Edmund C. P Hull, Robert Slater Mair

Coffee Planting in Southern India and Ceylon

Edmund C. P Hull, Robert Slater Mair

Coffee Planting in Southern India and Ceylon

ISBN/EAN: 9783337005481

Printed in Europe, USA, Canada, Australia, Japan

Cover: Foto ©Andreas Hilbeck / pixelio.de

More available books at **www.hansebooks.com**

COFFEE PLANTING

IN

SOUTHERN INDIA AND CEYLON.

BEING A

SECOND EDITION, REVISED AND ENLARGED, OF "COFFEE, ITS PHYSIOLOGY, HISTORY, AND CULTIVATION."

BY

E. C. P. HULL,

AUTHOR OF "THE EUROPEAN IN INDIA," ETC.

London:

E. & F. N. SPON, 48, CHARING CROSS.
NEW YORK: 446, BROOME STREET.
1877.

[*All rights reserved.*]

TO THE MOST NOBLE

THE MARQUIS OF SALISBURY,

SECRETARY OF STATE FOR INDIA,

THIS VOLUME

IS

𝕭𝖞 𝕾𝖕𝖊𝖈𝖎𝖆𝖑 𝕻𝖊𝖗𝖒𝖎𝖘𝖘𝖎𝖔𝖓,

RESPECTFULLY DEDICATED.

INTRODUCTION.

SOME time ago, I received a communication from Messrs. Higginbotham and Co., of Madras, proposing that I should bring out a second edition of my work on coffee cultivation, published several years since, and now out of print. To this proposition I assented without much consideration, but on looking into my early and somewhat crude production, and being thus reminded not only of its many deficiencies and imperfections (making even due allowance for the date of its publication), but also of the numerous changes which had since taken place in the position of coffee cultivation, I began to regard the step with regret; a feeling which was not diminished, as it gradually became evident that instead of having merely undertaken to publish a new edition of an existing book, I had practically before me the task of writing a new book altogether, and that with very little time at my disposal for literary pursuits. Now that my work is accomplished, however, I begin to realize how much pleasure it has afforded me, by enabling me to recall many agreeable memories of days and friends in the past, of which I should not perhaps otherwise have enjoyed another glimpse; so that should the young planters and others who may read the following pages derive an equal proportion of practical benefit, in the shape of information on the subjects treated of, my time and labour will, altogether, have been far more than compensated for.

For the benefit of those who may ask, how one not now engaged in coffee planting can claim to be heard on the subject, I may explain, that I have never ceased to follow with interest the movements of an enterprise to which ten of the most impressionable years of my life were exclusively devoted, and with which I was directly connected for a much longer period; and there is perhaps no harm in adding, that for some years it was a necessity with me, as a regular contributor on this and kindred subjects to the Indian press, to keep myself *au courant* of all that occurred in connexion with them, as time went on.

Since 1865, other books on coffee-planting have, I believe, issued from the press, notably that by Mr. Sabonadiere; none of these, however, have I had the good fortune to meet with. Had the case been otherwise, no doubt the present volume might have been rendered more complete and valuable, at their expense.

The most remarkable change in the position of coffee-planting that has taken place of late years, has arisen from the falling off, from one cause or other, in the production of the staple in various parts of the world; and this, at a time when the tendency of consumption has rather been towards increase than otherwise. The natural result has been an enormous rise in price—coming, most opportunely, just in time to prevent the planters of Ceylon and Southern India from being utterly disheartened, by the (what would otherwise have been *ruinous*) devastations of the leaf-disease—a blight that for some years has brought down the Ceylon yield about 40 per cent. So much, however, has this calamity been thrown into the background by the advantage gained in price, that coffee property and land suitable for the cultivation, instead of being depreciated, have enormously increased in value.

More than normally prolonged seasons of drought, in some of the hottest districts of Southern India, have at length forced on the planters a conviction that a change in the system of cultivation (from that ordinarily pursued in Ceylon and other more humid climates) must in future be adopted, to enable the estates to undergo similar trials as they recur; which, it is evident, they must be expected to do, at more or less distant intervals. Recent researches, by Dr. W. W. Hunter of the Indian statistical department, based upon the entire existing records of Indian rainfall (which, however, extend over only some sixty-three years), seem to prove, that the seasons of minimum rainfall in the Madras Presidency (in which all the coffee districts are situated) have recurred in cycles of eleven years, corresponding to the periods of minimum sun's spots. Assuming this theory to be correct, and that the excessively prolonged drought which occurred in the Wynaad in the spring of 1876 corresponded with the end of the last of these cycles, the planters of that and adjacent districts would have fair grounds for the consoling expectation, that no similarly trying season is likely again to befall them for nearly a decade—an ample period, if well used, within which to adopt precautionary measures, such as providing shade and irrigation appliances, by which the effects of a dry season may be more or less mitigated.

Before concluding the estimates given towards the end of the work, I was fortunate enough to meet with my old friend Mr. W. Sabonadiere,[1] an experienced Ceylon planter, and to obtain from him information on several points, such as the present cost of land in Ceylon, of erecting stores, bungalows,

[1] Author of the "Coffee Planter of Ceylon."

&c., without which I might have found myself in some difficulty. My calculations have been framed with considerable care, and with a sincere wish to avoid misleading any one by flowery or over-sanguine representations. Possibly, nevertheless, they may *still* in some cases prove unduly favourable, but if so, I can honestly state my conviction that, in an equal number at least, actual experience under fairly favourable circumstances will yield more profitable returns than those set down; and such tables, it should always be borne in mind, are based on the assumption that circumstances *will* be fairly favourable, it being only under such circumstances that prudent men should think of investing their capital in this or any other cultivation.

No allowance has, it is true, been made for a high rate of interest on capital, and it will be evident that those who may have to take such an additional charge into account, must make up their minds to a much longer and more arduous struggle than is here shown, to free their property from incumbrance.

In an appendix will be found a chapter giving instructions for the medical treatment of Coolies and others on coffee estates, in the absence of professional assistance, written by my old and valued friend Dr. Mair, formerly of Madras, and this part of the work I commend to the estate manager as invaluable. Living in the jungle, far from doctors and apothecaries' shops, with a large number of comparatively helpless human beings dependent on his care, the man of good feeling will feel it a high privilege to be able to relieve the numerous cases of sickness and suffering which must constantly come under his notice; and those planters who thus thoughtfully regard the subject, will find in Dr. Mair's prescriptions, sufficient to enable them to become the instruments, not only of relieving much suffering, but probably also of saving many lives.

In order to be on the safe side, I have usually named in the text the authorities from whence extracts or quotations are derived; I may here, however, recapitulate those quoted in the original work:—

> Laborie's Coffee Planter of St. Domingo.
> Abridgment of ditto by Higginbotham.
> "W." Pruning.
> Wall on Manuring.
> Dr. Shortt's Handbook.
> Loudon's Encyclopædia of Gardening.
> Rhind's Vegetable Kingdom.
> Willich's Encyclopædia.
> Chambers' ditto.

I have also had the advantage of referring to Ferguson's Ceylon Directory (1875), a really marvellous compendium of useful information relating to that most charming and, for its size, richest dependency of the Crown.

CONTENTS.

CHAPTER I.

PAGE

Coffee—Botanical description—The Leaves—Blossom —Bark—Fruit—C. Mauritiana—C. Liberiana—C. Arabica—Origin—Introduction to Europe—Into Java—Holland—West Indies—Medicinal properties —Nutritive—Stimulant—Disinfectant—Discovery of Roasting process—Adoption in Arabia—Moslem opposition—Among the Túrks—In England—Mr. Edwards—Pasqua Rosee's Coffee-house—His hand-bills—Coffee leaves—Febrifuge properties—Method of preparing—Use in Sumatra—Their medicinal properties—Cheapness 1

CHAPTER II.

Coffee, Countries known in—Latitude it frequents— Introduction into Ceylon and S. India—Munzerabad—Discovered at Manantoddy—First cultivated by Europeans—So-called indigenous species in Neilgherries—Ceylon—Hangurankette—Sir Edward Barnes—His estate—Kondesalla—Durability of Coffee property—Position of the Enterprise in Ceylon—Labourers—S. India districts—The Wynaad—Manantoddy—The Neilgherries—Ootacamund—Labour—Elevation—Munzerabad—Coorg —Mercara—Game—The Natives—Rainfall—The

Shervaroys—Climate—Prospects for Ceylon and S. India—Slavery in Brazil—State of affairs in Java—Government monopoly—Diminishing production . 16

CHAPTER III.

Acquiring land in Ceylon—The upset price—Present value of forest-land—Rules for S. India compared—Property intrinsically less valuable—Why—Private titles more advantageous—Coffee Land Assessment—Rules in Coorg 31

CHAPTER IV.

Climate required for Coffee—High temperature not indispensable—Experiment in Germany—Temperate Climate required for profitable cultivation—Humidity—Elevation of 4000 to 5000 feet in Ceylon—Under 3000 feet in Wynaad—Results compared—Mean temperature required—Temperature of Ceylon hills—S. India districts—Land wind—Favourite elevation in Ceylon—Native Coffee-gardens—Below 1000 feet in Ceylon—Neighbourhood of Kandy—Change in the Climate—Temperature combined with moisture — Weeds — Black Bug — Elevation and Climate connected—Malaria—Fever—The Bamboo—Effect of clearings—The seasons—January to March—June—The Monsoon—N.E. Monsoon—Aspect—Wind — Effects— Remedial Measures—The Doombegas-tree 37

CHAPTER V.

Soil—Mr. Loudon's definition of soils for the cultivator—Organic matter—Friability—Absorbent power—Stagnant water—Vegetation a guide . . . 59

CHAPTER VI.

Collecting labourers—The labour difficulty—Causes of it—Coolies of the right sort—The Kangany or Maistry—The advance system—Firmly rooted—Causes—Losses not so frequent as might be expected—Usurious Kanganies—Contract labour—In Ceylon—In S. India—Malabar contractors—Hill-men—Ceylon labour Ordinance—Canarese coolies—Jungle tribes, alias "Locals"—Contracts—Imported labour—Tamil labour in Ceylon—Labour-field for Wynaad—The climate a difficulty—Author's experience in 1860—Engagements should be legally binding—Written agreements—Coolie agents—Food supply . 64

CHAPTER VII.

Tools and implements—Best quality desirable—The mammotie—The bill-hook—The axe—The crowbar—The quintannie—The reaping-hook—Erection of coolie lines—Bungalow—The bamboo—Jungle materials 85

CHAPTER VIII.

Young plants—Stumping—The nursery—Seeds—Seed-beds—Germination—Manure for seed-beds—Watering—Distance apart—Size of beds—The paddy-field bed—Irrigation—Old plants—Shade—Soil . . 93

CHAPTER IX.

The clearing—Mode of felling forest—Bamboos—Their uses—Felling bamboos—Lopping—Burning—The burn—Clearing—Pitting before clearing—Leeches . 99

CHAPTER X.

Lining out—Objects—Method—The rope—The base line—Lining square—West Indies and Java—Distance apart—Hexagons—Quincunx formation—Pitting—Depth desirable—The day's task—Work to be completed before wet season—Filling in—Women and boys 106

CHAPTER XI.

Planting—Stumps—Trimming the roots—Nursery plants—" With ball "—Continuance of rain needful—Old plants—Puddling—Disposition of roots—Method of planting—Care preferable to mere expedition—With the crowbar—The diamond dibber—Dibbling—Slit planting 114

CHAPTER XII.

Road-making—Recapitulation of works discussed—Time for road-making—Advantages of good roads—Cart-road—Subordinate roads—Frequency required—The road tracer—Marking out—The advance gang—Cost of estate roads—Blasting rocks—Method described 125

CHAPTER XIII.

Draining—Necessity for—Gradient of the trenches—Frequency of occurrence—Mr. Wall's opinion—Draining swamps—Mauritius grass. . . . 134

CHAPTER XIV.

Weeding—Weeds defined—Effects of—Methods of removal—Beginning early—Rapid multiplication—" White weed "—Hay—Weeding by hand—With the scraper—With the mammotie—Burying in—Weeding contracts—Rates 138

CHAPTER XV.

Supplying vacancies—Causes of vacancies—Prevention better than cure—Opening the pit—New soil desirable—Poonac—Strong plants required—" Supplies" put in early—Necessity of keeping them free from weeds 145

CHAPTER XVI.

Staking — Prevailing wind to be noted — Fastenings—Durability of stakes—Earthing up—Forest belts—Hedges, &c.—Exposed situations better not planted 148

CHAPTER XVII.

Shade necessary in hot climates—Planters unwilling to recognize this—Native gardens—Opinion changing—Jack-trees—Various advantages of shade—Objections—Diminished production—Reduced expenditure—Description of trees—Discrimination necessary—The Jack—In the Mauritius—Castor-oil plant—Plantains—Distance apart—Training . . . 151

CHAPTER XVIII.

Bungalows and lines—A permanent bungalow—Definition—Various materials—Stone and lime—Bricks — Criterion of quality—Brick-making — Clay required—Breaking-up soil—Moulds—Treading out—Moulding—Drying—Burning—The kiln—Tiles—Moulding — Burning — Wattle and dab — The uprights—The wattles—The "dab"—White ants—Timber white-ant proof—The supports—Laterite for building—Thatch—Cadjans—Straw—Shingles

—Splitting—Dimensions—Laying—Cost—Iron tile-sheets — Difficulties and drawbacks — Method of fastening—Description of bungalow required—Flooring — Asphalte — Plaster — Tiles—Boards—Sawing timber—Method of computing—Coolie lines—Site—Ventilation—Sanitation—Cowdung—Coolie gardens—Size of sets—Danger of fire . . . 160

CHAPTER XIX.

The pulping-house—The cherry loft—The machine platform—The cisterns—Water supply—The pulper—The sieve—The crusher—Revolving buckets—Butler's pulper—Letter of a Ceylon planter, 1860—The Disc pulper—Setting the pulper—Improvements—Iron barrels—Walker's patent punching—Gordon's breasts'—Letter from Mr. John Gordon—Stores—Iron stores—Objects required—Crop difficulties—Mr. Clerihew's system—Revolving fans—Hot-air apparatus — Barbecues — Macadam and plaster — Asphalte — Plenty of drying-ground desirable 184

CHAPTER XX.

Crop appearances—The blossom—The "set"—Ripening—Picking—Importance of allowing coffee to ripen fully—Green berries—Day's task—*Pro rata* wages—*System* required—Black berries—Iron spouting—Laying spouting—Immediate pulping necessary—Washing — Drying— Turning— Peeling— Sizing— Shipment 208

CHAPTER XXI.

"Topping"— Objects of — Proper height—In exposed situations—In sheltered situations—The true criterion—Economy of space—Argument against high plants—General mean height—Suckers—Time for topping—Method—Handling—Objects of primary branches — Secondaries — Open centres — Early handling—Pruning—Form of plant described by Laborie—General objects to be kept in view—Single branches — Suppression of unnecessary growth — Maiden crop — Knife pruning first season — Next year's wood—Tertiary branches—Criterion of good pruning—Regular handling, easy pruning—Women and children—Pruning neglected trees—Gradual reclamation —Violent treatment — Heavy pruning —Opening out thickets—Primaries not to be cut—Care and intelligence indispensable . . . 222

CHAPTER XXII.

Manuring—Its necessity early recognized—The objects of—Chemical constituents of plants—Mucilaginous and fatty fluids—Decomposition—Liebig's theory —Organic matter—Analysis of West Indian Coffee —Mineral constituents—Analysis of Ceylon plantation—Combustible constituents—Cattle dung—Duration of effects — Mr. Wilson's opinion — Sir Humphrey Davy on fermentation—English farmers view — Method of making liquid manure — Dr. Shortt's suggestion—Method with pigs—Another plan—Economizing transit with bulky manures—Cultivating grass—Putting out—On flat land—On slopes—Old method— Green vegetation—Woody fibres—Dead animals — Coffee pulp— Poonac — Bones — Castor-oil cake— Guano—Wood ashes — Lime—Sulphate of ammonia—Mâna grass—Ground thatching—Ceylon Prize Essays (1875) . . . 238

CHAPTER XXIII.

Diseases incident to plants—Classification by Tournefort—Enemies of coffee—Bug—The black bug—

Mode of propagation—Treatment recommended—The white bug—Affects dry situations—The borer—Its appearance in Coorg—Treatment—Probable causes—The leaf disease—Its character—Its effects—Its causes—Pellicularia—"Stump"—The rot—Grubs—Rats—Grasshoppers 263

CHAPTER XXIV.

Estimates—Difficulties in the way of accuracy—Cost of land—SOUTHERN INDIA, First year—Second year—Third year—Fourth year—Fifth year—Sixth year Seventh year—Balance-sheet.—CEYLON, First year—Second year—Third year—Fourth year—Fifth year—Sixth year—Remarks—Crop—Market value—Balance-sheet—General result 277

CHAPTER XXV.

Durability of coffee property—Question one to be faced—Age of estates in Ceylon—Planting fifty years ago—The legacy of pioneers—Native coffee gardens—Difficulties—Dangers to permanency—Diseases, &c.—Conditions of durability—Climate—Soil—Culture—The Author's opinion 303

APPENDIX.

Instructions for the Medical Treatment of Coolies and others on coffee estates until professional assistance can be obtained 313

IN

CEYLON AND INDIA.

CHAPTER I.

Coffee—Botanical description—The Leaves—Blossom—Bark —Fruit—C. Mauritiana—C. Liberiana—C. Arabica— Origin—Introduction to Europe—Into Java—Holland —West Indies—Medicinal properties—Nutritive—Stimulant—Disinfectant—Discovery of Roasting process— Adoption in Arabia—Moslem opposition—Among the Turks—In England—Mr. Edwards—Pasqua Rosee's Coffee-house—His handbills—Coffee leaves—Febrifuge properties—Method of preparing—Use in Sumatra—Their medicinal properties—Cheapness.

THE Coffee Plant (*Coffea Arabica*) belongs to the botanical family *Rubiaceæ*, and to the Class Pentandria Monogynia of *Linnæus*. In the Arabic language, *Kahwah* is the name given to the liquor made from Coffee; in the Turkish, *Capee*, of which last our own word is probably a corruption.

The Coffee plant may be best described as a shrub. Its appearance is graceful and attractive.

In its natural state, and under favourable circumstances, it will attain a height of from fifteen to twenty feet. In form it is slender, opening out at the upper part into long, drooping branches, which seldom grow to any great thickness.

The leaves in general appearance resemble those of the Portugal laurel, being of a dark shade, smooth and very shiny on the upper surface; in shape they are elliptical, pointed, and generally between three and four inches long (though, occasionally, they attain to as much as six inches in size). They are placed opposite each other, in pairs, and are connected with the branches by short foot stalks, each pair being usually from two to four inches apart from the next on the branch.

The blossom is white and small, not unlike that of the jessamine, both in scent and form. Botanically, it is described as axillary, sessile, calyx monopetalous, funnel-shaped, and cut at the limb into fine, reflexed, lanceolate segments. It comes out in groups; from four to sixteen flowers springing from the axil of the leaves.

The bark is smooth or nearly so, and of a greyish-brown colour.

The fruit or berries which succeed the blossom are at first dark green, but soon change their hue as they progress towards maturity,—first to yellow, then to red, until finally they become a deep crimson. When this stage has been reached they are ripe, and ready to be gathered. The external part of the berry, under the skin, is a pulp of mucilaginous, saccharine and somewhat glutinous character, which envelopes and closely adheres to two oval seeds, which, being convex on the one side and flat on the other, lie with the flat sides in contact, face to face. These seeds are commonly termed Coffee "*beans*," not from their resembling beans proper, but, as "Chambers's Encyclopædia" tells us, from the Arabic word *bunn*. The outer covering of the bean is a cartilaginous membrane, which, from its faint, straw-like tint and smooth, shiny consistency, has received the name of *parchment*. Inside the parchment there is another very delicate, semi-transparent skin, which adheres closely to the seed, and is called the "silver-skin."

There are other descriptions of coffee besides the *C. Arabica*, of which the *C. Mauritiana* is one which is said to have, when prepared in the same manner as the former, a bitter, unpleasant taste, and the property of being slightly emetic. Some botanists name only two distinct species, i.e., the *C. Arabica* and the *C. Occidentalis*, while others are of opinion that the differences between one kind and another are merely the effects of soil, climate and modes of culture, upon the *same* species.

A paper in *Blackwood's Magazine*, entitled "Beverages we infuse," has the following on this point:—"The *Coffea Arabica*, from its being the principal producer of coffee, is the chief and most useful species, but besides this others are cultivated in other parts of the world, on account of their commercial value, all of which, though now regarded as separate species, owe their origin to the *Coffea Arabica.*"

The attention of the planters of Ceylon and S. India has, during recent years, been directed towards the species of coffee grown in Liberia. in Western Africa. This species, which we may meantime call the *C. Liberiana*, possesses a larger leaf, and indeed is altogether of larger growth, than the *C. Arabica*. It is also understood to be capable of a higher degree of productiveness, and to possess the advantage of being suited for culture in low-lying situations with a high temperature, and in light, sandy soils where the *C. Arabica* would not flourish. It seems also to be hoped that the introduction of a new and naturally more robust species into South India and Ceylon, may, through the natural hybridism which it is to be presumed would follow, prove a means of combating the "leaf-disease," "bug," and other blights, the devastations of which have of late years proved so alarming and disastrous; or, failing this, that the more strongly-constituted new arrival may gradually with advantage supersede the older species altogether.

Experiments of this kind are always interesting in themselves, and worth trying, both from a commercial and scientific point of view.

The *C. Arabica* is a native of Caffa, a district of Southern Abyssinia, whence it was introduced about the beginning of the fifteenth century into Yemen, a province of Arabia, formerly known as Arabia Felix. It is said, however, to have been known long previously in Persia. The plant is also believed to be indigenous in the West of Africa, in the same parallel of latitude. It seems also a question whether it may not be indigenous in Peru; at any rate, a writer, from whom I shall quote later,[1] informs us it was known in that country long before the cultivation of the plant was begun in Brazil or the West Indies. The plant is stated to have been first introduced to the notice of Europeans by Rauwolfius, who brought some specimens to Western Europe in 1573, but Alpinus has the credit of having first scientifically described it in 1591. Others state that it is to the Dutch that Europeans are indebted for their first acquaintance with the coffee plant, and that this was brought about in the following manner :—

[1] Mr W. Branson's paper, read before the Society of Arts.

Some berries which had in the first place been procured at Mocha were, it is narrated, carried to Java, and there planted, a specimen plant being sent home to Amsterdam in 1690 by Governor Wilson. This plant bore fruit in the uncongenial climate of Holland, from which many young trees were propagated, and from this original, singular to relate, most of the gardens of Europe *and the East Indies* are supposed to have been furnished. Bishop Compton first cultivated the plant in Britain, in the year 1696. In 1714 a plant was presented by the magistrates of Amsterdam to the French king, Louis XIV.; this plant was placed at Marley, under the care of Jussieu, and from this source plants were forwarded some years afterwards to the French West India Islands, and from these all the coffee now found in that part of the world derives its origin.[2]

Coffee contains valuable medicinal properties, among others that of being anti-soporific, and hence useful in cases of narcotic poisoning. From the stimulating and enlivening effect of the beverage upon the system, one would suppose that it must contain a considerable amount of nutrition. Mr. Galton, however, in his "Art of Travel" denies that either tea or coffee contain any real nutriment. Opposed to this, we have, on the other

[2] Rhind's "History of the Vegetable Kingdom."

hand, the authority of a writer in *Household Words* (1851) for affirming that there is much nutriment in Caffeine, which is the oily principle we see floating on the surface of the pure beverage. The explanation of this conflict of opinion no doubt is, that although coffee may not perhaps be absolutely and technically nutritious, it possesses a function almost equally efficacious and valuable, namely, that of restraining the metamorphosis or waste of tissue in the human body. Coffee has frequently been found the best form of stimulant for administration to persons rescued from starvation by hunger or cold, and this is the more worthy of note that ardent spirits given under the same conditions often prove fatal. Captain Parry, we are told, when on his Arctic Expedition, put his starboard watch, which was on the *exposed* side of the ship, on coffee, and the port watch on rum; and the result was, that in course of time, the "coffee watch" were found to possess a vigour of health entirely wanting in the other.[3] Mr. Branson quotes Julius Fræbel in his "Seven Years in Central America," as saying :—" For the men accompanying the great mercantile caravans, coffee is an indispensable necessity. Brandy is taken as a medicine, but coffee is quite a necessary food, and is drunk twice a day. The refreshing effects

[3] Mr. Branson.

of this beverage in heat or cold, in rainy or dry weather, are extraordinary."

From all quarters testimony without limit might be accumulated to the same effect; and, in fact, which of us is not familiar with the grateful fragrance and invigorating qualities of a good cup of coffee, whether it be on the midnight journey, in the temperature of an Indian "hot season," or during exposure to the equally formidable winter of more northern latitudes?

As a disinfecting agent, roasted coffee is invaluable. Dr. Shortt of Madras tells us, "It is useful to purify any place having an offensive smell, or foul air." The coffee beans should be roasted in the vicinity of the room to be fumigated, and when brown, and while quite hot, placed in the centre, the doors and windows being meanwhile closed: by the time the coffee has cooled, the room will have been rendered thoroughly pure and sweet.

It is evident that the merits of coffee as a beverage would have remained unknown, but for the discovery of the value of the roasting process. For this discovery we are indebted to the Persians, who practised this method of preparing it, long before it was known to the Arabs. The name of the fire-worshipper who thus became a benefactor to mankind has not, unfortunately, been preserved.

It is stated that the Mufti of Aden, when on a journey to pay homage to his superior in Persia, saw the processes of roasting, grinding and boiling the coffee, which on his return he introduced into Arabia. There was considerable opposition raised by the "true believers" at first to the use of coffee, as, judging from its stimulating effects that it must possess properties akin to those of alcohol, they supposed it would properly come under the ban of the Koran. The Sultan, however, did away with this difficulty by issuing a proclamation authorizing its use, upon which booths for its preparation and sale were at once erected in all directions. The consumption of coffee among the Turks has ever since continued very great, which may be in some measure, perhaps, accounted for by their being debarred by their religion from the use of wines and spirituous liquors. So necessary did coffee soon come to be considered among the people, that the refusal to supply it in sufficient quantity to a wife was recognized as a sufficient ground upon which she might sue for a divorce.

The Turks drink their coffee very hot and strong, and without sugar; sometimes they add to the decoction, when boiling, a clove or two bruised, or a few seeds of starry aniseed, some of the lesser cardamoms, or a drop of essence of amber.

In England the use of coffee at first met with

violent opposition, as has indeed been the case with almost every new article introduced among our truly conservative countrymen. It was denounced as a "hell-drink," "hell-poison," and in other equally uncompromising terms, and a heavy tax was imposed on it by the Legislature. This tax seems to have been levied by *the gallon*, and it is thus not quite easy to see its exact incidence on the berry, as this would of course depend on the strength of the infusion.

The English owe to Mr. Edwards, a Turkey merchant, their knowledge of the art of preparing coffee as a beverage. This gentleman, about the year 1650, brought to England a Greek youth named Pasqua Rosee, who used to prepare the drink for his master. The latter, however, as the story goes, finding the novelty begin to attract too many visitors to his house, gave Pasqua his liberty, and enabled him to open a coffee-house on his own account in St. Michael's Alley, Cornhill, in partnership with an Englishman (a servant of Mr. Edwards' son-in-law). According to some accounts, this would seem to be the first coffee-house opened in this country, but other chroniclers relate that one had been established in Oxford some two years previously. These institutions flourished so exceedingly that it is said, in twelve months there were in London as many coffee-houses as in Constantinople, and from that time to the present they have succeeded in holding their own in the metropolis, the very word being replete with pleasant associations of the literature and refinement of the last two centuries. From the late Mr. Timbs' work on "London Club-houses," I take the following extract, being the original handbill by which Pasqua Rosee advertised his Coffeehouse in St. Michael's Alley:—

"THE VERTUE OF THE COFFEE-DRINK, *First made and publicly sold in England by Pasqua Rosee.* The grain or berry called Coffee, groweth upon little trees only in the deserts of Arabia. . . . It is a simple, innocent thing, composed into a drink, by being dried in an oven, and ground to powder, and boiled up with spring water, and about half a pint of it to be drunk fasting an hour before, and not eating an hour after, and to be taken as hot as possibly can be endured; the which will never fetch the skin off the mouth, or raise any blisters by reason of that heat. . . . . The quality of the drink is cold and dry (*sic*); and though it be a drier, it neither heats nor inflames more than hot posset. It so encloseth the orifice of the stomach, and fortifies the heat within, that it is very good to help digestion; and therefore of great use to be taken about three or four o'clock, afternoon, as well as in the morning.

It much quickens the spirits, and makes the heart lightsome ; . . . . It suppresseth fumes exceedingly, and therefore is good against the headache, and will very much stop any defluxion of rheums that distil from the head upon the stomach, and so prevent and help consumptions and the cough of the lungs. It is excellent to prevent and cure the gout, dropsy, and scurvy. It is known to be better than any other drying drink for people in years, or children that have any running humours upon them, as the King's Evil, &c. It is a most excellent remedy against the spleen, hypochondriac winds, and the like. It will prevent drowsiness, and make one fit for business, if one have occasion to watch, and therefore you are not to drink of it after supper, unless you intend to be watchful. . . . It is observed that in Turkey, where this is generally drunk, that they are not troubled with the stone, gout, dropsy, or scurvy, and their skins are exceeding clear and white. It is neither laxative nor restringent.

"*Made and sold in St. Michael's Alley, in Cornhill, by Pasqua Rosee, at the sign of his own head.*"

Mr. Timbs also tells us, that in the French colonies, where coffee is more used than among the English, gout is scarcely known.

It is not only the *berry* of the coffee plant

which contains medicinal virtue. I am informed that an infusion made of the leaves, has, in the absence of more powerful tonics, been found very beneficial. This is the less to be wondered at when we remember that the plant is allied to the family of the *Cinchonaceæ*, which yields us the invaluable specific antidote to fever, quinine.

It seems to be an unfailing rule of Nature, guided as she is by an all-wise and bountiful Providence, to allow no evil to exist within her realm, without providing a remedy near at hand; and doubtless the further we become acquainted with her ways, or, in other words, with SCIENCE, the more invariable this arrangement will be found; in support of this theory, it has been observed that coffee flourishes best in malarious localities, and where, consequently, fevers are prevalent.

The decoction from the leaves, the latter being previously dried in the same manner as those of the tea plant, yields a not unpleasant beverage, and one for which a taste might soon be acquired under favourable circumstances. The difficulty in preparing the leaves for use appears to consist in the necessity for preserving their greenish hue when dry, a secret said not in the meantime to be in the possession of Europeans; though a Dr. Gardner exhibited specimens of the leaves dried for use as coffee-tea at the Great Exhibition of 1851, and took out a patent to protect his method.

"Coffee-tea," as the infusion of the leaves may be called, is the common beverage of the natives of Sumatra, and it can, therefore, hardly be unwholesome, even if deficient in nutritious properties. Unfortunately, it does not appear to possess the deliciously aromatic flavour of the decoctions made from either the roasted coffee bean or from tea-leaves; rather, indeed, resembling, according to my judgment, what might be expected as the result of a mixture of both. In answer to this objection, however, it must be borne in mind, that the taste for some of the most valuable productions of nature has been an acquired one in the first instance, while in the end they rely for the favour in which they are held upon their intrinsic good qualities. When required for infusion the coffee leaves should be gathered fresh off the trees, and then dried in a pan over a slow fire until of a clear brown colour; during which process the *Caffeine*, or volatile oily principle (which is almost identical with that of the tea-plant, and known as *Theine*), becomes fixed. The leaves may then be put in the tea-pot, boiling water being poured over them, and the infusion drunk with milk and sugar, in the same manner as tea proper.

Though possessing slightly tonic and stimulant

properties, "coffee-tea" has not the same exciting effect as the decoction from the roasted bean; but against this it should be borne in mind, that it can be produced and sold at less than *one-fifth* of the cost of the latter. The price of prepared coffee leaves in Sumatra is about three halfpence per pound, and this price is remunerative to the planter. It could thus be very well imported and sold in England at twopence per pound! Dried coffee leaves contain about $1\frac{1}{4}$ per cent. of *Theine*, or $\frac{1}{4}$ per cent. more than the bean; they also contain more of another characteristic principle, Caffeic acid; the great difference in the properties of the two being, apparently, that while the bean contains about 12 per cent. of fat and 7 per cent. of sugar, the leaf possesses but little of either. While, therefore, evidently less nutritious than the bean, the product of the leaves would probably prove better suited to delicate digestive organisms.

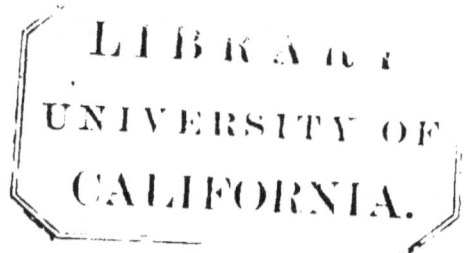

CHAPTER II.

Coffee, Countries known in—Latitude it frequents—Introduction into Ceylon and S. India—Munzerabad—Discovered at Manantoddy—First cultivated by Europeans—So-called indigenous species in Neilgherries—Ceylon—Hangurankette—Sir Edward Barnes—His estate—Kondesalla—Durability of Coffee property—Position of the Enterprise in Ceylon—Labourers—S. India districts—The Wynaad—Manantoddy—The Neilgherries—Ootacamund — Labour — Elevation —Munzerabad—Coorg—Mercara—Game—The Natives—Rainfall—The Shervaroys—Climate—Prospects for Ceylon and S. India—Slavery in Brazil—State of affairs in Java—Government monopoly—Diminishing production.

AT the present time coffee is to be found growing in Brazil, Peru and Central America, Java and Sumatra, Ceylon and Southern India, Africa (including Abyssinia, Natal, Gold Coast, Liberia, &c.), Arabia, Manilla, the Mauritius, in the West India Islands, and in the Islands of the Pacific. The plant is tropical, and has been observed to flourish best between the 5th and 15th degrees of latitude, north and south of the equator, and to affect mountainous regions; in other words, situations in which a temperate climate is to be met with within the tropics. My experience of coffee-planting having been gained in Ceylon and Southern India, the present work will be found naturally to refer more particularly to the cultivation of the plant in those countries.

By whom or at what date the coffee plant was first introduced into Ceylon and S. India, is not very clear; but there is little doubt this must have occurred *at least* a couple of centuries ago. It may probably have found its way eastward from Southern Arabia, in coasting craft, at a very early period; indeed, the natives of Mysore have a tradition that it was brought into the Munzerabad or Chick Moogloor districts by an Arab, between 400 and 500 years ago. Trees, then evidently of great age, were first observed in the Coorg territory half a century ago, and at Manantoddy in the Wynaad, a tree, then supposed to be fully thirty years old, was noticed about the year 1839 by Captain Bevan, Commandant of the place, who thought the circumstance sufficiently interesting to be specially reported to the Government of the day.

The systematic culture of the plant by Europeans does not appear to have been begun in India more than about thirty years ago, although I remember seeing it stated, in an old work dated 1802, that coffee had *then* been some time under cultivation in the *East Indies*. The reference here, no doubt, is to the Islands of Java, Sumatra, &c., which at one time all came under that denomination.

A gentleman residing in the Neilgherries informed me of the existence of what he believed to be an indigenous or at least a wild species of coffee, in the forests clothing those mountains, and which, he said, was well known to the Todars or aboriginal inhabitants. I must, however, doubt the correctness of my friend's impression, the probable origin of which is the growth of wild coffee plants in the woods, from seeds let fall by birds, squirrels, monkeys and other pillagers of the coffee plantations. It is quite common to find the forests in the neighbourhood of coffee estates in Ceylon, largely stocked with plants in the same manner.

Dr. Shortt in his work tells us, that coffee was introduced into Ceylon by the Arabs, prior to the invasion of that island by the Portuguese, and that the Dutch, after introducing it into Java in 1690, began its culture in Ceylon. He adds, that on the cession of the latter island by the Dutch, the cultivation was taken up by the Cingalese, and that during the British occupation of Ceylon the article was freely bartered by the Mahommedan traders at Galle and Colombo. The natives of Ceylon seem, in the first instance, to have cultivated the plant mainly, if not solely, with the view of obtaining its fragrant white blossom for the decoration of the temple shrines; hence it was first found largely grown at Hangurankette, some sixteen miles from Kandy, where there were at one time an important Buddhist establishment and a royal palace. From this centre, the plant had been propagated freely throughout the forest, covering the adjacent mountain slopes; and as soon as its value became known (after the Kandian dominion had passed into the hands of the English), the entire tract producing the precious plant was bought from the Government by a wealthy and intelligent native, at the then upset price of five shillings an acre. The fortunate proprietor, whose descendants still, I believe, hold the property, realized, as may be supposed, within a short time a handsome fortune by his sagacity.

Sir Edward Barnes, the energetic governor to whom is due the credit of having united Kandy with the coast at Colombo by a really magnificent carriage road,—which at the time produced a profound impression on the native mind, though now cast into the shade, and in great measure superseded, by the railway—was the first to bring British capital and energy to bear upon the cultivation of coffee on a large scale. His estate,

Gangaroowa, which was first planted about the year 1825, is still under cultivation, and up to the time the writer bade adieu to the island was being carried on by his son. It is situated within about four miles of Kandy, on the banks of the Mahavilla Ganga river, and faces the Botanical Gardens of Peradenia—a drive to which forms one of the earliest and most agreeable excursions of the visitor to the mountain capital. There are some other very old estates, planted probably about the same time, in the neighbourhood of Kandy, among which may be named Koondasalla.[1]

Such facts as these are encouraging to the intending cultivator, as tending to prove the *durability* of coffee property—a branch of the subject upon which I shall have more to say in another place.

While upon planting in Ceylon, I cannot do better than furnish the reader with some particulars as to the present position of the enterprise in that island. These are principally culled from that valuable compendium of information, "Ferguson's Ceylon Directory" (1875).

There are now 37 districts in Ceylon in which

---

[1] I believe I am correct in saying that Mr. George Bird, whom I had the pleasure of knowing for a short time before his death, in Kandy, in 1855 or 1856, was the first practical European planter in the island:

the cultivation of coffee is carried on, containing in all 1351 properties, of which 1215 are in course of cultivation; these are under the management of nearly 1000 European superintendents and assistants. The total extent of the above 1351 properties is 481,539 acres, giving an average of 360 acres to each; the total cultivated area, however, is only 249,604 acres, which gives an average of 205 acres to each of the 1215 plantations. The average crop per acre of land *in bearing*, has ranged during the 20 years from 1856 to 1875, from the highest point 5·07 cwts. per acre in 1868, to 2·75 cwts. in 1874—the general average for the 20 years being rather under 4·25 cwts. per acre. The largest estate in Ceylon is Hunasgiriya, with 1986 acres of land under actual cultivation.

The number of labourers employed on the plantations is about 220,000, drawn from Southern India, chiefly from the districts of Madura, Tinnevelly, Tanjore and Trichinopoly, though Mysore furnishes a considerable contingent. These Coolies are brought over by "Kanganies," or native "Gangers," who have received money advances from the estate managers to enable them to furnish funds for preliminary expenses to each Cooly who enrols himself under their guidance. The usual time for their arrival in Ceylon is between May and October, and for their return home between

January and April. Many Coolies remain two or three years in Ceylon on the same estate, while others will only remain one season: on most estates it is usual for about one-third of the gang to return to their country every year, in rotation. The ferry by which they cross at Manaar (should they take the North road homewards) is under Government management; and vessels are also provided enabling them to return by Colombo to Tuticorin, Negapatam, &c., on payment of a small fare. The Legislature has enacted just and impartial provisions regulating minutely the relations of these labourers and their employers, by which both master and servant are greatly benefited.

Cingalese labour is available for contract works, such as felling and clearing, sawing, building lines, stores, &c., and is thus far efficient and satisfactory. The Cingalese are also excellent carpenters.

The coffee crops are principally cured at Colombo, which is the port of shipment and possesses a large number of curing establishments, with machinery and appliances of a highly elaborate description.

The planting districts of SOUTHERN INDIA are the *Wynaad*, *Neilgherry* districts, *Coorg*, and parts of *Mysore*, *Travancore*, and the *Shervaroy Hills*.

The Wynaad.

The Wynaad is a district of the Madras Presidency in the Collectorate of Malabar, about 70 miles long, and averaging about 25 in width. It lies above the Western Ghauts, within the 11° and 12° of north latitude, and is bounded on the north and east by Coorg, Mysore, and the Neilgherries. It is, for the sake of convenience rather than officially, divided into north, south and south-east Wynaad. The district contains no town deserving of the name, though Manantoddy in the north, Culputty in the south, and Goodaloor in the south-east division, would perhaps be so styled by their inhabitants. The principal of these, Manantoddy, was formerly garrisoned by a native Infantry detachment, under the command of a European officer, and figures in the despatches of Colonel Wellesley, written in the time of the wars between the British and Hyder Ali and his son Tippoo Saib; no troops have, however, been kept there for some years now. The Cutcherry, Police and Post-offices, with the Travellers' Bungalow, are the principal buildings, but there are besides three or four European residences situated on eminences in the immediate neighbourhood, a good native bazaar, one or two general stores kept by Parsees, and finally a club-house, which is the *rendezvous* of the planters from the surrounding districts, when business, or the desire for a little social recreation with their friends, leads them to visit the place.

North Wynaad communicates with the western coast by three roads, known respectively as the Terriout, Cotiaddy, and Perria Ghauts; the last-named, leading to the port of Tellicherry, being by far the most accessible and generally used. South Wynaad is connected with Calicut by the Tambracherri Ghaut. North and South Wynaad are connected with each other by two roads, one by way of Culputty, and the other *viâ* Terriout; there is also a road to Mysore, and one to Ootacamund *viâ* Goodaloor.

The coffee crops are conveyed to the coast for curing and shipment, those from the northern division to Tellicherry, and those from the south to Calicut, principally on pack bullocks.

The NEILGHERRY HILLS are a spur of the Western Ghaut range, running eastward, and form a bold and lofty group of mountains containing the culminating elevation of this part of India at upwards of 8000 feet above the sea level. The chief town is Ootacamund, the sanitarium *par excellence* of the Madras Presidency, this contains many commodious European residences, a club, hotel, and European as well as native shops. Ootacamund, and the adjacent stations, Coonoor and Wellington, are resorted to each hot season by large numbers of European families from the low country, who here, within twenty-four hours' journey of Madras (the railway now extending to the very foot of the Ghaut), find a climate unsurpassed, perhaps, in the world.

Ootacamund is approached by four ghauts or passes, the Coonoor, Kotagherry, Seegoor, and Neddiwuttum or Goodaloor Ghauts; the mountain slopes adjacent to these approaches being covered with coffee plantations on every side. Labour is not over abundant, the climate being found rather too cold and wet for the natives of the low countries, but many advantages of soil and climate render the district eminently suited for coffee cultivation, which, as well as that of tea and cinchona, is carried on successfully and on a large scale. Some of the plantations are situated as much as 6000 feet above the sea; in fact, at a greater elevation than I have seen coffee cultivated elsewhere. The port of shipment is Calicut, to which the crops are conveyed a considerable part of the distance by water.

Munzerabad is the principal district in which coffee-planting is carried on in Mysore; plantations were here begun as early as thirty years ago. The port of shipment is Mangalore.

Coorg is a district some sixty miles in diameter, situated above the Western Ghauts to the south of

Mysore. It is a native state, the administration being controlled by a European officer or superintendent, who is responsible to the Supreme Government at Calcutta. Its capital, Mercara, or as it is pronounced by the natives, "Mudkerry," is situated about 4500 feet above the sea, and contains a travellers' bungalow, several European residences, a fort garrisoned by native infantry, Protestant and Roman Catholic churches, and a very considerable bazaar. Mercara is planted on the very summit of the mountain, being approached by three excellent carriage roads, one from the coast *viâ* Veerajenderpett (Tellicherry and Cannanore being equally fifty miles distant), another from Mangalore, also distant fifty miles, and the third from Mysore.

There are several coffee estates in the immediate vicinity of Mercara, while within a few miles on the slopes of the hills lie thousands of acres of plantations, whose area is constantly being increased.

Labour is drawn chiefly from the Mysore, as is the case in the Wynaad, but is cheaper and more abundant, the district being apparently preferred by the Canarese to the latter one, owing, no doubt, to the cheapness of food grains.

The lower parts of the district are covered with bamboo jungle interspersed with forest trees, the higher lands being clothed with a dense and luxuriant forest. The soil is on the whole rich and fertile. The country abounds with game, including bison, sambur, deer, pea-fowl, &c., and the natives, a pleasant, high-spirited race, are all keen sportsmen, seldom going abroad without a fowling-piece and stock of ammunition.

Veerajenderpett is the chief town or village of the lowlands, its market supplying the wants of the inhabitants of the surrounding district in food and clothing. It promises to become a place of note, having regard to the large number of European planters settled down in its neighbourhood.

The natives of Coorg are very well disposed towards the English, whom they look upon as their deliverers from the Mysoreans, who in former times, under Hyder Ali and his son, used constantly to be making warlike inroads upon their country, slaughtering the inhabitants and carrying off their cattle. In our wars with the Mysore, the Coorgs rendered the British commanders important services.

The annual rainfall of Coorg is very great, being about 150 inches, occurring principally between the 1st of June and the 1st of October.

The SHERVAROY HILLS are situated in the centre of the Madras Presidency, being about equidistant from Madras and Beypore. The coffee plant is said to have been first introduced upon their slopes about the year 1820, by a Mr. Cockburn. Its cultivation has not, however, made great progress so far, nor is the yield large. Possibly these hills may be situated too far from the sea-coast, the climate being thus too dry for the successful prosecution of coffee cultivation; but I am inclined to think that by the judicious use of shade, such, for instance, as that of the jack-tree, this difficulty might be overcome. Dr. Shortt, one of the residents of Yercaud on the Shervaroy Hills, informs us, in his work, that there are 5000 acres under cultivation.

The town of Salem, containing some 40,000 inhabitants, is situated at the foot of these hills, and as the Madras and Beypoor railway passes the town, great advantages in connexion with the supply of labour as well as transit are afforded to the district.

In a paper read some time ago before the Society of Arts, by Mr. W. Branson, on the present condition of the growth of coffee, he reviews the prospects of South India and Ceylon as coffee-producing countries, as compared with those of Brazil, Java, &c. Mr. Branson lays it down as a fixed principle, that the total extinction of slavery and forced labour in whatever part of the world is only a question of time, and that the freed African is physically incapable of becoming an industrious labourer in a tropical climate. In support of these conclusions, he instances the entire collapse of the planting industry in Jamaica (an island at one time producing an annual crop of 13,000 tons), in consequence of the abolition of slavery. He consequently argues that in Brazil, which is at present the largest producing country (yielding a crop of 250,000 tons, or *half the world's supply*), and which is entirely dependent on slave labour, the enterprise must eventually diminish, if not die out altogether. Already a struggle has begun in that country in reference to the slave question, the Government, led by its enlightened emperor, being in favour of manumission, which is, however, vehemently opposed by the cultivators. The difficulties which must necessarily accompany a discussion of this kind are already being felt, and the exports for some years past have fallen off 200,000 bags per annum. Mr. Branson next glances at the state of affairs in Java, the annual yield of which may be roughly stated at 80,000 tons. Here, we learn, the cultivation is carried on by tribute, or partially forced labour. The Government hold a monopoly of the land, each family being allotted its farm on condition of planting and keeping in bearing 650 coffee trees, and gathering and delivering this crop into the Government warehouse, in return for a payment of thirty-five shillings, which, as the crop is about two cwts. only, amounts to seventeen shillings and sixpence per cwt. The Government in addition, carries on a further cultivation directly on its own account, by means of Malay labourers. "Under this system," says Mr. Branson, "so little in accord with the progress of civilization, the limit of production has been passed, and the yearly export is now 100,000 bags less than that of ten years ago." He thus sums up his conclusions:—"The difficulties connected with labour in Java and Brazil have a constant tendency to contract their production, so that whether this decreases, or the world's consumption increases in the ratio of the last twenty years, but one conclusion can be arrived at. Ceylon and Southern India will rapidly become the most valuable and important coffee-growing countries in the world, offering every year an ever-widening field for British capital and enterprise."

CHAPTER III.

Acquiring land in Ceylon—The upset price—Present value of forest-land — Rules for S. India compared — Property intrinsically less valuable—Why—Private titles more advantageous—Coffee Land Assessment—Rules in Coorg.

IF land is required in Ceylon, should it belong to Government, application must be made at the Court of the Agent, or Chief Revenue Official of the district or province in which the land is situated. Within a reasonable time after this application has been sent in, the block within the specified boundaries will be gone over by the Government surveyor—if indeed this had not been done previously—and carefully surveyed. Should there be grass-land adjacent, a certain proportion of this will be included with the forest-land, and an advertisement will then be published in the *Government Gazette*, and in the newspapers, giving the name of the applicant, and naming a day for the sale of the entire tract by public auction, at the Cutcherry or Civil Court of the district. The "upset" price fixed by the Government for forest-land is £1 per acre, but so great has been the competition among buyers of late years, that really suitable and desirable forest cannot now be secured at anything like this price. Up to 1865 land had begun to change hands freely at prices as high as £8 per acre; while, since then, owing to the high prices ruling for coffee in the European markets of late years, even this sum has frequently been largely exceeded, in some cases from £15 to £25 per acre having been paid, prices which cannot but be looked upon as highly speculative. The purchaser becomes a freehold proprietor, the land being subject to no taxes or restrictions of any kind.

These Government rules will thus be seen to be fair and liberal in a country where, in pursuance of an enlightened and energetic policy, as displayed in the construction of railways, roads, and bridges, and in careful protective legislation, much has been done to add to and render permanent the value of the land thus disposed of.

In Southern India, at least in some parts of it, the state of the case is somewhat different. In the Wynaad, for example, which is to a large extent but badly provided with roads available for wheeled traffic, its rivers in many cases unspanned as yet by bridges, and sometimes even without ferries (so that a few days' rain not unfrequently suffices to render the country untraversable¹), and with a general absence of facilities for the transport of the crops to the coast; where, also, the planter has many other difficulties to encounter, all of which of course tend to render property less valuable, and the prospects of profit from the cultivation of the soil less assured, the terms on which land is to be obtained are, strange to say, far more tedious and complicated. Here application must be made to the collector, the names of the streams, or paddy fields, or other boundaries of the required land being at the same time stated: in course of time inquiries will be set on foot by the Revenue Department as to the title of the land, and should all be found to be satisfactory, it will eventually be advertised in the *Malabar Gazette*, and subsequently put up to auction at the nearest Cutcherry. The upset price is the cost of survey, but there is an

¹ The original work contains the following note, written in 1865. In the monsoon of 1864, the tappals (letter-carriers) were prevented from reaching Manantoddy for fourteen days by the flooding of the river, the raft, or "pandy," having been washed away, and all communication consequently with the coast, *viâ* Culputty, cut off. Later on in the same season communication was again interrupted for several days by the same cause. This will show how the Wynaad was situated in regard to communication at that time; since then no doubt there have been improvements effected, though even up to this time the district is far behind Ceylon in communications as well as in other particulars.

D

annual tax of 2 rupees per acre, which can only be compounded for by payment of 25 years' tax (50 rupees per acre), besides the cost of survey and any additional sum to which the bidding may have been run up by competition.

In view of these terms, the demand for Government land in the Wynaad has been less than for that owned by private holders. Many of the more important temples were originally largely endowed with lands, and as these have hitherto remained uncultivated and useless, the trustees of these endowments, as well as other native proprietors, have usually been found willing to dispose of suitable tracts of forest to intending planters at about 10 rupees per acre. The titles thus acquired have in general been found good, and land thus obtained is free of tax *until under cultivation*, when an assessment of 2 rupees per acre begins to be levied as on land bought from Government.

This annual tax, of 2 rupees per acre on all coffee land in full bearing, is somewhat unfair in its incidence, no consideration being given to the amount of crop yielded; it might, with advantage, be replaced by one more on the principle of the export duty levied in Ceylon of 8 annas per cwt. at the port of shipment.

In Coorg, the rules for the sale of waste lands are very favourable to the man of small means. If the land has not been already surveyed, the estimated cost of survey must be deposited with the superintendent, to whom application must be addressed. Should there subsequently prove to be a surplus remaining when the work has been done, this will be refunded to the applicant. Orders will now be given for the required survey, a date being fixed for the sale, the same being notified by public advertisement.

The upset price is 2 rupees per acre, including all surveying expenses. On the appointed day the land is sold to the highest bidder above the upset price, subject to an assessment, after four years, of 1 rupee per acre, and after nine of 2 rupees, annually.

The successful bidder is required to pay down on the day of sale 10 per cent. of the price, and the remainder within thirty days. Failing this, however, i.e. "if the purchase shall not be completed by the 30th day from the day of the sale," the purchaser may have further grace allowed him at the discretion of the superintendent, paying 12 per cent. interest on the balance of purchase-money; "without prejudice, nevertheless, to the right of resale, if not paid within one year."

At one time the Coorg Government made *free* grants of land, subject only to the condition that a certain area should be brought under cultivation within a specified time, and that then the valuable timber on such cultivated portion should be paid for at a nominal valuation, as estimated by an official.

CHAPTER IV.

Climate required for Coffee—High temperature not indispensable—Experiment in Germany—Temperate Climate required for profitable cultivation—Humidity—Elevation of 4000 to 5000 feet in Ceylon—Under 3000 feet in Wynaad—Results compared—Mean temperature required—Temperature of Ceylon hills—S. India districts—Land wind—Favourite elevation in Ceylon—Native Coffee-gardens—Below 1000 feet in Ceylon—Neighbourhood of Kandy—Change in the Climate—Temperature combined with moisture—Weeds—Black Bug—Elevation and Climate connected—Malaria—Fever—The Bamboo—Effect of clearings—The seasons—January to March—June—The Monsoón—N.E. Monsoon—Aspect — Wind — Effects—Remedial Measures—The Doombegas-tree.

THAT the coffee plant can be induced to grow, and even bear crop, in countries where frost and snow prevail in winter, is proved by the following narrative from "Dr. Willich's Encyclopædia," on the authenticity of which, he says, the reader may fully rely: "A nobleman in Germany found, in a bag of raw coffee, twenty green berries, resembling oblong cherries, and each of which contained two beans. In March, 1788, he planted them in a common garden-bed, two inches deep. In April it snowed, and was so cold that the windows were covered with ice for two days. Notwithstanding this unfavourable prospect, five of the berries appeared above ground in the latter part of June, and all the rest previous to the middle of July. They grew rapidly, being in a shady situation, and a soil somewhat sandy but well manured. In September of the same year they had attained a height of about six inches, and dropped their small leaves during Michaelmas. During the winter he covered them with a little hay, and afterwards with snow; both of which were removed in the fine weather of April. In this simple manner they were defended against the severity of German winters, and in the fifth year four of the little trees produced together seventy-six berries. By the inattention of the gardener two of the plants died in the very hard frosts of 1798; yet the remaining eighteen were all in full blossom in the ensuing spring, and yielded in autumn three pounds and a half of coffee berries, the flavour of which was not inferior to that imported from the island of Martinico."

It is thus evident that great warmth of climate is not absolutely essential to the mere existence of the plant; our object, however, goes much further than this, being to cultivate it in a climate where it will not only *live*, but flourish and bring forth fruit abundantly, and experience has clearly shown that this is only to be found within the tropics. It is not, however, to be understood that a high temperature is required in order that the most favourable conditions may be brought about. What *is* necessary is a climate characterized by neither extreme of heat or cold, and possessing a fair amount of humidity all the year round.

If invited to be more precise, I would specify 60 and 80 degrees of Fahrenheit in the shade as the limits of temperature; and with regard to humidity, I would stipulate that there should be no month in the year entirely without rainfall, and that from 100 to 150 inches should be distributed throughout the twelve.

At an elevation of between 4000 and 5000 feet above sea-level, in Ceylon, one sees, supposing the situation to be not unduly exposed to wind, fields of dark, ever-green, luxuriant coffee-trees, so well clothed with foliage that not a square yard of bare ground is visible for acres. Such situations have what may fairly be called an *exceedingly* humid climate: probably hardly a week passes without rainfall, while at certain seasons this occurs without intermission for weeks together; even after a fair bright noon-day a dense white mist will frequently settle down towards evening, wrapping all in obscurity, and saturating vegetation with moisture. The temperature here will probably seldom rise above 70° in the shade, at other times falling as low as 50°. The general result is, that although the trees have a gloriously healthy appearance, they bear hardly any crop.

Turn from this picture to the Wynaad, say to an estate some few miles inland from the Ghauts, with an aspect facing eastward towards the Mysore plateau, and at an elevation of something less than 3000 feet. Here will be found a climate possessing great heat, and entirely deprived of rainfall during a considerable part of the year. True, there are showers in the spring months, while a perfect deluge may be looked for while the monsoon lasts, during the months from June to August inclusive, but it is strictly correct to say that there are several months every year during which not a drop of rain falls—droughts of four or even five months being not unusual. Day after day the sun blazes forth ; to use the powerful language of Scripture, "the heavens are as brass and the earth as iron ;" the soil opens in fissures, the jungles become parched and bare, and all nature seems to gasp for moisture. The effect of this ordeal upon the coffee is at once apparent; the plant, although not by nature deciduous, beginning first to droop, and finally losing nearly all or much of its foliage year after year, until eventually it falls a prey to the effects of exhaustion in one form or other.

The foregoing have been brought forward as two opposite representatives of climate; the first being characterized by too great a degree of humidity for successful coffee cultivation, as is shown by the fact that although the plants produce a redundance of wood and foliage, their productiveness ends there, the crop being at all times nearly absent, or very deficient; while, in the second case the long dry season tends ultimately, though gradually, to kill the plants.

It would, therefore, seem natural to infer that somewhere between the two, we shall meet with the exact climate most conducive to the growth, productiveness, and longevity of the coffee plant; and this appears to be fully borne out by experience.

The climate of the mountain districts of Ceylon owes its humidity in great measure to insularity of position. The continual warm exhalations which ascend from the land create a vacuum, into which a corresponding influx of atmosphere from all points of the compass is constantly attracted, and this atmosphere must ever be charged with the moisture evaporated by the sea, which is in due course once more condensed and poured down upon the hills and valleys in the form of dews and rain;

the temperature of the island being also regulated and cooled by the same process.

The coffee districts of Southern India, on the other hand, having the sea on one side only, and a wide stretch of bare level country on the other, have a less temperate, that is to say, a hotter climate, and are visited by but little rain except at those seasons when the prevailing wind comes from the ocean, namely during the south-west monsoon, which extends over less than half the year. During the north-east monsoon months, the wind passes over hundreds of miles of a country scorched with the rays of a sun at this season nearly vertical, and is thus converted into a furnace blast burning up all before it, and which under the term "land wind" is commonly recognized as injurious alike to animals and vegetation.

The effect of the difference brought about by these causes between climates of Ceylon and south-western India, is evident enough in the vegetation of the two countries; it being observable that plants which flourish in Ceylon at an elevation of say 3000 feet, are not found on the mountains lining the Indian continent, until we have attained a level of some 4000 or 4500 feet; and due allowance must always be made for this difference in treating the question of elevation, in connexion with coffee or other cultivation in the respective localities.

The favourite and most fruitful coffee districts in Ceylon some years ago were, and probably still are, those situated at an elevation ranging from 2500 to 3500 feet, although there are coffee estates under cultivation at all elevations, from about 500 to over 5000 feet, while native gardens may be met with, sometimes bearing good crops along the coast actually at sea-level. In these cases, however, the plants will invariably be found growing under the shade of the jack, cocoa-nut, or other suitable trees, without which protection all chance of their thriving permanently would be out of the question. These native gardens are, moreover, limited in extent, and are generally richly manured, and often well watered during the dry season.

The foregoing conclusions will be found further borne out in those districts of Ceylon in which coffee cultivation has been attempted below 1000 feet elevation, such as Cornegalle, Kaigalle, &c.; abandoned properties on every side bearing evidence that humidity and rainfall have been insufficient to neutralize the high temperature. In the neighbourhood of Kandy there are properties which, even at 1800 feet above sea-level, seem to owe their present existence chiefly to shade and irrigation. On some of them powerful irrigating machinery and appliances are kept constantly in operation during the dry season.

Of late years, new districts have been opened up in Ceylon, which would formerly, owing to their great elevation, have been looked upon as next to hopeless; while some of the more elevated properties, which formerly yielded little or no crop, are said to have of late years become more fruitful, owing apparently to an increased temperature and diminished atmospheric humidity, brought about by the constant extension of forest clearings in that island. This fact would seem to make the prospects of the low-lying districts appear more discouraging than ever, i. e. in the exact proportion that the change has benefited those which had previously suffered from cold and wet.

On the supposition, then, that a mean elevation of between 2500 and 3500 feet will be found the most eligible climate for coffee in Ceylon, it would thus appear that an elevation equally suitable in Southern India is to be looked for at from 3500 to 5000 feet; while in the Neilgherries we find the cultivation successfully carried on, and the plant eminently productive at as high as 6000 feet. The limit must, however, always be sharply drawn at that point where frost begins to occur, even though it be only at night and during but a short period of the year.

Coffee can always bear a considerable warmth of climate, provided the humidity be proportionate;

indeed a hot climate will probably produce the heaviest crops *provided it be sufficiently humid.* Such a climate, however, will probably prove very malarious and inimical to the health of the planter and his labourers—a drawback not to be disregarded ; while the growth of weeds will also probably be so rapid, as to cause a considerable increase of outlay in cultivation and abnormal deterioration of the soil. So great is the influence of climate upon the growth of weeds, that while in some districts two monthly weedings will be found necessary, in other and colder situations one such operation every five or six weeks will be found sufficient.

High, wet situations, again, prove in many instances strongholds of the blight known as "black bug," which may probably be taken as some indication that the trees are deficient in healthy tone and vigour.

From the foregoing, it will be seen that the questions of elevation and climate are so intimately connected that it is impossible to treat them apart ; elevation alone being capable of rendering cool and temperate a climate within the "torrid zone" or tropics—and a temperate climate within the tropics being indispensable to the successful cultivation of coffee. This is so far fortunate for those engaged in the pursuit, and is no doubt one of the principal reasons of its being so favourably regarded by young Britons on the look out for a sphere of enterprise abroad. In fact, the climate which is most favourable for coffee, is that in which an Englishman will find little to complain of, except in some cases malariousness. The latter quality, it must be admitted, prevails to some extent in certain districts, though principally in those which are deficient in elevation. Thus, in Ceylon, fever is prevalent during certain seasons, particularly in Cornegalle, a district which, it will be remembered, is referred to above as one of those in which coffee has been planted at an insufficient elevation, while in Hewahettie, Rangalla, and other districts which lie at about 3000 feet elevation, the affection is but little known. Similarly in the lower districts of the Wynaad, Coorg, &c., malaria obtrudes its influence unpleasantly during the spring months, while the higher Neilgherry districts are almost entirely free from it.

It has been remarked, that fever may be always looked for in those districts where the bamboo flourishes, and that as soon as one gets out of the region of the bamboo, the limit of fever is also passed. This is probably simply a question of elevation, the bamboo ceasing to find a congenial home at 3500 feet above the sea. It is also satisfactory to know, that the clearing away of forest necessitated by coffee culture, has had the effect of rendering the climate in many districts much more healthful than formerly. A curious proof of this is found in the case of an estate not far from Kandy, which many years ago acquired the ominous appellation of the "white man's grave," that part of the country being now almost as free from malaria as the town of Kandy itself.

At from 3000 to 4000 feet in Ceylon, and some 1000 feet higher in S. India, the temperature is seldom other than mild and agreeable. Exertion is still a pleasure to the European, and the planter, free from the depressing languor which eventually settles down upon his countrymen in the plains, pursues with cheerfulness, not to say enjoyment, the arduous out-door duties inseparable from his calling, and commonly returns to his native country after a term of years, with health but little impaired, to enjoy the fruits of his industry and enterprize. European flowers and fruits flourish often to perfection in these situations in addition to those of the tropics. Thus, the high-roads are often bordered by luxuriant hedges of the rose, laden with magnificent white, pink, and crimson clusters, charming the eye, and charging the breezes with their delicious perfume. Scarlet geraniums, fuchsias, &c., flourish in almost equal profusion; while pineapples, oranges, limes, citrons, mulberries, loquats, guavas, and other fruit-trees yield their produce freely with but little nursing or persuasion. Any one taking the trouble to keep a garden, can easily keep himself supplied all the year round with vegetable marrow, cucumbers, cabbages, lettuce, potatoes, tomatoes and capsicums, besides many pleasant and wholesome vegetables purely indigenous and unknown elsewhere.

In general terms the *seasons* may be thus described. During December, January, February, and March, the winter months, the rainfall is trifling; the thermometer may range from 75 to 80 in the shade at noon, the temperature being so cold and invigorating from sunset to sunrise, that indoors fires, and at night blankets are by no means unacceptable. April and May are also pleasant months, though the occasional showers and thunderstorms alternating with hot sunshine, which now precede the south-west monsoon, render the atmosphere, if more favourable to vegetation, unfortunately less healthful to man. The coffee plants, previously somewhat enervated by the long continuance of comparatively dry weather, now begin to assume a more vigorous appearance. The thunderstorms referred to, accompanied by heavy falls of rain, generally come on in the afternoon after hot sunshine, and a considerable evaporation of miasma ensues, causing in some situations a general tendency to fever, dysentery, &c., among the natives, whose meagre diet and consequent comparatively weakly physique probably account for their being more subject to such influences than the European, who is not only naturally more robust, but fortified against them by being better fed, clothed, and housed.

Early in June, or earlier in some parts, heavy masses of cloud begin to gather on the south-west horizon, fitful squalls arrive from the same quarter, and finally a day or two of driving mist, accompanied by angry thunder crashes, usher in the "burst of the monsoon." This is the great atmospheric phenomenon of the eastern tropics. Sheets of rain fall with a vehemence and persistency unknown in temperate latitudes: the wind roars day after day through the forest, the sky is overcast, while the sun, as if exhausted with his previous exertions, appears to have made up his mind to withdraw permanently behind the interminable masses of rolling vapour—the climate in fact is completely metamorphosed. With short "breaks" of fine weather, like angels' visits, few and far between, this state of things is continued till August, when pleasant peeps of sunshine make animated nature smile once more after the beneficial, though to all appearance stern ordeal it has passed through. Towards the end of August the weather becomes settled, and a condition of the atmosphere more in accordance with popular ideas of the tropics, again resumes its sway.

Later on, the north-east monsoon comes in and brings with it considerable rainfall. This is experienced, however, more in Ceylon than in Western India. In the former island it occasions a second "wet season," which sometimes extends with intermissions from October till near Christmas—adding, as may be supposed, considerably to the difficulty of gathering in the crop.

The point next in importance after elevation is *Aspect*, for although it will very probably not be practicable to get land exactly to one's mind in every particular, it is perfectly permissible in this as in other matters, to approach as near to perfection as circumstances will allow.

Many drawbacks it may become a necessity to submit to, but there is one which must be sedulously avoided, i. e. a bleak and exposed aspect, this being one of those evils that can neither be mitigated nor remedied. The monsoons which, as has been seen above, blow incessantly for three or four months together, are assailants which coffee bushes cannot withstand. Not unfrequently large fields of windblown coffee have had eventually to be abandoned in despair, after years of persevering and expensive culture, and if the planter has unfortunately selected a block thus circumstanced—that is to say, fully exposed to either monsoon—such will probably be the wisest course to follow.

Wind injures the plants in various ways. Sometimes its effects are at once recognizable in the pinched, stunted, and almost frost-bitten look both of the wood and leaves, the former being hard and small, the latter crumpled, dwarfed, and tipped with yellow. In other cases, the trees will be found denuded of leaves, on the side on which they are assailed, forming on the opposite one a growth somewhat like that of boxwood. In situations where the soil is soft and yielding, the wind, even if failing to strip the trees of leaves, does equal mischief by working the stems in the ground, so that in a short time a funnel is formed round the neck of the plant, and this being continually chafed, in process of time the bark is worn off, the roots are loosened, and the plant dies. A plant thus affected is said to be "wind-wrung." Should it, however, be rescued before the bark is entirely worn off, the plant will sometimes recover, though its growth will of course have been seriously interfered with, and it will be extremely liable to be attacked by "bug," "worm," or any other blight prevalent in the locality.

In wind-blown situations, however, if the mischief

is not too pronounced, partially remedial measures may be adopted, as will be shown elsewhere, and this is the more fortunate, that when a block of forest is far inland it is not always easy to ascertain from its aspect how far it may be sheltered from certain prevailing winds; indeed, a very small clearance of forest lying adjacent, will occasionally alter the direction of the wind so much, that it will only remain to remedy as far as possible what could not have been anticipated. Thus, an estate which for many years may have remained quite sheltered, has been known suddenly to become seriously affected by a belt of jungle having been cleared on a neighbouring estate, or by a new estate having been opened in the neighbourhood.

That wind should prove an enemy to the coffee plant is hardly surprising, it being inimical to every species of vegetation, even grass, unless of a particular kind, not thriving when exposed to it. All will at one time or other have seen the farmer's crops laid low by a single night's storm; what then may be expected from a continuous gale lasting through many weeks by night and day. The only exception I ever heard of to the general rule, is the Doombegas-tree of the Ceylon forests, which is said to flourish most luxuriantly in situations where the atmosphere is habitually the most boisterous; the abundance of this tree may, if this be so, possibly be some criterion as to the degree of shelter enjoyed by any particular locality.

There are vast tracts of forest in the high lands of Ceylon, and all along the crests of the Western ghauts of Southern India, which would be admirably adapted for the culture of coffee, tea, cinchona, and probably other valuable products, but for their being exposed to the full violence of the monsoon, a circumstance which will no doubt insure their preservation. This appears to be one of those wise providential arrangements which an advancing science enables us to recognize, it being well-known that the wholesale destruction of forests is one of the greatest misfortunes that can happen in countries within the tropics, whose welfare and prosperity are in every case to a very large extent dependent upon rainfall. This fact was either unknown or disregarded in many parts of the world until within recent years, but every one now understands that disforesting exercises an important effect upon the climate, reducing atmospheric humidity and rainfall, and still further diminishing water supply by causing the springs and streams to dry up. It may, therefore, be supposed that were the forest tracts above referred to, to be gradually cleared away for the purpose of cultivation, the results to the country at large would be disastrous, while the coffee planters would themselves be the first to suffer from the altered character of the climate. The clearing away of forests has further the effect of rendering climates more subject to storms and hurricanes, and the country to inundations on occasions when the rains *do* occur.

So important has this subject appeared to the Indian Government, that a Commission was at one time appointed for its consideration, the result of which has been that several useful enactments have been passed in the Madras Presidency, having for their object the preservation of a certain extent of forest in each district above a certain elevation; the native head men throughout the country being also obliged to see to the planting and due cultivation of young trees, such as banians, mangoes, jacks, &c., along the main roads passing through their districts.

Having described the ruinous effects of wind, and as the strongest and most continuous wind comes from the south-west, it will be evident that this aspect is the worst that can be chosen; neither would it be wise to select one directly opposite, this being exposed for some months of the year to the north-east monsoon. Northerly or easterly facings are perhaps the best, not being directly exposed to violent wind for any lengthened period, the latter also getting the benefit of *the morning sun*, a circumstance to which experience attaches much importance. We all know how a gardener in Northern Europe loves a southern aspect; this is because it is the *sunny side*, and also because it is sheltered from the bleak north winds. In Southern India, however, the cold winds come from the south. Any one who has made the long sea voyage to India will find it hard to forget the dreary gales encountered when rounding the Cape of Good Hope: the wild disturbed sky, the chilly atmosphere, and the groaning timbers alike betokening approach to a region cold, bleak and inhospitable. When, therefore, we consider that the south-west monsoon collects its forces in such a quarter, we can hardly be surprised that its influence on tropical vegetation should be injurious, even were the invasion characterized with less headlong violence.

The next point to be considered is what is technically termed the "lay" of the land. That there are estates situated on surfaces greatly differing in character, yet all apparently yielding results equally satisfactory, might at first sight appear to argue this subject as unimportant; but similarly an inference might be drawn that elevation was of slight conseqnence, from the fact that some estates situated at 1000 feet above the sea and others situated at 5000 appear to be equally profitable, which, however, simply arises from one drawback being often compensated for by some equivalent advantage of another description. I have always been of opinion that some of the most productive estates which have come under my observation, have owed their fertility to "lay" as much as to any other favouring circumstance.

Among the many different dispositions which the uneven, ever-varying surface of a mountain district presents, I will describe some which appear to be the most favourable for a coffee estate. Slopes are, of course, more or less the general feature observable, and they are to be recommended owing to their incapacity to retain sufficient moisture to render the soil stiff or sour. They are also favourable, owing to the soil having become enriched by the deposit of decayed vegetable matter which the rains must have left on their surface from the hills above; though once the land has been cleared this liability to "wash" becomes a drawback, as matter that might have been retained while the surface was covered with a close and minute vegetation, or by a layer of decayed leaves, is in danger of being floated off, once the soil is bare and disturbed.

A level plain lying at the base of high hills, will be likely to contain a rich surface soil, more especially if the hills which command it have been clothed with forest vegetation, as the product of the decayed leaves, &c., falling during ages, will have been partially at least washed down and deposited on it, forming in course of time a deep rich loam. There is also the advantage that the soil thus made is retained, while should there be sufficient declivity to admit of the superfluous moisture escaping, nothing will remain to be desired. One will sometimes come upon a tolerably level stretch of land along the banks of some mountain stream, and this would be a particularly desirable formation, any danger of stiffness of soil arising from want of drainage being thus obviated. Marshy land is quite fatal to the coffee plant, while a soil stiff and heavy in wet weather will be hard and impervious in the dry season, either condition being equally unfavourable.

An estate formed by the opposite sides of a gently sloping valley, provided the outlets are not towards the unfavourable aspects before described, would promise well, as each side would shelter the other, and the stream which would in all probability flow down the centre might be made available for curing operations.

One splendid property with which I was acquainted, consisted of a number of knolls or mounds rising from a broad plain, extending along the foot of a mountain slope and bounded on the other side by a running stream. Its great productiveness was always ascribed, as in great measure due to this remarkable conformation, the soil, as might be expected, being remarkably rich, while, at the same time, sweet and friable.

To sum up, from my own experience I would recommend a preference, when practicable, for moderately gentle slopes towards the base of a hill range, intersected by numerous ravines, or "nullahs," with running streams, and facing as much as possible in an easterly or northerly direction. Such a lay as this will not only be found entirely suitable, but, fortunately, is one generally not difficult to meet with in countries whose scenery is mountainous. Steep slopes are to be avoided, in consequence of the great difficulty at all times of entirely preventing the soil being washed away by the rains. Gradual slopes on the other hand are preferable to flats.

CHAPTER V.

Soil—Mr. Loudon's definition of soils for the cultivator—Organic matter—Friability—Absorbent power—Stagnant water—Vegetation a guide.

THE question of soil is one which admits of a good deal of discussion, though this need not be made a primary difficulty of by any one about to open an estate of ordinary dimensions. Commonly speaking, when the soil is dark in colour, loose, and full of roots, it is rich in organic matter, and therefore good for coffee, which is a hardy plant not on the whole difficult to please in this particular.

Planters whose estates yield heavy crops, and at the same time happen to have a light red or yellowish soil, will probaby argue in favour of that particular colour, others may have seen the best results in conjunction with a chocolate-coloured soil, others again with black. The best criterion, however, as to the quality of the soil is the luxuriousness or otherwise of the vegetation it produces in its original state. For instance, in forests which, in addition to a large growth of timber, have a dense close underwood, and which abound in creepers, mosses, ferns, &c., it may be safely concluded the soil is good.

In making an excavation in land, it will be generally noticed that the first stratum is of a dark colour, and that the shade lightens as we proceed in depth, until it gradually becomes a yellowish composition of sand, gravel, or clay, as the case may be; the thickness, then, of the upper stratum, which is the real *soil*, is the gauge of the probable productiveness of the land.

The practical cultivator on a large scale but rarely possesses a knowledge of the chemical constituents of soils, and often manages to get on tolerably well without it; but the following remarks, however, in reference to this subject from Mr. Loudon's work on "Gardening" may probably be found useful:—

"The leading soils for the cultivator are the clayey, sandy, ferruginous, peaty, saline, moist or aquatic, and dry. Plants are the most certain indicators of the nature of a soil, for, while no practical cultivator would engage with land of which he knew only the results of a chemical analysis . . . yet every one who knew the sort of plants it produced would be at once able to decide as to its value for cultivation.

"The true nourishment of plants is water and decomposing organic matter.

"Vegetable or animal matters, when finely divided, not only give coherence but likewise softness and penetrability: but neither they nor any other part of the soil must be in too great proportion.

"A certain degree of friability or looseness of texture is also required in soils, in order that the operations of culture may be easily conducted; that moisture may have free access to the fibres of the roots; that heat may be readily conveyed to them; and that evaporation may proceed without obstruction. These are commonly obtained by the presence of sand. A great proportion of sand, however, always produces sterility.

"As alumina possesses all the properties of adhesiveness in an eminent degree, and silex those of friability, it is obvious that a mixture of these two earths would furnish everything wanted to form the most perfect soil *as to water and the operations of culture.*

"The power of soil to absorb water from the air is much connected with fertility; when this power is great the plant is supplied with moisture in dry seasons. . . . The soils most efficient in supplying the plant with water by atmospheric absorption, are those in which there is a due mixture of sand, finely divided clay, and carbonate of lime, with some animal or vegetable matter, and which are so loose and light as to be freely permeable to the atmosphere. The absorbent power of soils is always the greatest in the most fertile.

"The absorption ought to be much greater in warm or dry countries; on declivities than in plains, or in the bottoms of valleys. The productiveness of soils is likewise influenced by the nature of the subsoil, or stratum on which they rest. When soils are immediately situated on a bed of rock, they are much sooner rendered dry by evaporation than when the subsoil is of clay and mud. A clayey subsoil will sometimes be of material advantage to a sandy soil. A sandy or gravelly subsoil often corrects the imperfections of too great a degree of absorbent power in the true soil.

"Stagnant water may be considered as injurious to all land plants, by obstructing perspiration, and thus rendering their roots and submerged parts diseased."

I think we may gather from the foregoing very interesting remarks, first, that luxuriant vegetation is an indication of rich soil, and also that the natural growth of certain plants may indicate the constituents of the soil. Might we not go a step further, and say that in seeking a soil adapted for successful coffee culture, it would be wise (as it would in many cases be practicable) to observe carefully the character of the vegetation on land adjacent to some highly productive plantation already under cultivation, in order to use this as a guide. Other land producing the same kind of plants would doubtless turn out equally well adapted for coffee.

Further, soil to be *rich* must contain suitably admixed proportions of sand, clay, and decomposed organic matter; and next, due proportions of coherence, friability, and power of evaporation and absorption, the latter being especially necessary in hot or dry climates.

CHAPTER VI.

Collecting labourers—The labour difficulty—Causes of it—
Coolies of the right sort—The Kangany or Maistry—
The advance system—Firmly rooted—Causes—Losses
not so frequent as might be expected—Usurious Kanganies—Contract labour—In Ceylon—In S. India—
Malabar contractors—Hill-men—Ceylon labour Ordinance—Canarese coolies—Jungle tribes, alias "Locals"—
Contracts—Imported labour—Tamil labour in Ceylon—
Labour-field for Wynaad—The climate a difficulty—
Author's experience in 1860—Engagements should be
legally binding—Written agreements—Coolie agents—
Food supply.

WHEN about to open a new estate, the first step should be to secure a gang of coolies. This is not always by any means an easy matter; indeed "the labour difficulty" is one of the most serious problems the planter has to encounter. It is a constant source of anxiety in whatever part of the coffee districts he finds himself, and fortunate will he be if at any time during his career he is able to secure the exact number of men he wants at the time he wants them. The difficulty experienced by planters generally of obtaining sufficient labour, notwithstanding the high wages they are willing to pay, is partly due, no doubt, to the easy-going disinclination of Asiatics of the lower orders to engage in permanent hard labour, and partly to the universal cheapness of food. In 1826, it was calculated a family of five persons in the Bombay Presidency, could live comfortably for one month on a sum not exceeding two rupees, eight annas, or say for about one shilling per head, and although this is hardly the case now, I have nevertheless calculated that a coolie in Ceylon can easily feed and clothe himself on less than two-thirds of his earnings, and a coolie in the Southern India districts on less than one-third. Such being the case, and having regard to native character and temperament, it is not very surprising that the labouring classes should be somewhat indifferent to the openings for money-making offered to them in return for tolerably hard work in the coffee districts; or that those of them who have been induced to give their services should, in large numbers of cases, be willing only to reside on the plantations for short periods. Coolies, in fact, have no ambition, and as a rule but little desire for wealth. So that their wants from day to day are supplied, and provided they have a few rupees to take home to their villages, they care for no more—why should they? Of course there are exceptions;

smart thrifty fellows with good health and spirits who seem to enjoy work, and who try to make as much money as they can: these are always to be seen with a neat bright-coloured jacket on their backs, and a gay handkerchief round their heads. Such are the men to get hold of, if one can. Eventually, they develope into good "Kanganies" or "Maistries," and some of them after a time arrive at the dignity of a full-blown "Head Kangany," on a salary of fifty rupees a month, and with a following of from two to three hundred men. But these instances, as it will be readily supposed, are the exceptions rather than the rule.

In order to form the nucleus of a gang, it will be necessary to secure the services of a "Kangany" or "Maistry," which can generally be done through the assistance of some planting friend, or employment may be offered to some native or Eurasian "writer" or conductor, on condition that he succeeds in bringing together a suitable gang of labourers. A sum of money will no doubt have to be paid him in advance to aid him in accomplishing this, and it will of course be desirable, if possible, to obtain from him some proper security for its repayment.

When one remembers what the temptation must be to an uneducated native of the lowest class, previously without a rupee in his possession, and brought up from childhood to regard *expediency* as the one principle by which to regulate his actions, on suddenly finding himself, as an entire stranger (for this is frequently the case), and without having produced any security or guarantee whatever, entrusted with a sum of money sufficient to support himself in comparative ease and comfort for several years, it appears a puzzle how "the advance system" could ever have been allowed to attain the proportions it has arrived at. It requires, however, but a short residence in the East to convince the new comer that he will get only a little way without having to conform to the universal practice. Should you require a pair of boots, the maker must have an advance before he sets to work; a coat made, and the tailor prefers the same demand. In nine cases out of ten were the person receiving the advance to abscond, he can with the utmost ease place himself beyond the reach of apprehension. Let us suppose, for instance, a Ceylon planter to have given a Kangany 100 rupees with which to repair to Trichinoply, Madura, or even Mysore, many hundred miles distant on the adjacent continent, and there collect a gang of labourers, what probability can there be, in the event of this man's absconding, of his being arrested and brought to justice? unless, indeed, the planter himself may possibly think it worth while to spend a month or more in travelling over India for the sake of prosecuting him; the delinquent may, in this case, be ferretted out, but even then this is by no means certain. It seems improbable, however, now, that this system of advances will be done away with in our time; in many cases the Indian ryot is too poor to leave his home without assistance, while he also requires a few rupees to leave behind with his female relatives and parents. The Kangany at least always makes this the ground of his claim for an advance, and without it he will not stir, and this, although he may have a good round sum of his own laid by somewhere, which he could quite as well make use of for the purpose, were he disposed to do so. The explanation, in cases where the borrower has no dishonest intention, is that he wishes to have as much capital at command as possible, since he manages to extort a heavy rate of interest privately for his own benefit from those among whom it is distributed.

Kanganies commonly receive advances of two, three, and even five hundred rupees in this way, and heavy losses under this heading have often to be written off on the estate books. It must, however, be admitted that these losses are by no means so frequent as might be expected. Sometimes the Kangany is an old hand belonging to the estate, and has proved himself worthy of confidence during previous service; sometimes, again, he or his friends give security for his return and due repayment. The exorbitant interest which the Kangany occasionally extorts from the poor coolies for the few rupees he lets them have (out of his master's purse), sometimes creates great dissatisfaction in the gang, and leads to grumbling and desertions—the true cause of which the unfortunate planter may probably never discover, the Kangany of course endeavouring to put him off the scent as much as possible. The unpleasantest part of this is, that in all probability the Kangany has led the victimized coolies to believe that this frightfully usurious interest is being levied for the planter's benefit and by his orders.

Contract labour should always have the preference where available, since it saves supervision and anxiety. In Ceylon, no difficulty is experienced in obtaining trustworthy and efficient contractors to undertake felling, clearing, hut-building, &c. These men, being well up to their work, merely require general instructions, and to be supplied with implements and food for their men. Such contracts are not uncommonly merely verbal, and even advances are sometimes dispensed with by Cingalese contractors, until work has actually begun. The usual plan is to pay so much per acre for felling alone, and a further sum for clearing and burning, accounts being squared when the land is finally handed over ready for culture.

In South India a more elaborate course is usually followed, a contract being signed on stamped paper in the presence of witnesses, and an advance of part payment made at once in order to render the agreement binding. There are indeed several points to be attended to, to render these agreements valid in law. It is, I believe, first necessary to state the amount of work, next the rate of remuneration, the date when work is to be commenced, when it is to be finished, and finally the amount of advance. The value of the stamp must be proportionate to the amount of the advance, and without an advance no contract of the kind is binding, according to Indian law. These formalities having been complied with, breach of contract is criminal and punishable by imprisonment. Notwithstanding all this elaborate procedure, however, I have not found the contractors in S. India at all more punctilious as to the fulfilment of their engagements than the Ceylon felling contractors— indeed, the contrary has been my experience. Along the Malabar Coast, so-called native contractors can be found ready to pledge themselves to the performance of any sort of work, under any penalty, always provided the amount of advance proposed appear sufficient to compensate for any little risk they may run of subsequent prosecution and conviction as defaulters. Europeans can sometimes be met with willing to undertake contracts of this kind, but they themselves are usually as much affected by the difficulty of getting labour as those desirous of employing them.

To render any system of contracts really satisfactory, those undertaking them should be able and willing to give some material guarantee or security for their due fulfilment, and natives seldom are either able or willing to do this. Europeans will seldom consent to do so, knowing how much their success depends on the uncertainties of the labour market.

In regard to the class of coolies to be engaged, the planter is seldom in a position to pick and choose ; he must accept those he can get ; and the first who come, and all who come, are generally received without much question. Hill-men are of course the most suitable and desirable, coffee plantations being always more or less in mountainous situations, and consequently sickness and dissatisfaction would be greatly avoided by the minimised change of climate which would thus be experienced.

In the Wynaad districts, especially, is the supply of labour fluctuating and unreliable, being as a rule unequal to the demand, while the planter is moreover weighted with the disadvantage of being often unable to retain in his service those coolies whom he has actually secured, often by means of heavy money advances,—the coolies having a tendency to abscond or to change from estate to estate on very trivial pretexts. It is much to be regretted that the Madras Government has not yet endeavoured to provide against these difficulties by drawing up a suitable Labour Ordinance, similar in its provisions to that which has been found to work so advantageously in Ceylon. At present the coolies are perfectly free *in law* to come and go as they please, not being required to give any notice before leaving, unless, indeed, they should have signed a written agreement, which is seldom the case, as they usually object to doing so. By the Ceylon Ordinance, on the other hand, a day's labour is held, in the absence of a declared understanding to the contrary, to constitute an agreement for a month ; a month's notice being always given and required before coolies leave an estate. With this rule, which no one ever dreams of complaining of or regarding as an injustice to the coolies themselves, the planter's interests are protected from mere native caprice, and he can calculate beforehand to some extent what labour he will have available at a particular season, as it is most important he should be able to do.

The Canarese, or Mysore, coolies come into the Wynaad usually between April and July, in gangs, under the leadership of a "Maistry" as in Ceylon, and return to their villages, almost *en masse*, between January and March; a much smaller number remaining on the estate than is the case in Ceylon under like circumstances. This is partly to be accounted for by the wonderful cheapness of food in their native country, which enables them to subsist after their return, for many months, on the savings of a few weeks' wages earned in the planting districts. The common food of the Canarese people is a grain named "raggee," much resembling millet, and four annas worth of this (one day's wages in the Wynaad) will support a man for a week! Animal food is but little used, except on high occasions. Another reason for the shortness of the season during which the Canarese are willing to remain at work, is their being required to return for the harvesting of the grain crops in their own village.

There is, however, another class of labour in the Wynaad and the adjacent districts, which stands the planter in good stead *as far as it goes*. This is drawn from the local hill-tribes inhabiting the jungles of the district in a semi-wild condition. These hill-tribes, who are to be found nearly all over India, are understood to be the remnants of the aboriginal inhabitants. In the Wynaad they are known as the Errawers, Adyars, Cooroombers, Punyars, Croo-chers, &c. This class of labour, however, is very desultory and uncertain, although a few of the smaller estates are entirely carried on by its means. These people are frequently hereditarily attached by families to some native owner of rice-fields, and yield a certain amount of service in ploughing, sowing and reaping, in return for food and protection during the more inclement seasons. It is probable that originally they were the slaves of the superior natives, whom, consequently, they are accustomed to look upon more as their natural employers than the European settlers. It thus happens that when rice cultivation is in progress in the village, but few hill-men can be induced to remain on the coffee estates; although, as soon as ploughing, sowing, or the ingathering of the rice crop is over, they return to offer their services to the planter, who, as a rule, is only too glad to avail himself of them.

These simple people excel in such operations as felling and clearing jungle, which, especially where the bamboo prevails, require not only patience but also considerable skill. They are also very expert in the construction of buildings in the native style, both being branches of labour in which the Canarese and Tamil labourers succeed but poorly. On estates where large extensions are the order of the day, the labour derivable from all the above sources combined has been generally found quite inadequate, more especially as at the very season when a large gang is most required by the planter for opening up new land, the different classes of labourers enumerated are employed in the cultivation of the rice-fields. In order, therefore, to meet this difficulty,. the planter has to fall back on contracts, undertaken by natives from the adjacent coast of Malabar. These contracts, although usually made at high rates, are nevertheless sufficiently remunerative when successfully carried out. Unfortunately, however, but too often the contractor, after having obtained a large cash advance, fails to carry out his undertaking, and, in some cases, absconds with the advance at the outset. Such are some of the difficulties the Wynaad planter has in the meantime to contend with, arising, as it will be seen, for the most part, in connexion with the labour question.

A coffee company formed some years ago, with the object of cultivating land in the Wynaad on an extensive scale, being fully convinced of the impossibility of proceeding without some additional labour supply, tried the experiment of introducing coolies from the same districts of S. India, whence the Ceylon, Mauritius, and W. India labour markets are supplied; but notwithstanding every effort to render the imported labourers comfortable and contented, the Tamils could not be induced to settle down. The climate did not seem to suit them; numbers were attacked by fever, and in the end the majority took the earliest opportunity of returning homewards. I am still, however, decidedly of opinion that labour of a more reliable kind and on a more extensive scale than is at present available will have to be obtained, to render coffee planting in the Wynaad largely successful. This is a subject worthy the attention of the entire planting community.

One of the causes to which I attribute the success of the Tamil labour in Ceylon, is the distance by which, once arrived there, the coolies are separated from their homes. In the districts round Kandy, they find themselves compelled to make up their minds to stay for the season at any rate; consequently they feel their dependence on their employer, and philosophically set about making themselves as comfortable as possible. Having a long journey before them when they wish to return homewards, they recognize beforehand the desirability of being able to save a substantial sum out of their earnings, and consequently try to make as much money as possible while on the estates.

Another vital consideration doubtless is, that they are, as a rule, well housed, regularly provided with an ample supply of food such as they have been accustomed to, and at a price they can easily afford to pay. In fact, the arrangements altogether made for their accommodation have a completeness and system about them which show forethought and organization, and they are thus inspired with confidence. The Tamil labourer going over to the coffee districts of Ceylon, knows as well what lies before him as the Irish reaper coming over to England in harvest time. All this is the result of combined action, intelligently directed, on the part of the Ceylon planters, who, as a rule, work together in such matters with great unanimity, gathering periodically at their "Association Meetings" in large numbers, to consult and determine for the general good; and in order to bring about a similarly satisfactory state of things in the Wynaad, the planters there must follow the example set in the older and more prosperous settlement.

In choosing a new field of labour supply for the Wynaad, I would suggest one at a *distance*, so that the immigrants may be prepared on arriving in the district to settle down contentedly, and to take sufficient interest in their new abodes to render them cleanly and comfortable. They should be encouraged to cultivate for themselves a few vegetables, for which purpose plots of ground adjoining the lines should be allotted. In fact, all possible inducement should be held out to them to look upon the plantation as their *home* for the time being. Contentment, and this feeling of being settled, will go a long way towards preserving them in good health and spirits.

A gentleman some few years ago deputed by the Ceylon Planters' Association to visit Ganjam, and report on the labour supply available in that district, submitted on his return a report both satisfactory and promising as to its capabilities.

No doubt the feverish climate of the Wynaad at present, and especially of those parts of the district which face the Mysore plateau, will prove the great obstacle in the meantime (and that the climate is malarious during the spring months cannot be denied), but this difficulty can be neutralized to a considerable extent by the use of certain precautions. In the first place, the coolie lines should only be erected on dry, elevated situations, protected from easterly winds. Care must be taken to see that there is a good supply of water in the immediate vicinity—*well-water* being preferred to that of a running stream; cleanly habits should be enforced on the coolies as far as possible, in regard to their persons, their huts and surroundings; and above all, they must be supplied with abundance of good wholesome food of the kind they have been accustomed to. It is unnecessary to add, that proper medical treatment and hospital nursing should be provided when sickness makes its appearance, a due supply of suitable medicines being always kept in the manager's bungalow in readiness for such cases.

The following experience will show what may be done by attention to the simple principles of sanitation, in even the most malarious localities. It was about the year 1860, that I went down to undertake the management of an estate in the Cornegalle district, some 14 miles from Kandy. The district bore an unenviable character for feverishness, and when I arrived on the plantation my first impressions were anything but reassuring. My predecessor, who met me to deliver over charge, was a Eurasian who had had some direct interest in the property, but the other proprietors being dissatisfied with his management had bought him out. The "lay" or formation of the land was peculiar, the lower part forming a sort of uneven basin, and the remainder running up the sides of a steep narrow valley or gorge. At, or near the lowest part of the property, all the buildings, including the coolie lines and bungalow, had been erected, the elevation here not being more than 400 or 500 feet above the sea, while the saddle or brow at the head of the valley rose some 1500 feet higher. The coffee had been so much neglected that large patches had disappeared entirely in the encroaching growth of jungle, and that which remained had grown into a perfectly wild condition, and was overgrown with weeds and creepers. In reply to my inquiry as to the healthfulness of this place, the former superintendent's replies were at any rate straight-forward; about 40 per cent. of the coolies, he informed me, had died of fever in the previous year; the words he used, I well recollect, being that they "died off like rotten sheep." Quinine and other remedies he had tried, but found them of no avail. I at once saw that vigorous action would be required, and my resolution was soon formed. I engaged some Cingalese carpenters and contractors, and erected a strong comfortable set of lines, large enough to house all the coolies on the place, and surrounded with a wide cool verandah, on the very top of the gorge. This spot formed a sort of bridge or saddle, from which one looked down on the low part of the estate on the one side, and on the villages of the "low country" on the other; while before and behind the mountain rose up some 800 to 1000 feet higher, so that through the passage or opening there was nearly always a fresh breeze passing one way or other. In the immediate neighbourhood of the new lines moreover, there was a copious stream of clear water, so that altogether the situation was as desirable a one as could well have been chosen. The great objection of course was the long steep ascent from the larger part of the estate, and the poor coolies, enervated and disheartened, at first flatly refused to take up their abode in this eagle's nest. They urged various objections, first that the climb of a mile and a half up 1500 feet after their day's work would kill them, next that the site of the new lines was too cold, and so on. Laughingly saying that it was better for a few to die, if it could not be helped, of fatigue, than for all to die of fever (which they certainly would do unless they changed their quarters), I gave them plain notice that next day they must be prepared to remove up the hill or take the consequences. Next morning about eight o'clock I went down to the *old* coolie lines, and calling out the Kanganies asked if all were ready to migrate; but further remonstrances and objections being the only response, and seeing that the time for half-measures had passed, I now told them that they would do well to take their goods out without further ado, as in ten minutes the lines would be in a blaze. I then took a burning faggot and held it ready to fulfil my warning. This had the desired effect; in ten minutes the pots and pans and blankets were outside, and the thatched roof was enveloped in flame. Making a virtue of necessity, the whole gang now marched up the hill. I took up my own abode about 500 feet higher than the new lines on the mountain side, the general result being that during the two years I remained on the estate subsequently, although I had occasion largely to increase the number of the gang, there were *no deaths* from fever. Sickness there was from this cause, but not to an extent to cause alarm, or that could not be made to yield to ordinary remedies and nourishment.

If labourers are imported at great expense and after much trouble and anxiety, it is only fair that their engagements should be recognized by law, and rendered binding so as to protect their employers against desertion. It is equally desirable for the labourer himself that the exact tenor of his relations towards the planter should be clearly defined by the Legislature.

Coolies should, as far as possible, only be recruited among agriculturists and persons accustomed to out-door labour; natives who have been previously making their living in such occupations as weaving, spinning, cheroot-making, &c., also loafers, horsekeepers, &c., from military cantonments, are quite unsuitable for estate work, and should be rejected.

In all cases where coolies have been induced to sign written agreements, the greatest care should be taken to ascertain that these have previously been properly and clearly interpreted and explained to them, and to insure this the fact should be attested on the back of the contract by some trustworthy and responsible person; and if possible, this attestation might be made in the presence of a magistrate or justice of the peace. This is compulsory by the Ceylon Labour Ordinance, and it will always be a satisfaction to the planter himself to feel assured that the coolies have not been inveigled into his service by false representations; more especially as the class of persons who make their livelihood by collecting coolies on commission, are frequently adventurers without character or principle, who do not scruple to make all kinds of absurd promises, caring for nothing but the head-money, and being quite indifferent as to whether the people they have engaged remain at their destination or not, once the commission has been paid. It is only natural that coolies should become troublesome and discontented, when, on arriving at the estate, they find themselves to have been grossly deceived by false representations, the nature of the work upon which they are to be employed being entirely different, and the wages they are to receive far smaller than they have been led to expect; nor is it greatly to be wondered at that they are often unable to discriminate between the knave by whom they have been duped, and the innocent planter whose representative he seemed to be. In such cases, continual difficulties and unpleasantness may be expected on the estate, often ending in the desertion of the entire gang, the planter often to the last remaining in entire ignorance of the real cause.

In the Wynaad, it is at times a matter of no small difficulty to obtain adequate supplies of suitable food for natives imported from the rice-growing districts. What they require is " boiled rice," i. e. rice that has been soaked and dried before separation from the husk; this is not generally used in the Wynaad and adjoining districts, the inhabitants of which live principally on raggee, with a certain proportion of "raw rice," (i. e. rice which has simply been separated from the husk without the process above referred to). The latter appears to agree with natives who do not make it their staple food, but with those who do, it has a tendency to produce dysentery, &c. In the event of any systematic importation of labour from such districts as Ganjam or the South Indian plains, it will be essential to import rice from Bengal, Ganjam, Chittagong or elsewhere, as is done in Ceylon. This could be landed at Tellicherry, Cannanore, or Calicut, or at Madras, and thence sent by rail to Bangalore, and by bullock-cart to Mysore and Manantoddy. This want, however, would very soon be supplied by the various enterprizing agency firms established on the Malabar coast.

CHAPTER VII.

Tools and implements—Best quality desirable—The mammotie—The bill-hook—The axe—The crowbar—The quintannie—The reaping-hook—Erection of coolie lines—Bungalow—The bamboo—Jungle materials.

THE tools or implements necessary for opening up and carrying on the cultivation of a coffee estate are of various kinds, and differ in many respects from those used in corresponding operations in Europe. They should always be made of the best materials, the metal being wrought iron, edged and tipped with steel, and of the most approved shapes and dimensions, in order to get the work satisfactorily done, even though the first outlay may be greater than might be incurred by the purchase of second-rate articles. This will reduce the cost of sharpening and repairs, and the coolies will work much more cheerfully and efficiently than would otherwise be the case. The old adage is, "bad workmen make bad tools," but it has often appeared to me equally true that bad tools spoil good workmen.

The *mammotie*, which is used on all occasions and for all purposes for which in England a spade, a pick, a hoe, or a shovel would be required, is a heavy, short-handled hoe, something between the spade and the adze. It has a haft from three to three-and-a-half feet long; if required for digging, the blade should be heavy, sharp, and deep, and not too wide; a depth of nine inches from the haft-socket to the edge, and a width of six inches will probably be the best dimensions; if, however, it is required for such purposes as surface-scraping, shovelling loose earth, sand, &c., the *wider* the blade is the better, and the dimensions may be as much as ten inches wide by, say, eight or nine only, deep. It is obvious that for labourers who invariably go barefoot, the spade as used by the European workman would be quite useless.

The *bill-hook* is principally required for cutting down jungle and underwood, lopping the branches of felled timber, dressing stakes, shingles, &c. It should have a long, curved, heavy blade, and be provided with a haft or handle, either six or eight inches, or three or four feet long, at the option of the labourer, or according to the description of work for which it is required. The bill-hook in common use among the Cingalese, has a handle about four feet in length, and is much curved or hooked in the blade; that used by the local jungle tribes of

Southern India has a similar blade, but is usually attached to a short handle. The best form for general estate purposes is a moderately-curved blade under a foot in length, sharpened on the inner side, a cylindrical socket being provided, into which a haft of any required length may be inserted at pleasure.

The *axe* most commonly used for felling has a long, narrow head with a round socket, into which the haft can be inserted—axes made in the English manner for *square*-headed hafts being troublesome to fit. For the planter these should be of better material, if anything, than ordinary, many of the trees to be operated upon being hard and close-grained, qualities which very soon begin to break up inferior implements.

The *crow-bar* should be flattened into a sharp, spade-like blade at one end, and be pointed at the other. It is useful for picking out stones among roots, for using as a lever in moving weights, loosening earth, and for excavating, cutting roots, &c., in narrow, deep pits where there is not space for the free use of the mammotie.

Quintannies or *mattocks* will be found useful for digging in ground more than usually hard and stony. This should be in all respects similar to the mammotie, but of heavier metal, and deeper and narrower in the blade; more, in fact, resembling a carpenter's adze, only of course much stronger as being intended for much rougher work.

A few *grass-hooks* or *sickles*, some *pick-axes*, the same as used in England, a *cross-cut saw*, a *grindstone*, and perhaps a few other articles will complete the list of what is required to start with.

Having got the coolies together and provided the necessary appliances, operations may be at once begun. The first undertaking will be the erection of dwellings for the planter and his people; and, for this purpose, a small piece of land should be specially cleared in the first instance. This spot should be chosen with the greatest care and deliberation. It should be in a dry, healthful, and tolerably elevated situation, be provided with a good supply of pure, wholesome water, and be conveniently placed with regard to the future estate and the nearest public road.

To make the clearing a party of men or boys, provided with bill-hooks, should be first sent in to cut down all the underwood and saplings, these being followed the day after by men with axes to fell the heavy timber. In felling trees, it should never be forgotten that though two or three men with axes can, in a few hours, bring down a monarch of the forest, the growth of many centuries, the act, should it afterwards prove to have been ill-advised, though it may be regretted, can never be remedied or repaired. This is a consideration of the greatest importance, and the more so that an opinion is now beginning to be generally adopted that in certain districts the wholesale felling of the forest has been altogether a mistake from the cultivator's point of view, and that plantations now become extinct would have been flourishing to this day had the forest shade been at least partially retained, instead of having been ruthlessly done away with by means of axe and fire. As a matter of health, comfort, and taste also, it is most desirable to leave, at any rate, some of the more picturesque and symmetrically-formed trees standing about the spot chosen for the planter's bungalow and coolie lines.

Five or six weeks after the felling and lopping, that is as soon as sufficiently dry, the *débris* should be set on fire, so as to get the ground clear. The "coolie lines" may be run up in a very short time, from the natural materials abundantly at hand on all sides. It is very important to provide the coolies with proper shelter and accommodation, and the planter should remember that although he may be willing to undergo hardship and to "rough it," the coolies should be made as comfortable as possible according to their accustomed mode of life. The great thing is to guard against sickness and keep the gang in good heart, from the outset. They will then give the estate a good name, say it is *lucky*, and labour difficulties will subsequently be much diminished. It is not, however, necessary to put up coolie huts of an expensive or even permanent character at this period. The great object is to have well-drained and well-ventilated dwellings, capable of keeping out any amount of wind and rain.

In localities where the bamboo flourishes, the erection of a house is a simple and expeditious matter. The process would surprise a European artisan, inasmuch as no nails are required, nor indeed anything in the way of material but such as the adjacent jungle affords. Bamboos are seldom used for the principal supports of the house, owing to their liability to destruction by minute borers; though, indeed, bamboo posts, *if cut down near the roots*, and previously left to soak some time in water, will be found exceedingly strong and durable. The natives always cut bamboos for building purposes when the moon is on the wane, as they then contain less sap, and are, consequently, less liable to early decay. The walls of native houses in bamboo districts are made of bamboo laths some two inches wide, interwoven basket-fashion, the interstices being afterwards plastered up with mud. In every jungle there are different fibres or "jungle ropes" to be found (and which are well known to the natives), with which all fastenings can be effected;

while grass will no doubt be found in the neighbourhood for thatching purposes.

Coolie lines are usually in the form of one long building partitioned off into different apartments; each apartment being ten or twelve feet square, opening into the general verandah, which should be five or six feet in width, and extend along the entire building. Two or more persons will generally occupy one room of the above dimensions, provided they are of the same caste; it is much the best plan, however, to leave the coolies to make these little dispositions and arrangements among themselves. Each married couple should of course be allowed to appropriate a room to themselves.

A temporary bungalow for the superintendent will be the next undertaking. This will probably be no more than a simple parallelogram partitioned off into three rooms, or perhaps only into two, with a verandah along the front, a portion of which at each end can be enclosed to serve as store-room, or pantry and bath-room. A porch may be added as a finishing touch, giving architectural effect to the structure! A building of this kind may be made comfortable enough with a little care and ingenuity, and if good stout posts are used, and the walls are kept well plastered with mud, and afterwards (as also the clay floors) regularly washed with liquefied cow-dung, will stand for many years. This is a consideration, inasmuch as when the "pucka" bungalow is subsequently put up, the original one can still be utilized as a stable, store, or out-house.

In districts where the felling and clearing can be done by contract, the manager will be in a position to employ his permanent gang of coolies in the erection of the above buildings, while the contractors are proceeding with their operations.

CHAPTER VIII.

Young plants—Stumping—The nursery—Seeds—Seed-beds—Germination— Manure for seed-beds —Watering—Distance apart—Size of beds—The paddy-field bed—Irrigation—Old plants—Shade—Soil.

IN Ceylon, abundant supplies of coffee plants of all sizes are generally to be found growing wild in the forest, in the vicinity of old estates—the product of seed pillaged and subsequently sown by tribes of monkeys, wild cats, squirrels, &c. These plants having grown up in the shade, are generally lanky and straggling, and consequently require, before being planted out on the estate, to be "stumped," i. e. cut down to within some six inches above the roots. These stumps are then very independent, and usually come on well, throwing out shoots within three or four weeks from the time they are put into the ground. The best size of stump is the thickness of a common pencil; these throw out shoots and take root more quickly than larger plants, while those that are younger and thinner are more liable to be burnt up by the sun, should the season be more than usually dry.

Where wild plants, however, are not to be had merely for the trouble of collecting, others can frequently be got from native gardens at a trifling rate per thousand. When plants are obtainable in sufficient numbers in either of these ways, a nursery is but little required; but in case the planter should not be so fortunate as to find his wants thus supplied, it will be advisable to begin making a nursery at once.

The best time of year for this is the end of October, when a few bushels of fresh coffee seed of the new crop can be obtained from some neighbouring old estate. A bushel contains about 40,000 berries of cherry coffee, and as most berries contain two beans, the number of seeds will be not far from 80,000; but allowing ten per cent. for peaberries and imperfect beans, we ought to get about 70,000 plants in the nursery from one bushel of parchment.

Seeds should be carefully selected, as far as possible from healthy trees only, and should not be picked until fully ripe. They should be pulped by hand, so as to avoid the injury which would be incurred by a certain percentage in being passed through the pulping machine. The seeds are better not washed, but may be shaken up with wood ashes, to dissolve the saccharine pulp adhering to them, and thus prevent fermentation. They should then be *slightly* dried, when they will be ready for the nursery.

The seed-beds should be dug up to the depth of a foot, all roots and stones being picked out. The surface must then be nicely smoothed over, when the beans may be placed in straight drills and at equal distances from each other, being then lightly covered over with fine mould. Over this a layer of rotten leaves may be spread two inches thick, the bed being then well watered at least once every three days, if the weather be dry, until germination takes place. In about six weeks the seeds will begin to force their way above ground, and to send a root downwards, and the layer of decayed leaves may then be gently and carefully removed.

The following correct and interesting description of the process of germination I found somewhere, though I am unfortunately unable to give the name of the writer :—" Let the seed with its parchment be laid only upon a wet soil, and you will see it open itself a little. A pedicle peeps out, an extremity of which leans towards the ground. Here two radicles are seeking and soon grasp their nurse. The other extremity rears itself up, loaded with the whole seed. In a short time two follicles almost round, and of a thin yellow colour, unfold themselves from the very substance of the seed, and shake off the parchment. The stigma or fissure seemed to mark their separation on the flat side of the seed; and on the round side they seemed to be perfectly blended together; but now they part of themselves. Thus it is the seed itself which spreads out into these two follicles, which turn green by contact with the air. From between them a small top rises. Its point is acute, and divides itself into two leaves of lanceolate form. The sapling rises again and again, still in the same manner, bearing its leaves two and two, or axillary, at equal distances, &c."

In all cases where the nursery is made in virgin soil, manure will be unnecessary, and indeed is better dispensed with, as being calculated to introduce grubs likely to prey upon the seeds; but in old nurseries, after the first year or two manure will be required. This should be given in the form of compost, or the produce of the stable or cattle shed, *old* and *well-rotted*, and a moderate quantity will suffice thoroughly broken up and dug in.

Watering should be done in the morning or towards sunset, and not during the heat of the day, as wetting the plants during sunshine will prove fatal.

The seeds may be put in about one inch apart at first; the plants being afterwards, as they increase in size, thinned out. The beds should not be more than three and a half or four feet wide, so that a person standing on either side may be able easily to reach the centre, without stepping off the footpath. Weeds can thus be easily pulled out, and the beds watered without any mischief being done. They may be either raised above the level of the surrounding paths, or the reverse, each method having its advantages in different localities. In damp situations the beds should be raised for dryness, while in very hot localities they should be depressed in order that they may retain as much as possible of the moisture they receive. Some planters prefer nursery-beds made after the fashion of paddy-fields, that is to say, perfectly level and surrounded by raised borders or "bunds," to admit of their being irrigated at pleasure. The drawbacks to this method, however, are, that the rush of water when it is let in carries the seeds in a heap before it, and also that the water after subsiding is apt to leave the ground hard and stiff. Once the plants have taken root and are well above ground, irrigation is the cheapest and most expeditious method of supplying them with moisture, and is not so objectionable except where the soil is inclined to be stiff and clayey.

If the plants are intended to remain in the nursery for a second or third season, they should be allowed space, and be at least three or four inches apart. If grown in straight rows at right angles, it will always be easy to ascertain the number of plants in each bed by simple measurement. Thus, a bed three feet and a half wide by twenty-eight in length, with plants at four inches apart, would contain about 1200, or sufficient to cover an acre planted at six feet by six feet.

When the climate is hot, it will be necessary to erect a "pandall," or awning, to protect the young plants from the sun during the dry months. This may be done in a very rough manner, by laying green branches out of the jungle over a framework. The shade must, however, be removed on the approach of the rainy season, otherwise the drip will prove injurious to the plants, which, moreover, will be strengthened by such sun and air as they are likely to get at this time of year.

In order to keep up the nursery from year to year, seedlings can be raised in fresh beds, and then transplanted into it, after it has been well dug up and enriched with a little rotten dung or compost. The soil of the nursery is just as well *not to be too rich*, otherwise the plants will be apt to suffer from the change if put out into one of poorer quality. Some planters are strongly of opinion that the seedlings should be brought up in the *same soil* as that in which they are afterwards to dwell, and that, consequently, plants brought from a distance are less promising than those raised on the spot.

CHAPTER IX.

The clearing—Mode of felling forest—Bamboos—Their uses—Felling bamboos—Lopping—Burning—The burn—Clearing—Pitting before clearing—Leeches.

I HAVE somewhere come upon the following description of a newly-felled clearing in Ceylon :—
" The sun was high in the horizon, when we found ourselves at a turn of the road in the midst of a clearing ; the spot we had opened on was at the entrance of a long valley of great width, on one side of which lay the estate we were bound to. It was not difficult to fancy one's self in the recesses of the Black Forest ; pile on pile of heavy dark jungle rose before us. Before us were, as near as I could judge, fifty acres of felled jungle in thickest disorder ; just as the monarchs of the forest had fallen, so they lay heap upon heap, crushed and splintered into ten thousand fragments. To me it was a pretty as well as a novel sight to watch the felling work in progress. Two axe-men to each tree if small, three and sometimes four to

larger ones; their little bright axes flung back far over their shoulders, and then dug deep into the heart of the tree. I observed that in no instance were the trees cut through, but each one was left with just sufficient of the heart to keep it standing. On looking round I saw that there were hundreds of them treated similarly; my planter-friend assured me that if the trees were to be at once cut down, a few at a time, they would so encumber the ground as to render it impossible for the workmen to have access to the adjoining trees. They (the workmen) were, however, finally ranged in order; all being ready, forty bright axes gleamed high in the air, and then sank deeply into as many previously all but severed trees, which at once yielding to the sharp steel groaned heavily, then slowly bent forward until they fell with a stunning crash on the trees below them; these having also been cut through previously, offered no resistance, but followed the example of their upper neighbours, and fell booming on those beneath. In this way the work of destruction went on from row to row; only those fell, however, which had been cut, and of these not one was left standing."

Felling bamboos is a more laborious and tedious operation. The bamboo, with which the whole of the interior of the Wynaad, Coorg, and Mysore districts abound, is the most useful of plants. It grows in groups or clumps of some twenty or thirty to upwards of a hundred stems; these clumps are planted about at irregular distances, sometimes scattered at broad intervals over open grass-land, but at others more closely ranked, and in company with other descriptions of timber, forming a complete forest. In either case the bamboo lends a most picturesque character to the landscape, its foliage being peculiarly light and graceful, conveying at a distance somewhat the idea of masses of ostrich plumes. Its long, straight, cylindrical stem is universally used by the natives for building purposes, for which it is peculiarly well adapted. Vessels for holding water, measuring grain, &c., bottles, buckets, spoons, baskets, shovels, mats, and many other articles are also fashioned from the bamboo.

In some parts of India, where this useful tree is less plentiful, the planters having regard to the many purposes to which it can be applied do not destroy it when making their clearings, reserving it for use as required. It is, however, generally supposed among the Wynaad planters, that the vicinity of bamboos is injurious to coffee, a theory I am almost inclined to support.

In order to cut down the bamboo clump, the thorny branches which, proceeding horizontally from the upright stems form a dense and most formidable *chevaux de frise* extending to a height of some fifteen or twenty feet, have to be removed in detail by means of the bill-hook, so far as to leave a clear space of some six feet from the ground within which the workman may make his attack. Each stem is then cut completely through about five feet from the ground, and again down near the roots, the piece thus excised being removed. By this means access is obtained to those next inside. When all have been cut through, with the exception of one or two, the bill-hook is dug deep into these, and the entire clump comes crashing to the ground. It is important to see that the stems are completely severed, as a very slight connecting ligament will suffice to enable the prostrate stem to retain its vitality, a contingency which will quite prevent its destruction when the torch comes to be applied later on. After the bamboos have been felled any other trees that are to come down are felled over them, in order that their weight may condensate the prostrate piles, and so contribute to rendering the burn more effectual.

As soon as the felling is over, all the branches of the fallen timber which have a straggling or upward tendency, are lopped off and made to lie as close as possible. This should be done before the leaves have fallen, otherwise the prospects of a good burn will be diminished. In fact, it will be better with this object to have a small gang from the first engaged in lopping, following a day or two after the felling gang.

About a month after the felling and lopping operations have been completed, the clearing may be set fire to. Should it be on the slope of a hill, as is most frequently the case, the best plan is to apply the torch at different spots about seventy or eighty yards apart, in parallel lines across its face, beginning near the top of the hill. If the ground is level, fires may be applied at more frequent intervals still, beginning near the centre. The burn should not be commenced till between twelve or one o'clock in the day, in order that the dews of the previous night may have evaporated; and fine weather will of course be chosen as far as possible.

Though a "good burn" is almost always eagerly desired by the young planter, in order that the subsequent operations may be rendered more easy, there is little doubt that a fierce fire is more or less prejudicial and injurious, calcining as it does the organic constituents of the first inch or two of surface soil. Were it possible to get rid of the mass of timber and brushwood by some other means, this would be most desirable and advantageous; but as this can hardly be done without greatly increased labour and expense, the proposition will seldom be entertained, more especially as neatness and regularity of planting can hardly be secured unless the ground is tolerably well cleared in the first instance. I have somewhere seen it suggested, that the fallen timber and brushwood should be piled up in rows, and left to decay, the coffee plants being placed in lines intervening, but this would be impracticable. In the first place, strongholds would thus be formed, of which all manner of weeds and green jungle would at once take possession, and which it would be impossible to eradicate.

Should the fire not have cleared the land sufficiently, the superabundant timber, branches, &c., will have to be cut up, piled in heaps and refired.

The injury done to the surface soil by burning, could to a great extent be obviated by "lining" and "pitting" the land before the forest is felled. By this means the surface soil would be, in great measure, covered over with the earth taken out of the pits, and thus protected from the fire. On the other hand, of course, the lines cannot be marked out with mathematical accuracy or regularity, and the estate will subsequently suffer to some extent in appearance, though it is a question how far this drawback is worth considering, compared with the advantage gained.

I remember once, when in Ceylon, lending a neighbouring planter some spare labourers to line and pit for him in an uncleared forest. The coolies, however, suffered so severely from the attacks of jungle leeches, that it became impossible for them to continue their work. These leeches are one of the greatest pests met with by the planter in the forest districts; frequenting shady, damp situations, they lie in wait for and at once attack every passer-by, laying hold, in batches of half a dozen at a time, of the calves of the leg and ancles. They are smaller than the medicinal leech, and must have some poisonous property, their bite causing intense itching and irritation, and being even apt to fester and produce troublesome sores. To protect themselves against this annoyance, planters and others whose calling necessitates their frequenting damp jungles, are obliged to wear "leech gaiters," a kind of over-all stocking of linen or cotton material, going inside the boot, but tied over the trousers below the knee. The best remedy for the acute itching caused by the bite of the jungle leech is to rub in common salt; or, should this fail to give relief, to burn the part with caustic.

CHAPTER X.

Lining out—Objects—Method—The rope—The base line—Lining square—West Indies and Java—Distance apart—Hexagons—Quincunx formation—Pitting—Depth desirable—The day's task—Work to be completed before wet season—Filling in—Women and boys.

IN order to admit of large gangs of labourers working together on an estate without confusion, and to enable the employer more easily to check the amount of work done by each person, as well as to economize surface to the utmost, by having the largest number of plants on a given area, each with its due share of ground, the land is "lined" as soon as cleared. That is to say, the place for every plant is carefully marked out by means of pickets placed at equal distances, and in perfectly straight parallel lines throughout the plantation. This gives an appearance of order, regularity, and neatness very pleasing to the eye. The work is done in the following manner:—In the first place, the pegs or pickets must be provided; they should be from two and a half to three feet long, and sufficiently strong to bear being well driven into the ground with a mallet; a coolie should be able to make from three to four hundred of them in a day. A rope must now be procured, and marked off with strips of coloured cloth at the proper distances, say every four, five, or six feet, according to the distance intended to be observed between the plants. A couple of measuring rods, with which to regulate the distance between each line, will complete the apparatus required.

The rope having been previously *well stretched*, and all being in readiness, an intelligent man should be put in charge of each end. It is usual to run the lines straight up the face of the hill, i. e. conforming as much as possible to the greatest declivity of the general lay of the land, a peg being driven in opposite every mark on the rope. A coolie with one of the measuring rods should now mark out a base line, planting pickets in a straight line at right angles to the direction taken by the rope, so that when the first vertical line has been marked out, the rope may be moved on to the next of these, and so on. Care should be taken in measuring a cross or base line, that the rod is held perfectly *level* and horizontally, as well as at a perfect right angle, otherwise, of course, the distance will become diminished, and the lines instead of continuing to run parallel will gradually converge.

Other and more complicated systems of "lining" are frequently adopted, but the simpler the method the better with coolies. In order to line square, or to make perfectly rectangular lines, it is necessary to use three ropes, marked with strips of cloth, two of them being laid parallel with each other, at say sixty yards distance, and the third stretched from one to the other at the corresponding marks.

The measurement between the marks on the rope should be constantly checked and readjusted, as the more the rope is used the more it will stretch, the spaces between mark and mark being consequently increased.

In the West Indies, and also in Java, the space left between each picket appears to be usually from ten to twelve feet. In Ceylon and Southern India, however, the distance most commonly observed is from five to six feet; very often the plants being five feet apart in the lines, and each line six feet distance from the next. Plants are very seldom grown more than six feet apart every way, or closer than four feet. These distances, however, must be decided by the situation, climate, elevation, and the nature of the soil. The object to be always kept in view, is that with the greatest convenient number of trees in a given space, none shall incommode or interfere with the growth or sustenance of its neighbour. In cold or exposed situations, where the plants cannot attain any great size, close planting is necessary; the reverse being the case where the climate is warm and humid and the soil productive, and consequently likely to produce large bushes. It is desirable that the branches of the plants should as near as possible touch without being intertwined, so that the ground may be well covered; and this for more reasons than one, not omitting the checking of weed-growth; at the same time, this cover should hardly be of sufficient density to exclude the light and air entirely from the soil.

An acre planted at 6 feet × 6 feet will contain 1210 plants.
„ 6 „ × 5 „ „ 1452 „
„ 5 „ × 5 „ „ 1742 „
„ 5 „ × 4 „ „ 2178 „
„ 4 „ × 4 „ „ 2722 „

"It has been demonstrated," says the *Farmer's Magazine* (vol. vii. 409), "that the closest order in which it is possible to place a number upon a plain surface, not nearer than a given distance from each other, is in the angles of hexagons, with a plant in the centre of each hexagon. Hence it is argued that this order of trees is the most economical, as the same quantity of ground will contain a greater quantity of trees by 15 per cent. when planted in this form than in any other."[1]

[1] Loudon's "Encyclopædia of Gardening."

Another method is termed "quincunx," the plants in every *alternate* line being opposite each other. This, however, is hardly to be recommended to the coffee planter, as it will be quite beyond the understanding of the coolies, and consequently lead to much delay, annoyance, and trouble. Moreover, from the ruggedness of the surface in forest clearings, with large logs, stumps and boulders strewn in every direction, it will be next to impossible to preserve a form of this kind with any degree of exactness. It is recommended by Laborie,[2] on the ground that while the rows are approximated the plants are still kept the same distance apart. This, however, is of course only partially true, as is apparent from his next remark, to the effect that "this method has the inconvenience of narrowing the passage for the labourers, *the boughs also suffering from it in the extremities.*"

After the land has been "lined" and picketed, the next work to be undertaken is "holing" or "pitting"—one much more tedious and laborious. At every picket a hole of from 18 to 24 inches wide and deep has now to be dug, in which the plant is afterwards to be placed. No pit should be less than 18 inches deep, though in loose, open soils depth is less necessary than in those which are on a substratum of gravel or clay. The object of a deep

[2] Abridged coffee planter of St. Domingo.

pit is to enable the tap-root to descend easily to a point at which moisture can be obtained, however much the surface may be dried up by heat and want of rain; and there are, of course, some situations where the soil proper is sufficiently deep and loose to enable the tap-root to accomplish this without any previous excavation. It will not, however, be prudent to calculate on this, and as a general rule the deeper and wider the pit is made the better for the plant; although some pretend that if the former be too deep, the plant being unable to send its roots down to the undisturbed stratum, will not have a sufficiently firm hold to steady it against the assaults of wind. This argument, however, I consider unworthy of attention.

An ordinary coolie can make on an average from 25 to 30 pits of 18 inches cube per diem. This is equivalent to removing about 101 cubic feet of soil, which is the same displacement as caused by only 12 pits of 24 inches cube, though it would be as easy, probably, to dig 18 two-feet pits as 30 of a foot-and-a-half, owing to the greater difficulty of excavating in depth in proportion as the lateral space is reduced. Where the ground is hard or gravelly, or much bound together with roots and stones, the day's task per coolie will of course have to be proportionately reduced.

It should always be remembered that a *narrow*

pit may be remedied by subsequent digging and trenching, but a shallow one never; it is better, therefore, to be on the safe side as to depth. It not unfrequently happens that a flat stone below the tap-root in dry weather causes the death of the plant, whereas had the excavation been a few inches deeper this would have been detected and removed.

It will thus be seen that "pitting" is a slow and tedious operation, and indeed it is the most arduous of all the works undertaken in the formation of a plantation. This should be borne in mind when the extent of land to be cleared in a single season is being decided on, a larger area being sometimes cleared than the number of labourers available will admit of being pitted and planted. Pitting should begin as soon as possible after the land has been cleared, say in January or February, and may be continued up to the end of June, or until the rainy season sets in. Each coolie should be provided with a sharp heavy mammotie, and a crowbar or "digger" flattened at one end. This spade-like blade of the latter is useful for digging down the sides and bottom of the pits, while the pointed end is used for picking out stones.

After the pits have been left open for a certain length of time, they should be "filled in." This is done by scraping into them the dark soil from the surrounding surface, the red gravelly or clayey earth which will probably have been taken out from the bottom of the pit being rejected. Care must be taken to avoid stones, and it will be safer also to exclude roots, weeds, &c., which are apt to generate grubs, and so endanger the roots of the plant. The pits should be filled in in wet weather, or at least while the ground is moist, so that the sides may not be hard or caked, as otherwise the roots of the plant will have difficulty in penetrating beyond its limits.

Women and boys ought each to be able to fill in sixty or seventy pits a day. Should the land be on a slope, only the soil above the pits should be scraped in, the lower side being carefully preserved intact as a retaining wall. Careful supervision will be necessary, the coolies being naturally disposed to shovel in the loose earth previously taken out. By digging in the soil round the sides of the pits, not only is the surface mould, rich in organic matter, supplied to the tender roots of the young plant, but the area of the pit itself is extended; moreover the walls or sides of the pit after exposure to the sun and air for some time will probably have become encrusted, and unless thus broken in would be apt to operate much in the same way as a flower-pot, restricting the liberty of the roots in their search for nourishment.

CHAPTER XI.

Planting—Stumps—Trimming the roots—Nursery plants—
"With ball"—Continuance of rain needful—Old plants
—Puddling—Disposition of roots—Method of planting
—Care preferable to mere expedition—With the crowbar
—The diamond dibber—Dibbling—Slit planting,

"PLANTING," or the actual operation of putting out the young trees, is the most important work of all, and should be most carefully executed, as on its success depend the prospects of the estate.

Stumps, as described in a previous chapter, are hardier and safer in a general way than whole plants, more especially in uncertain weather. They will strike readily, even without rainfall for some little time after being put in, provided the ground has become sufficiently moist to prevent their being burnt up. The roots should be previously trimmed with the knife, and the stump cut smoothly off some six inches above them. The object of pruning the roots is that any ends which have been bruised or torn during the removal of the plant from its original home, may be cleanly dressed; and also that no feeders or lateral fibres may be left of sufficient length to become doubled or twisted in the planting. The tap-root should not be cut short, but only just *tipped*, a length of nine inches being sufficient, the laterals or feeders being about four inches in length. Should there be two tap-roots, it will probably be as well to amputate one of them.

It has been observed, that stumps cannot be used with success in districts where a long period of drought may be expected to succeed the wet season—as is the case in some parts of Southern India.

If small nursery *plants* still furnished with leaves, &c., be selected for use in preference to stumps, more delicate treatment still will be necessary. They should be taken out of the nursery-beds on a dark, rainy day, the surrounding earth being in the first instance gently prized up and loosened with a crowbar, and each plant carefully removed with as much soil as can be got to adhere to the roots. This should then be pressed gently round them between the hands, the plants being then put in baskets and carried off for distribution, one being laid gently down at each pit. In very wet climates, where a long continuance of uninterruptedly rainy weather can with certainty be calculated on, all this care to remove the plants, "with ball" as it is termed, is less necessary, though it is always desirable.

There is some diversity of opinion as to the size and age at which nursery plants are best suited for being put out. It is not, however, a question that can be settled by any fixed rule. Much must depend upon the conditions of time and place and climate. In Ceylon, for example, where the planting season is frequently interrupted by bursts of sunshine, entire nursery plants are usually looked upon as somewhat precarious, and they should never be put in without a good ball of earth round the roots. This, again, makes putting them out a slow and tedious operation, during the course of which favourable weather may slip away, and an opportunity of getting a large area planted up be lost. Ceylon planters consequently, in general prefer stumps, which can bear being kept longer out of the ground, and are less likely, provided the ground itself be moist, to be injured by the appearance of sunshine immediately after they have been put in.

When dull, rainy weather can be depended on as a continuance for some little time, nursery plants of the second year are the most satisfactory, and if quickly put in under the system above recommended, "with ball," will hardly appear to suffer any check from being transplanted. Should a few hours' sunshine intervene, however, before they have taken root, the danger is they will at once begin to droop and lose their leaves, if not die altogether.

Nursery plants of the first season are still more unsafe, if there is a long dry season to be undergone within the first year, as their roots will not be sufficiently deep to obtain for them the necessary moisture. Moreover, they are somewhat too easily choked up with weeds, which unfortunately cannot *always* be kept down, especially at low elevations and in bamboo or "chena" lands.

If it is intended to put out plants that have grown for *three* years in the nursery, I should recommend their being cut down to stumps in the beds, in the December or January before the planting season; they will then throw out "suckers," which by the time July has come round (say six months later), will be nine or ten inches high. When these plants are put out, a couple of the most promising suckers may be selected, the rest being *pulled* off. These two (being those nearest the roots) may then be suffered to grow together for a month, after which the weaker of the two may be taken off, the other being left to develop into the tree. I have tried this plan *most* successfully, in one case having been able to pick a maiden crop of two to three cwts. per acre off plants that had hardly been eighteen months in the ground.

It is almost superfluous to say, that no plant should ever be kept out of the ground an hour longer than is unavoidable; there are, however, times when some lapse of time during removal from the rearing-beds to the clearing cannot be avoided. In these cases, the plants may be preserved by means of "puddling;" that is, by dipping the roots, or even the whole stump and roots, in a composition of stiff earth or clay and water of the consistency of gruel. In this way not only is the natural moisture of the plant retained, but an additional supply is likely to be absorbed from the atmosphere. Mr. Loudon remarks on this subject, "When the plants have been brought from a distance, Pontey strongly recommends "puddling" them previous to planting; if they seem very much dried, it would be still better to lay them in the ground for eight or ten days,[1] giving them a good soaking with water every second or third day, in order to restore their vegetable powers; for it well deserves notice that a degree of moisture in soil sufficient to support a plant recently or immediately taken from the nursery, would, in the case of dried ones, prove so far insufficient that most of them would die in it."

In putting in the plants great care must be taken

[1] This, it must be remembered, refers to a cold, damp climate, and would be quite unsuited to the tropics.

to see that the roots are laid straight out, and in their natural position, and also that the tap-root is not doubled up or bent at the end.

The best method is as follows: a boy or girl having laid down at the pit the plant intended for it, a man provided with a mammotie follows. He strikes the blade of this three or four times deeply into the pit, breaking and chopping up the mould. A stroke is then given as deep as the mammotie will go into the centre of the pit, the handle is then drawn back, the blade remaining buried in the earth; by this means a space is created behind the blade, and into this the labourer introduces the plant with his disengaged hand; having seen that the tap-root goes down straight to the bottom of the opening, he then raises the mammotie gently, allowing the mould to fall naturally round and among the roots, and finally presses in the earth with his other hand. In order to make *sure* that the tap-root and feeders are not bundled up, the plant should be drawn slightly upwards, and the earth may now be firmly trodden down, until the surface round the plant is quite smooth and flat.

I again quote Mr. Loudon in connexion with this subject : " On very steep slopes which have been pitted, the following rules ought to be observed in planting : to place the plant in the angle formed by the declivity and surface of the pit, and in finishing to raise the lower margin of the pit, whereby the plant will be made to stand as if on level ground, and the moisture be retained in the hollow of the angle. . . . Green, or unpractised hands, are apt to double the roots ; . . . a careful man, however, will become if not a speedy, at least a good planter in one day, and it is of more importance he should be a sure hand than a quick one."

It is worthy of attention that in planting with a stake or crowbar, as is sometimes attempted, coolies are apt to "hang" the plants, namely, to press the earth round the *throat* of the plant only, while a vacuum is left round the roots below; indeed, where the soil is stiff, and only a deep narrow hole has been made with the crowbar, this can hardly be avoided. The result is that, although for a week or two the plant may bear a healthy appearance, it dies as soon as hot weather begins. For this reason *narrow, pointed* implements should never be used for planting. In Europe, an implement called the "diamond dibber" is often used. It is thus described : " The plate of the dibber is made of good steel, and is four inches and a half broad where the iron handle is welded to it ; each of the other two sides of the triangle is five inches long ; the thickness of the plate one-fifth part of an inch, made thinner from the middle to the sides, till the edges become sharp. The length of the iron handle is seven inches, and sufficiently strong not to bend in working, and six-eighths of an inch square ; the iron handle is furnished with a turned hilt, like the handle of a large gimlet both in its form and the manner of being fixed on." This implement might probably be found convenient for the actual operation of planting, being used in accordance with the instructions given above, in reference to the mammotie ; the latter, however, I am inclined to think, is equally suitable, and has the additional recommendation of being better understood by the coolies.

It will be evident that if pitting could be dispensed with, an estate might be opened and planted up at a greatly reduced expense, and in comparatively little time ; consequently the experiment has often been tried, the plants being simply "dibbled in," and this in some few cases has seemed to answer fairly well. The objects of pitting are mainly to give free scope to the roots of the plant, while young and tender, and to prevent their being interfered with by the original forest roots or stones. Should this end be otherwise gained, however, by means of some special peculiarity in the nature of the soil, or if they can be secured by other means ; in other words, should the surface soil be deep and open, should it not be bound together by roots, should it be void of stones, and should there not be a gravel or clay sub-soil within a couple of feet (a happy combination not likely to be often met with), then, perhaps, pitting may be dispensed with.

In bamboo districts, where a dense jungle will spring up within a few weeks after the land has been cleared, the ground becoming thickly clothed with a crop of fine and luxuriant hay, it will be evident that the surface must be little other than a web or mat of roots, and "pitting" is consequently absolutely indispensable. Even on forest-land, and where after a good burn the blackened surface will remain clear of vegetation for a long period, "dibbling" will, in the vast majority of cases, be most inadequate and unsatisfactory. This may be easily proved by digging a pick into the ground, when it will, in all probability, either be met with a stout resistance or be found firmly held by a tangled mass of forest roots and stones, among which a coffee plant unaided would have but a poor chance. Dibbling should therefore never be adopted except as a last resource, and unless the land possesses an unusually deep, friable soil, and where it will be practicable, at an early subsequent date, to loosen the soil round each plant by digging or trenching. In any case dibbling with the crowbar is a very objectionable system, as the hole formed by this implement being produced simply by centrifugal pressure, the sides which ought to be broken and free, are, on the contrary, thus rendered peculiarly hard and impervious.

The best method appears to be what is called in Scotland, "slit" planting. This might be done by an implement exactly similar to the diamond dibber before described, only that it should be several inches broader, and have a handle some three feet in length, instead of seven inches. "The operator," to quote once more from Mr. Loudon's work, "makes three cuts crossing each other in the centre at an angle of 60 degrees, the whole having the form of a star; he inserts the implement across one of the rays a few inches from the centre, and on the side next himself; then bending the handle towards himself and almost to the ground, the earth opening in fissures from the centre, in the direction of the cuts which had been made, he, at the same time, inserts his plant at the point where the spade intersected the ray, pushing it forward to the centre, and assisting the roots in rambling through the fissures. He then lets down the earth by removing the spade;"[2] and it is then trampled down smooth.

---

[2] It must be borne in mind, however, that all these quotations from Mr. Loudon's valuable work have special reference to the formation of forest plantations in Europe; which is a very different matter from planting a compara-

In cases where dibbling is adopted, the lateral roots should be cut closer to the tap-root than would be proper were they to be planted in pits.

tively delicate exotic shrub like coffee, which would very soon be choked and obliterated if left unaided to fight its way among the natural wild vegetation of the land.

CHAPTER XII.

Road-making—Recapitulation of works discussed—Time for road-making—Advantages of good roads—Cart-road—Subordinate roads—Frequency required—The road tracer—Marking out—The advance gang—Cost of estate roads—Blasting rocks—Method described.

WE have now described all the primary operations in the formation of a coffee estate, and have at length arrived at the point where it becomes necessary to consider the various processes by which it may be kept in a state of efficient cultivation. This we shall do, as far as possible, in the order in which they would in all probability force themselves upon the attention of the planter.

It may be well, however, first to recapitulate briefly the works already treated of in their due order.

First, we have had a description of *felling* and *clearing;* next of building *coolie lines* and temporary *bungalow*, and of making the *nursery*. The season for beginning operations is October, or the early part of November, while the foregoing should have been finished by the middle of January.

The felled land should be burned off early in February, and *cleared* up AT ONCE; it should then be immediately *lined*, the *roads* being next traced out. Then comes the *pitting*, which may be continued till the middle of June, by which time the rainy season, and consequently the only safe time of year for *putting in the plants*, will have arrived. This wet season extends more or less through June, July, and August. The land must now be carefully *weeded*, once every month, every weed being rooted out, by hand if possible, carried away and burnt.

After the first weeding (or, if this can be done by women and children, while it is going on) the able-bodied men may be employed in opening up the roads that had previously been marked out, and in making drains to prevent "wash."

About six weeks or two months after the plants have been put in they should be carefully gone over and examined, all that have evidently died or are not looking well being taken out, and their places being supplied with good healthy plants or stumps. Of course, however, this will only be done provided suitable *planting weather* continues.

Having got thus far without special instructions being laid down for road-making, the subject might seem to have been overlooked. The seeming oversight, however, is due to the opinion I have always held, that while the roads may be traced, that is marked out, as soon as the land has been lined, their actual excavation should be postponed until it has been planted up. Owing to the limited duration of the rainy season, pitting and planting must have been completed by a certain date; it is better, therefore, that the planter should be able to devote his entire attention and all his available labour to these operations in the first instance. When they have been disposed of, it will be time enough to turn his men on to other works which are able to wait. Once the rains commence, the *sooner* the plants are in their places *the better*. Early planting is most desirable, as upon it a maiden crop may often depend.

Good, well-traced roads not only greatly facilitate the working of an estate, but give it a tasteful appearance. They are also useful as drains in preventing the soil from being washed down the hill-slopes by rainfall. A good cart-road will ultimately be a desideratum, and a trace suitable for one, say at a gradient not steeper than one in fifteen, should be first marked out, so that the space it will occupy may not be uselessly pitted and planted. This should go right through the centre of the estate like an artery, passing of course the spot intended for the stores, pulping-house, &c.; it should also cross the boundary of the estate at the point nearest to the main highway, with which it will afterwards have to be connected. The principal object of this road will be to facilitate the transport of crop and manure, and as it will not be required for these purposes during the first two years, it need not be cut to *its full width* at the outset unless labour happen to be unusually plentiful. Other roads of less width should next be traced, extending to all parts of the plantation, and all converging towards the store, where the crop will eventually have to be brought in, and where usually the coolies will be mustered morning and evening before proceeding to the various works. There should also.be an easy communication between the bungalow and the store, and between the former and the main entrance to the estate.

When engaged in crop-picking, the coolies are accustomed to deposit their sacks on the nearest road, filling them from time to time from smaller bags which they carry tied round their waists; consequently the distance between one parallel road and the next should not be great, or much time will be lost in passing backwards and forwards. The distance may be limited to 100 or 150 yards, which will allow of a line of from fifty to seventy-five plants between road and road. Some may consider too much of the land will thus be taken up for roads, but I do not think there is much waste. The coffee is always much finer and more fruitful for some distance below a road, and moreover roads are excellent stays and preservers of the soil, the wash being less destructive the oftener it meets with such interruptions.

In order to insure an easy and equable gradient, the roads should be carefully traced out by means of a suitable road "tracer." This is, in the first place, a brass telescopic tube, forming the base of a triangle, suspended by the apex from the side of a pole, so that it shall swing just at the level of the eye; below the tube runs a steel plate with graduated scale and weight, exactly similar to the arm of a platform weighing machine. By shifting this weight along the scale, the tube to which it is attached is of course swung at the incline or gradient required. At the end of the tube next the eye is a small perforation no larger than a pin's head, at the other a larger square opening, across the centre of which, horizontally, a thin wire is stretched. The pole being held upright, and the weight adjusted so as to give the required gradient, a coolie is sent on some ten or fifteen yards in the proper direction, bearing a *second* upright pole, with a cross-piece attached at exactly the same height as the tube on the first one. This second pole must now be held upright on the ground in such a situation that the

K

person following with the first contrivance, and looking through the small orifice of the tube, shall find the horizontal wire (at the end furthest from the eye) exactly bisecting the cross-piece held before him. A picket must then be put in, and the advanced pole moved on to another station, the tracer being moved up to its previous place, and so on *da capo*.

A man should now follow with small pegs, six inches in length, and drive one into the ground up to the head close to each picket, in order that when the road is dug out of the bank or slope above, the correct level may be arrived at; the earth thus excavated being banked up below or outside the peg, so as to give additional width of road-way.

When a road is being made through a clearing, it will be advisable to send a gang of men with axes, cross-cut saws, and strong bars and levers, one or two days in advance, to cut through and remove the prostrate timber and stumps; the gang with mammoties, pick-axes, &c., following to dispose of the earth-work.

A cutting of four feet in the solid (which, with the banked-up earth-work, should give a roadway of some six feet or more in width) will, if made by the estate hands, cost some £10 or £12 per mile, exclusive of blasting, or anything extensive in the way of building up, bridges, &c.

In *blasting rocks* bad accidents frequently occur through the inexperience of estate coolies, and often of their employers; it will, therefore, be useful and appropriate to give here some instructions as to how the work may be done safely.

Several implements are required: first, "jumpers," for boring the holes, generally octagonal steel bars, sharpened at the end like a stonemason's chisel; next, some good strong hammers, and long-handled iron scoops or spoons for cleaning out the bores, as the stone dust accumulates in them.

Coolies are usually tasked to make 36 inches of bore *per diem;* but, unless practised hands, they will hardly be able to keep up to this; indeed, in hard, granitic rocks, one will often have to rest satisfied with 20 to 24 inches.

As soon as the bore is finished, it should be cleaned out with the scoop, and carefully wiped throughout its entire length with tow. Once perfectly clean and smooth, the ramrod comes into requisition; this is generally made of iron, though some metal less liable to cause ignition by friction would, if sufficiently hard, be safer and more satisfactory. Down the side of the ram-rod runs a groove, to receive the fusee, while the process of loading is going on.

A ball of clean dry tow or torn "gunny" cloth

having first been thrust down into the bottom of the bore, the charge of large, coarse-grained blasting-powder is poured in. This should be in the proportion of one inch of powder to six or eight inches of bore. The fusee now comes into requisition, and should be cut of a length exceeding the depth of the bore by about six inches; one end of it, i. e. that which is to go into the bore, should be untwisted and opened out for half an inch or so, so that the powder it contains may be unmistakeably brought into communication with the charge it is intended to explode; it should next be carefully straightened, and then put down *along the side* of the bore, well into the charge at the bottom. A piece of torn gunny cloth or tow must now be pushed quietly down, as a wad, over the powder. A supply of soft, porous sandstone, free from quartz or flinty grits, and broken up into pieces of the size of peas, or say of the little finger-nail, must now be in readiness; this should be sprinkled with water till moist, and a small quantity (about a tea-spoonful or more at a time) put in and beaten down with the ram-rod, *gently at first*, but continuously, until quite firm and close. This must be gone on with until the bore is filled up, the ram-rod being vigorously hammered home, with increasing strength the greater the depth of the gravel loading over the powder, until the whole has become a homogeneous composition as hard and close as the original rock itself, or nearly so.

Now remove all implements, coats, &c., to a distance; open out the protruding end of the fusee into a flat, spoon-like form, and into this pour a few grains of powder to insure ignition; next, *apply the fire-stick, and* GET OUT OF DANGER!

CHAPTER XIII.

Draining — Necessity for — Gradient of the trenches — Frequency of occurrence — Mr. Wall's opinion — Draining swamps — Mauritius grass.

NEARLY all coffee estates being situated more or less on hill slopes, their surface soil is liable to be washed away during the heavy rains of the monsoon. In order to prevent this, recourse must be had to continuous trenches or drains dug across the face of the slope, and the more frequently these occur the better.

These trenches will not merely prevent the soil from being carried off, but will benefit the land in other ways, as will soon be evidenced by the appearance of the plants in their immediate neighbourhood. The trenches should be pretty *nearly* level, especially if near each other, though a slight gradient will be desirable in order to allow the gradual escape of surplus rainfall; otherwise they will be constantly in danger of overflowing or bursting, and thus causing damage. The fewer the trenches, i.e. the greater the distance which separates them, the greater, as a matter of course, will be the quantity of soil and water to accumulate in them, and the more frequently will they require to be cleared out and kept in order. The greater the declivity, the more danger will there be of their *facilitating* the escape, not only of the surplus rain-water, but of the soil which they have collected, and which escape it is their object to prevent.

If they can be made every ten or fifteen yards, in parallel lines across the hill, so much the better—in fact, they cannot occur too closely, in my opinion; and the gradient should never be greater than one in twelve; though one in twenty or thirty will be even better, what is wanted is to allow the *surplus water* to run off into the nearest ravine or nullah, *not the soil*. In width they may be from fifteen to eighteen inches, and in depth not less than one foot on the lower side. After a heavy fall of rain a few hands should always be sent round to clear them out with the mammotie, and make good any breaches.

This is a *most important* work, and upon the attention paid to it, the duration and value of the estate will positively depend, as I have endeavoured to show in another chapter.

Mr. George Wall, for many years one of the leading planters of Ceylon, writes upon this subject as follows:—"I have no hesitation in saying, that surface draining is the most profitable operation in connexion with coffee cultivation. It not only directly accomplishes a most important object in preventing the washing away of soil by heavy rains, but it also prepares the way for modes of cultivation which would otherwise become impracticable.

"It is surprising to see the indifference with which planters witness the loss of thousands of tons of their best soil, by the wash of heavy rains; and whilst they use their most strenuous efforts to improve their soil, they scarcely do anything to prevent its being carried away. True economy suggests that whatever we may do to improve it, we ought at least to preserve the soil we have. Draining, systematically and judiciously carried out, is an effectual preventive of wash."

Coffee should never be planted in swampy or sour soils until they have been well drained, otherwise the plants will soon die, from the roots becoming rotted. Draining swampy ground, however, is another thing altogether from surface draining to prevent wash, and is seldom likely to pay, unless labour is cheap and plentiful. In such cases, the trenches should be two feet deep, and have an outlet for the water, in fact, *they cannot be too deep*. Even after being thoroughly drained, swampy ground will seldom grow good trees, the soil being generally left very stiff and clayey—defects that can only be remedied by burning, an expensive and tedious operation; or by adding sand to it in sufficient quantity.

A more provident and profitable use for swamps will be found in planting them up with the succulent grass known as "Mauritius grass," an excellent item in the fodders required for the cattle-shed. In such situations this grass finds a congenial home, and flourishes luxuriantly—reference has been made to it elsewhere.

CHAPTER XIV.

Weeding—Weeds defined—Effects of—Methods of removal— Beginning early— Rapid multiplication—" White weed "—Hay—Weeding by hand—With the scraper—With the mammotie—Burying in—Weeding contracts—Rates.

WEEDING is a work of the first importance, and must be attended to from the very outset. And this for several reasons; in the first place, the plants cultivated ought to have the soil reserved for them entirely, whatever is abstracted from it by other vegetation being just so much waste of power. Moreover, weeds, growing as they do close together over the whole surface, have a peculiarly exhausting effect upon the soil, from which they draw off moisture and organic matter. They also smother the objects of culture, depriving them of light and air, and preventing the ground from being enriched by the dews and by the *atmosphere*. Weeds, especially those of the grass description, also bind the soil together, and render it less penetrable by the roots of the plant it is desired to cultivate. Every shrub, plant, or herb not expressly intended for growth, is a weed, and must be treated accordingly.

Weeds on coffee estates are usually removed either by being pulled up by the roots, scraped away by means of a piece of hoop iron, or by the hoe, or by being dug up. They can be subsequently destroyed by being buried or burned. Too often, however, they are merely left to rot on the surface of the ground.

By beginning to weed early, much subsequent loss and expense will be avoided, and the work should be systematically and carefully pursued once a month, *or oftener if necessary.* Unfortunately, however, this is not always practicable, owing to scarcity of labour, and hence it is estates are often seen so deplorably over-run. Within the first month or two after a clean burn, on forest land, the number of weeds should be so small as almost to admit of their being *counted;* one springing up here and there, but each isolated and independent. If, then, these are taken up *before they have run to seed,* and if the whole estate is subsequently gone over in the same way, once a month *unfailingly,* it can easily be kept permanently clean at a very trifling expense; *but,* once allow the isolated weed-plant to run to seed, and for every *one,* soon a hundred will appear; and if these hundred go also to seed, then we may expect for every hundred, ten thousand more; and so on until the surface is covered so closely that not an inch of soil is to be seen. I have counted twenty young "white-weed" plants in Ceylon spring up on a single square inch of ground. Never was there a subject to which the proverb about the *stitch in time* might be applied with greater appropriateness.

In bamboo districts, where the prevailing weed-pest takes the form of grass, matters are even worse, this being propagated *from the roots* as much as from seed; and within an incredibly short space of time, unless great care is taken, the planter will find to his dismay, his estate turned into a luxuriant hay-field, the coffee steadily waning away under the influence of the irrepressible invader. And here it may be remarked, that seldom will finer hay crops be met with than are sometimes to be seen covering estates in the districts alluded to. The thing to be regretted is their being so entirely in the *wrong place*.

Of the different methods of disposing of weeds above mentioned, each has to be adopted in turn under particular circumstances.

Weeding by hand is *par excellence* the proper method, and provided it be begun at the proper time, and afterwards unremittingly followed up, no difficulty will be found in adhering to it; that is to say, on forest clearings, where the soil is not naturally sown with grass, and produces only "sow-thistle," "goat-weed," and other tall plants. The labourer may be provided with a pointed stick or a small bit of hoop, to help him in eradicating obstinate roots, while a small sack should be tied round the waist, into which he can stuff everything he gets hold of, especially everything that is in flower or running to seed. The contents of these sacks may be emptied into receiving pits dug at convenient distances, or on the road—being in the latter case at once destroyed by fire. By religiously adhering to this method the planter is enabled to avoid all unnecessary disturbance of the surface soil, a faithful promoter of wash. This, it will be evident, is most of all to be considered on steep slopes.

If the weeds have once been allowed to get the upper hand, however, this prudent and efficient method will become less and less practicable, and as soon as the ground has become sown, and small weedlings begin to spring up close together over the surface, the *scraper* comes into requisition. The weeds are too minute and too numerous for eradication by hand, and the only alternative is to scrape them out wholesale. The great objection to this is, that you not only scrape away the weeds but the first inch or more of valuable surface mould, which will be very apt to float away with the first heavy rain that falls, especially when the land is steep. Repeat this process every few months, and the effect upon the property in loss and deterioration of soil may be imagined. Nevertheless, after a certain point has been passed there is no alternative. Weeding-scrapers are made and sold by the ironmongers, but being merely pieces of hoop iron, about fifteen inches in length, bent round at one end, and pointed at the other, any bit of hoop bent into the required shape will do equally well.

Unfortunately, however, there too often comes a time, when even the hoop-scraper is insufficient to meet the necessities of the case. When, for instance, the estate has become over-run with grass, the mammotie must be used. Nothing much more serious can befall an estate than that this should become unavoidable, on steep slopes of course particularly. On level fields, where wash is not to be apprehended, hoeing freely and deeply will on the other hand be highly beneficial, by opening up the soil to the sun and air, *except* in the dry season, in districts which suffer from drought, when for this very reason it ought to be avoided. In damp, cold climates, digging up the soil tends more than almost anything to improve its character; especially stiff, clayey soils. Without digging up, indeed, stiff soils altogether cease to absorb either air or moisture after a time, or having absorbed them remain too retentive.

"*Burying in.*"—When weeding has, from one cause or other been long neglected, and the weeds have got beyond control, and are high and dense, this method of disposing of them may be adopted with advantage; a wide, shallow pit being made, and all the weeds for several feet round being dug into it and covered over.

A not uncommon, and in many respects a most advantageous practice, is to give out weeding contracts to canganies, or native overseers, at so much per acre per month. In these cases the contractor has to provide and pay his own labourers, and is usually bound to weed over the land let out to him once a month. On clean forest land, where this system has been in vogue from the first, the cost is often as low as from one to two shillings an acre; but on old estates, which have been allowed at one time or other to get weedy, and are consequently more or less stocked with seed, it will be as much, sometimes, as 4*s.* an acre monthly. The great advantages of contract-weeding are, that a special gang being permanently devoted to the work, there is less risk of its being at any time interrupted; also that the onus of providing this part of the labour gang is taken off the shoulders of the superintendent ; thirdly, that the latter is saved the labour and anxiety of supervision ; and, finally, that the cost is less than would be the case under a system of day-work.

CHAPTER XV.

Supplying vacancies—Causes of vacancies—Prevention better than cure—Opening the pit—New soil desirable—Poonac—Strong plants required—" Supplies " put in early—Necessity of keeping them free from weeds.

IN newly-planted clearings, as well as in old fields of coffee, a certain percentage of the plants may always be expected to die out from one cause or other, and it becomes necessary to fill up regularly and promptly the vacancies thus occurring. The causes of the plants dying out are various : some do so from bad planting, such as being put in with the roots doubled up, some from the tap-root having come upon a slab-stone at the bottom of the pit, and being thus prevented from sinking further into the soil ; others from the attacks of insects, grubs, &c. ; from being smothered by weeds ; from drought, swampiness of the land, or from inherent disease.

Old plants are naturally more subject to decay than young ones, and consequently our attention is here more particularly required to the filling-up vacancies in old fields.

Prevention is always better than cure, and it is

the more important that every precaution should be taken to guard against "failures," that "supplies" (as they are called) will seldom if ever do as well as young plants put in virgin soil. Failures in new land can be almost entirely guarded against by honest pitting, careful planting, and a close examination of the plants which are to be put in; subsequently their number may be kept at a minimum by keeping the ground free from weeds, and by good draining, manuring, and pruning.

Notwithstanding every care, however, a certain number of vacancies will occur from time to time, and they must be filled up in the following manner: —The original pit, having been re-emptied, should be *enlarged* an inch or two all round, and especially in depth. This should be done in the dry weather, the pit being left open for some time, and only filled in when the time for planting has arrived. In most cases it will be desirable to refill the pit with the soil which has been taken out of it—this having probably, in the first instance, been surface mould, though no doubt its organic constituents will in great measure have been consumed if the pit has been already occupied for some years. Where the vacancy is in the midst of old trees, a large pit is necessary to protect the new plant from being interfered with by their roots; indeed, it might be well to isolate the young plant by making a ring trench round it, say six or eight inches wide and a foot deep. When practicable, it will always be desirable to put a basketful or so of new soil from the forest into the pit near the top. Where this cannot well be managed, and where the land requires renovation, a few handfuls of pounded poonac should be mixed with the surface mould; or, what is better still, a basketful of rotten dung or compost.

Good, strong, healthy plants must be chosen for this duty, either from the forest or the nursery: if the former, they must be "stumped;" but well-formed nursery plants, with three or four pairs of primaries, and say twelve or fifteen inches high, put in just as they come from the beds, with a good ball round the roots, are greatly to be preferred where steady wet weather can be calculated on for some time.

"Supplies" ought to be put in *early* in the wet season, so as to give them every advantage, their circumstances being (it should be remembered) less favourable than those of plants on virgin land. What they want is *a good start* before the dry weather comes round.

Before leaving the subject it may be well to state that it will be useless to incur the expense and labour of filling-up vacancies, unless the ground in which the young plants are placed is to be kept perfectly free from weeds.

CHAPTER XVI.

Staking—Prevailing wind to be noted—Fastenings—Durability of stakes—Earthing up—Forest belts—Hedges, &c.—Exposed situations better not planted.

IN situations where the plants are exposed to wind, the sooner they are provided with supports the better—at any rate as soon as they have reached a height of ten or twelve inches, and begin to throw out sufficient leaves and branches to present a resisting surface.

For small plants of the first season, the "lining" picket may be used for this purpose; but for larger plants a good stout stake will be required, from three to three and a half feet long, sufficiently strong not to bend, and well pointed so as to penetrate the ground easily.

Should the wind prevail especially from any one quarter of the compass, the fact must be duly noted, the stake being always posted on the *windward* side, by which means chafing and consequent injury to the stem and branches will be effectually avoided. The stake should enter the ground about six inches from the plant, and at such an angle as to come in contact with the stem at about half the height of the plant. It should be driven deeply into the ground with a mallet, so as to afford a firm and efficient support, care being of course used not to cause more injury to the young roots than is unavoidable.

The plant must now be attached to the stake by means of a broad band of some vegetable fibre, looped in the form of the figure 8, the stem occupying one opening, and the stake the other. The ligature must not be *tied* round the stem, otherwise it will cut into the bark as the growth of the plant goes on. I have seen cases where the bark of the coffee-tree has grown completely *over* the band, the plant being thus eventually killed.

Stakes of good durable wood will generally last from two to three years, and by the end of this period the plants should have obtained a sufficiently firm hold of the ground to be independent of artificial support.

For fastenings, strips of aloe leaf, the inner bark of many descriptions of trees, natural green jungle rope, or coir yarn may be used, whichever may be the most easily obtained.

Should the plants have got worked in the ground before having been provided with support, they should be comfortably earthed up five or six inches from the ground, in addition to being firmly secured.

Belts of jungle are sometimes left standing in likely situations, to protect the coffee from the wind, but opinions differ as to the probable advantage of this course, some planters holding that more harm is likely to result than good, the wind being thus frequently concentrated into eddies or whirlwinds, instead of taking its natural and more equable course. This, however, is a question which can only be decided by local circumstances in each case. It is not uncommon in Europe, when plantations have been made in exposed situations, to put in edges, or rows of some hardy quick-growing shrub, to protect the plants during the first few years; and I remember a case in which a Ceylon planter constructed a wall or barrier of posts and brushwood, some eight feet high, along the most exposed part of his estate, with the same object. All operations of this kind, however, are costly and laborious, and seldom productive of much permanent benefit; and as the result of experience, I believe it will probably *be wiser not to plant land where they are required.* At the most they can only mitigate the evil complained of. In moderately sheltered situations, staking combined with low topping ought to be sufficient to secure the stability of the plant; where they are not, the situation has little to recommend it for coffee culture.

CHAPTER XVII.

Shade necessary in hot climates—Planters unwilling to recognize this—Native gardens—Opinion changing—Jacktrees—Various advantages of shade—Objections—Diminished production—Reduced expenditure—Description of trees—Discrimination necessary—The Jack—In the Mauritius—Castor-oil plant—Plantains—Distance apart—Training.

IT appears to me that the past history of coffee cultivation in the East, if carefully looked into, conclusively proves that in hot climates and where prolonged seasons of drought may be expected to recur, coffee will not flourish permanently except under shade. The plant appears to affect shade universally in a state of nature, never being found growing wild (as far as my experience goes) except under the protection of its parent trees, or in the depths of the forest. This is the more remarkable, that the seeds are commonly deposited by wild animals and birds quite as freely on the open grass lands adjacent to the plantations as in the forests.

It seems curious that a fact like this should not from the first have forced itself into notice, but, so far from its having produced any influence, planters generally have all along shown great unwillingness to recognize the advantage of shade under any circumstances; and those few wise enough to adopt it, in such districts as Munzerabad and elsewhere, have been looked upon as quite old-fashioned and fanciful. The reason of this perhaps is the fact of the native gardens being always under shade, the tendency of the European planter being to regard with the utmost contempt all idea of instruction coming from such a quarter.

This of course is a great mistake. Were the coffee-plant a product of Northern Europe, like ourselves, the prejudice might be intelligible; but inasmuch as it is a strictly tropical plant, the European might be supposed to be eager to learn something of its habits and requirements from native experience, and to follow the native method as closely as possible in the first instance—experimentally at any rate. That the natives were right in adopting shade is clear enough. Their gardens are nearly always found in hot, low-lying situations, or precisely those in which the plants might naturally be expected to die out most rapidly from exhaustion; and yet, protected by fine old Jacks and other wide-spreading trees, they will often be found stocked with coffee of time immemorial growth, and which is still vigorous after having outlived generations of proprietors ; while the plantations of Europeans in the neighbourhood, upon which far greater solicitude and labour have been expended, but which have been left fully exposed to the sun, have long since passed into decay and been abandoned.

Of late years, however, the planters of the low-lying districts have had a series of stern, practical lessons on this subject, and these have not been without effect. I believe it will be found that by far the larger number of the estates that have "gone out," and been abandoned during the past thirty years, have been situated in such districts. The "Borer," "leaf disease," or some other enemy have here been conspicuous, and are seen to be *the immediate cause* of decay; but a grim suspicion has at the same time been gaining ground that these have had the way prepared for them by predisposition, and that their visitations might possibly have proved less fatal, had not the trees been left in a miserably weak condition by periods of prolonged and unmitigated drought ; in other words, that the "Borer," &c., have perhaps only hastened that decay which in any case could not have been long deferred.

It is very significant that whenever Jack-trees are found, as is often the case, standing here and there upon these abandoned properties, there will also inevitably be found a surviving remnant of the coffee-bushes clustered round them as it were for protection—all traces of the rest having disappeared.

The question as to the particular locality in which shade is required is one of climate, and has been alluded to in connexion with that subject, and it is always to be remembered that the present remarks are only applicable under those particular circumstances where the climate is such as to render shade necessary, and not universally.

The advantage to be derived from shading coffee in hot climates, may be summed up as diminished exhaustion, and consequently increased longevity of the plant; reduced cost of cultivation; a conservation of the nutritious properties of the soil, and an actual increase of these properties. Moreover, the cover given to the ground causes the surface vegetable matter to decay more rapidly, rendering it thereby more suitable for assimilation by the young roots of plants. Then the continuous fall of decaying leaves adds organic matter to the soil; and as these have originally been formed to a considerable extent from constituents furnished by the sub-soil (i.e. provided the tree be a sub-soil feeder), there is a positive gain of matter to the surface which the roots of plants such as coffee would otherwise never have been able to come within reach of. In addition, however, the value of estates growing large quantities of useful timber is being permanently increased, it being clear that a time must arrive when, owing to the constant progress of forest clearing, timber, whether for fuel, building purposes, or cabinet-making, will become greatly more scarce and valuable than at present.

What, then, on the other hand, are the objections to shade? The sole drawback, as far as I am aware, is that coffee under shade yields a smaller crop than that in open ground but otherwise similarly circumstanced. The exact falling-off cannot be stated, as this will depend on the density of the shade and the heat of the climate. In a *very* hot climate the yield would be but little diminished, while in a comparatively cool, moist one, shade would operate more unfavourably. Let us suppose, however, that in a climate where an efficient shade is really *required*, the crop is thereby reduced by one-third or even one-half; the result in this case merely is that, in the course of ten years, the coffee without shade would have produced a total of say 50 cwts. of cured berries per acre, while under shade the same area would perhaps have yielded no more than 30 or 40 cwts. In the first case, however, the trees will be well-nigh "pumped out," whether from exhaustion pure and simple, or sped on by "Borer," &c., while in the latter they will probably show no signs of exhaustion, but be ready to all appearance to go on bearing a crop of 3 or 4 cwts. per acre every year till doomsday. The question then arises, which of the two cases is the more desirable?

A consideration of by no means trivial importance, also, is that the cost of weeding will be *much* smaller under shade than in open clearings.

Now comes the question as to the description of shade to be provided. It is a well-known fact that certain trees exercise a prejudicial influence on particular plants in their neighbourhood, while seeming actually to benefit others. This is probably due in part to the excretion given off by the roots (by a process perhaps similar to that which prevails in the animal kingdom), and which, while actually useful as manure to one description of plant, may be no less noxious to another. Again, some trees, instead of delving down for their sustenance into the sub-soil, prefer spreading their roots abroad near the surface, and thus abstract nourishment and moisture which cannot be spared them. Some trees also exhale gases injurious to other vegetation. This is the case in a marked degree with the elder, the walnut, and the laburnum of Europe; and with the orange, lemon, citron, &c., of the tropics. All these points have of course to be considered.

I am strongly in favour of the *Jack* as the tree best suited for providing shade for fields of coffee. In the first place, its presence, so far from being prejudicial, seems to be actually beneficial to the coffee-plant; next, it is a sub-soil feeder; then it produces a fruit much valued as food by the natives; its timber is also valuable, whether for cabinet-making or building purposes; and, finally, it flourishes best precisely in those situations where its shade is most required. Known to botanists as the *Artocarpus integrifolia*, the Jack grows to a large size; it resembles and belongs to the same family as the bread-fruit tree. The timber, when newly cut, is of a light yellow colour, possesses a beautiful grain, and is capable of a high polish, not greatly inferior to that of mahogany or satin-wood, both of which it also resembles to a certain extent in grain and colour, after having been polished. The fruit is as large as a pumpkin, and weighs from twenty to thirty pounds, containing from 200 to 300 seeds, which, though somewhat unpleasant in smell when raw, are converted by being roasted or boiled into a wholesome and agreeable farinaceous food, always much appreciated by the coolies.

The *Loquat* tree is planted along the road-sides on many of the estates in the Wynaad and elsewhere, and coffee appears to thrive well under it; but, so far as I am aware, the wood is not of any value, which at once places it at a disadvantage in competing with the Jack. The loquat yields a pleasant fruit, in size and appearance much like the yellow plum.

The Jack is said to bear transplanting badly, and it will therefore be necessary to deposit two or three of the seeds a couple of inches below the surface, wherever a tree is desired to grow. The most healthy of the plants can afterwards be selected.

I remember once meeting an old French gentleman from the Mauritius, who informed me that a plant of very rapid growth is used for the purpose of shading the coffee and sugar plantations in that island. I have not, unfortunately, been able to ascertain its name, but my informant gave it as his opinion that by its aid coffee might be successfully cultivated in India *on the plains!* The castor-oil plant (*Ricinus Communis* or *Palma Christi*), which grows from six to ten feet high in a year, bearing a crop (from which the oil is expressed) in the first year, might perhaps be found useful in some cases, as it requires but little care in cultivation; but I do not strongly recommend it for being grown with coffee, it being apparently a surface-feeder, and consequently likely to draw off much moisture from the soil, while it would not prove very serviceable, its foliage not being luxuriant.

Plantains or Bananas are planted for shade in St. Domingo, and at any rate these will not injure coffee among which they may be planted; probably in hot climates, and for the first few years, until Jack-trees have had time to grow up, they might prove useful.

Trees for shade should not be sufficiently near each other to prevent a free circulation of air, or entirely to exclude the sun's rays, a certain amount of both being necessary to produce vigorous coffee. They may, however, in hot situations, be grown tolerably close together in the *first* place, it being easy to thin them out to the required extent afterwards, as they increase in size. In order to make the trees throw out wide leafy heads, and thus form a sort of natural canopy or awning over a large space, they should be trained to single stems till ten or twelve feet high, all lateral branches being kept off. This system will also tend to produce large straight *timber* (which is a consideration to be kept in view).

CHAPTER XVIII.

> Bungalows and lines—A permanent bungalow—Definition—Various materials—Stone and lime—Bricks—Criterion of quality—Brick-making—Clay required—Breaking-up soil—Moulds—Treading out—Moulding—Drying—Burning—The kiln—Tiles—Moulding—Burning—Wattle and dab—The uprights—The wattles—The "dab"—White ants—Timber white-ant proof—The supports—Laterite for building—Thatch—Cadjans—Straw—Shingles—Splitting—Dimensions—Laying—Cost—Iron tile-sheets—Difficulties and drawbacks—Method of fastening—Description of bungalow required—Flooring—Asphalte—Plaster—Tiles—Boards—Sawing timber—Method of computing—Coolie lines—Site—Ventilation—Sanitation—Cowdung—Coolie gardens—Size of sets—Danger of fire.

SUBSTANTIAL, comfortable buildings not only add to the value of an estate, but contribute largely to the health and contentment of those residing on it. As soon, therefore, as all the more immediately necessary works have been disposed of, and a time of slackness begins to set in previous to the coffee coming into full bearing, the manager's attention should be directed to the erection of a bungalow for himself, and of lines for the coolies; these to be of a "pukka" (complete or permanent) character, and to supersede the rude, temporary structures which have probably been in use up to that time.

Permanent buildings are really more economical in the end than temporary ones, the latter requiring constant repairs and renovation, and thus involving considerable outlay year after year.

A "Bungalow" is said to be strictly defined as a dwelling such as Europeans usually occupy, of one storey, and provided with a verandah. This, in fact, is just the sort of house the planter requires. Of course, however, it may be constructed of various materials and in different styles, and as it is a comparatively costly undertaking, and closely concerns the health and comfort of the superintendent, the plans and estimates should be carefully gone into beforehand.

The walls may be either of stone and mortar, bricks and mortar, or of bricks or stone with mud (the bricks being either burnt or sun-dried); or of wattle and daub; of laterite and mortar, or of wooden boards.

The strongest houses are, of course, those made of stone and mortar; but then they are also the most expensive and tedious to erect, involving usually a great outlay for collecting and carrying the stones, of which a much larger quantity is required than would be the case with other materials, inasmuch as walls of undressed stone cannot very well be less than a foot and a half thick. Where the walls are of stone, all the door-ways and window openings should be arched; the arches being made of bricks, should they be procurable. The cost of a bungalow of these materials can only be determined by the facility with which the stone can be collected.

Bricks, in my opinion, are the most desirable material for estate buildings. They give sufficient strength, are easily transported and used, and, above all, are cheap, and can be made almost anywhere. A common mason will lay from 400 to 500 large-sized (say 7 lbs.) bricks per day; eight of these will just make up an ordinary coolie load, and their dimensions will probably be about $10\frac{1}{2} \times 5\frac{1}{4} \times 3\frac{1}{2}$ inches.

The evidences of good bricks is their freedom from cracks, their hardness, which is evidenced by their giving out a ringing sound when struck, being of uniform size, and by their weight not being much increased by immersion in water.

A useful pamphlet on brick-making in the Madras Presidency has afforded me some useful hints as to their manufacture. The following are the dimensions therein recommended: Length, $8\frac{3}{4}$ inches, breadth, 4¼ inches, and thickness, 2 inches; each brick with its ¼ inch layer of mortar will then occupy a space of 9 × 4½ × 2¼ inches. Thicker bricks would be better, only that it is a difficult matter to get them equally well burned; as a smaller number would then be required, and they would be less easily broken. The earth best suited for the manufacture of bricks should contain a mixture of about five parts of pure clay to one part of sand; a composition of soil often found in a natural state. Almost any kind of earth, however, may be used, provided it is free from pebbles, and not too sandy.

The piece of ground, the soil of which is intended to be converted into bricks, having in the first place been cleared, should be broken up to the depth of a foot. If this is done a few months before the bricks are required so much the better. Water may now be turned in over-night and allowed to saturate the whole till morning, when the mud thus formed should be thoroughly worked up, kneaded, and finally trodden through for a couple of hours at least. More water may then be let in, the mixture being left till next day, when the tramping process may be repeated; if time is precious, however, as is sometimes the case, this may be done at once, until the mass is thoroughly homogeneous, and of equal consistency throughout.

The quantity of water must not exceed what is necessary to render the clay sufficiently plastic for manipulation and moulding.

The next step is to level off and clear a piece of ground immediately adjacent, on which the bricks when newly moulded may be laid out to dry.

The moulds should be of wood bound with iron, and made double, so as to admit of duplicate bricks being turned out together. The dimensions should be a trifle larger than the size the brick is intended to be, so as to allow for the shrinking in the kiln.

The clay may be trodden out either by coolies, or by bullocks, buffaloes, or elephants. The animals last-named do the work the most efficiently, but their services are not always to be obtained.

The prepared clay being in readiness, the mould must first be dipped in water, then placed on a wooden bench and well filled; the wet, soft clay being next well squeezed in; the top may then be smoothed over with the wet hand, any superfluous clay being removed. The mould may now be drawn to the edge of the bench, and its contents gently slipped on to a piece of board, and on this conveyed to the adjoining levelled drying-ground, and there deposited. The newly-formed bricks must now be allowed thoroughly, but gradually, to dry; and in order that the process may be a slow one, they should be protected from both sun and wind. When half dry each should be taken up, and any dirt or pebbles adhering to it scraped off, after which it should be again laid down, but this time upon the reverse side.

For burning the bricks a square piece of ground should be levelled, the bricks being laid on their flat sides in rows two deep, a space of one brick between each. This space must be filled up with firewood, with which the bricks themselves should also be covered to the depth of six inches; others must now be placed transversely in double layers as before, the spaces left being again filled up and covered with firewood; next, two courses of bricks must be ranged on their narrow edges, and above them nine inches of firewood. The clump may be raised in this manner to a height of six or eight feet, an extra layer of firewood one foot thick being allowed for every four layers of bricks, and a wall of unburnt bricks, cemented together with mud, being built round as the clump rises, to prevent the bricks from falling out as the wood is consumed. When all these arrangements have been completed, the wood may be lighted on the windward side, and (the top and sides being well sealed up with wet clay,) the whole mass left to burn itself out. A large clump of say 100,000 bricks will take a week to burn, but a smaller one will be ready in a shorter time. After the fire has burnt itself out, the pile should be allowed a week to cool before being opened, and the bricks will then be ready for use.

For tile-making, the clay should be prepared in the same manner as for bricks, being, if anything, more carefully tempered and worked up; a more tenacious character of clay being also desirable so as to give greater strength, the form being more fragile. Tiles are in the first instance moulded perfectly flat, being afterwards bent over a cylindrical piece of wood into the requisite shape, and then slipped gently off on to the ground, where they are left to dry.

Another method is as follows: the clay is dabbed within the mould or frame on a board previously sprinkled with brick dust, the superfluous clay being removed by means of a straight bar drawn clean over the face of the mould. The new tile is now slipped on to the back of one previously made (the latter having been plentifully sprinkled with dust to prevent cohesion), and thus acquires the requisite bend or curve; the newly-formed tile is now well sanded in its turn, and the next is placed on its back, and so on until a heap of twenty or thirty has been formed, when a new pile may be begun. These heaps are left till next day, when any deficiencies in their shape are carefully corrected, and they are then laid one by one on the ground to dry.

Tiles are burned in a circular kiln, and must be carefully packed *on end* for this purpose, and burned slowly.

"*Wattle and Dab*" (or "Daub") forms a cheap, convenient, and on the whole satisfactory substitute for masonry of brick or stone and mortar, and buildings thus constructed will stand for many years. The posts and cross-pieces may be either of sawn timber or taken green from the jungle. In the former case, the walls will of course present a much more even and angular appearance. A space of six inches should be left between the upright posts, each of which should be at least four inches thick. Lathes, or wattles from the jungle, must now be attached to these horizontally every six inches, on both sides and opposite to each other. These may be either tied with Coir yarn or jungle-fibre, or nailed to the uprights. This having been done, the spaces between the timbers should be carefully filled up with well-trodden clay, such as is above described as being requisite for brick-making. A good-sized stone may afterwards with advantage be stuffed into each square of mud, which will thus be still further compressed, and forced into all interstices; but this is not essential. As soon as the clay first applied has had time to harden, a further coating should be applied, covering the woodwork to the depth of an inch, both outside and in; and when this has become perfectly dry, the wall may be finished with a good coat of "chunam" plaster (mortar) from the mason's trowel, which may be applied in such a manner as to give an appearance quite equalling that of brickwork. The thickness of a wall of this kind will finally be about ten inches, or about that of a single brick— it will, however, probably be much stronger than a brick wall of the same thickness. Of course, however, the thickness may be increased to any extent by additional applications of clay or mortar.

I have seen bungalows constructed in this manner, still in excellent preservation after having stood for thirty years, and that too in localities abounding with white ants. This is partly accounted for by a remarkable provision by which these indefatigable little sappers invariably, when tunnelling through wood-work, leave a sufficient residuum or shell to prevent total collapse; while they also, it is stated, deposit a secretion as a sort of cement, by which this is materially strengthened; the object in both cases apparently being to guard against a destruction in which they themselves would be involved. However, even where walls of the above description have, owing to the operations of white ants, become in course of time totally deprived of their wood-work, it does not by any means follow that they have become dangerously weakened in consequence, clay or mud becoming excessively hard and solid by lapse of time, in the warm, dry atmosphere of the tropics. There are certain descriptions of timber which may be considered proof against white ants, such as "black-wood," "kino," "mutty," &c., while others may be in great measure rendered so by saturation with creosote and similar solutions.

All the posts used for the *corners*, as well as for the supports of the door and window frames, should either be of one or other of the above descriptions, or at least *charred* or soaked in some such preservative liquid, especially the part to be sunk underground. The uprights for these positions should also be strong, stout, and straight; they should be planted at least three feet deep in the ground, and in no case should they be more than six feet distant from each other; indeed, it will be safer to have one such support to every *four* feet of wall, and they will be none the worse for being of sawn timber, whatever the other timbers may be.

Weather-boards are too combustible a material to be used with safety in hot climates.

An excellent building material largely used in Ceylon and Southern India (principally found near the sea-coast, I believe) is "*Cabook*" or *Laterite*. This seems to be a kind of decomposed rock, or it may perhaps be better described as a clayey composition, which has the convenient faculty of becoming readily hard by exposure to the atmosphere. It is cut out some six to ten feet below the surface in blocks or bricks about 15 inches in length, by 9 by 6, with an axe or spade; these bricks becoming hard, in a few days make neat as well as substantial walls.

ROOFING may be variously made from thatch-grass or straw, "cadjans" (the plaited leaves of the cocoa-nut tree), shingles, tiles, or iron sheets, whether plain or corrugated.

A roof of thatch is generally the most ready to hand on a coffee estate, and as it makes the coolest house in hot weather, the warmest in cold, and is extremely healthful, it is the one most generally adopted. Like most other things, however, thatch, however excellent, is not without its disadvantages, amongst which are its liability to combustion, and the necessity of constant renewal and repair; the latter consideration rendering it by no means the least expensive in the long-run.

"Cadjans" make a very cool, water-tight, and on the whole neat-looking thatch, but are not much used except in the immediate neighbourhood of cocoa-nut plantations; neither these nor straw, however, are to be compared as thatching material with the magnificent lemon, ("*mana*,") and spear-grasses, which cover the hills of Ceylon and the Western Coast, growing to a height of from six to eight feet; they would, consequently, only be used as a substitute when the latter are not obtainable.

Shingles have much to recommend them for roofing. These are strips of wood split in proper dimensions, and nailed side by side, in the same way as slates on a house in England. If made from suitable timber they yield a neat, durable, and efficient covering; and, indeed, almost any hard, straight-grained wood will answer the purpose. They are made in the following manner. A straight-stemmed tree having been selected in the forest, not more than 15 or 18 inches in diameter, it is cut down and sawn into lengths of 22 inches, or 20 inches, as may be preferred. These lengths are now split into sections, so as to admit of these being again partitioned, according to the judgment of the workman, into the greatest number of thin boards of not less than 3 to 4 inches in width. Two men will be kept employed in felling the trees, and sawing them into the proper lengths, two in splitting up the blocks into shingles, and two more in dressing or finishing them.

For the splitting operation an implement is provided, in shape and character not unlike an enormous chisel, haft and blade being of one solid piece of iron; the blade should be about 6 inches square, and the handle 18 inches long, having a broad head or knob at the end. The block to be operated on having been placed upright on end, this implement is held in position by one workman while the second deals it a smart stroke on the head with a heavy mallet.

Each shingle should be from a quarter to one-third of an inch in thickness, and from three to five inches in width. After being split off they are handed over to be finished, all inequalities being removed as far as possible. They should then be stacked in a shed (or at any rate in some shady, protected spot), and, if made of green wood, allowed to season for some months before being used; unless this is carefully attended to they will soon crack and go to pieces, when exposed to alternate rain and sunshine on the roof. Six practised hands ought to be able to prepare 600 shingles per day. Shingle-making, however, is one of those works which should always be done by contract if possible.

Considerable care and judgment are required in putting on shingles. Each must be perforated with the gimlet 3 inches from the upper end, and nailed to the reaper with a small $1\frac{1}{2}$ inch nail or "sprig." Should the shingle split in being bored, it must be discarded, unless either of the divided parts is wide enough to be used of itself, in which case it should be turned to account A small space, say $\frac{1}{3}$ or $\frac{1}{2}$ an inch must always be left between each shingle, to allow for expansion when wet. The first, or bottom row, should be put on double, each one of the upper tier covering the division between two of the lower. This row may be allowed to extend some 4 or 6 inches beyond the ends of the rafters. Another row may now be commenced, the ends coming down to within 7 inches of the ends of the first, that is, over-lying just 15 inches of the first row, and so on. Arranged in this manner it is calculated that six or seven shingles of ordinary width will be required to cover every superficial foot of roof.

The cost of making shingles in Ceylon used to be estimated at about 9s. per 1000, and that of putting them on from 3s. to 4s.; add to this 4s. for nails, and thus (without allowing for transport charges) a roof may be had at a comparatively small cost, which will require little or no renewal for six or seven years.

Tiles have been previously referred to; they should only be used in localities where the best clay is obtainable. Once they are on the less they are interfered with the better, unless water begins to come in. It will be found necessary, however, to re-lay them from time to time, as they have a tendency to slip down and become displaced, especially should the slope of the roof be at all steep. They have the advantages of being durable and incombustible. Neither tiles nor shingles, however, provide so comfortable, dry or healthful a covering as *thatch*, according to my experience, whether for bungalow or coolie lines.

Iron sheets, both plain and corrugated, tarred and galvanized, are extensively used for roofing buildings of all kinds in the East. For *coffee stores*, where a maximum warmth and dryness is desirable, they are all that can be desired; they are also valuable from their durability and non-liability to combustion. As a material for dwelling-houses in a tropical climate, however, iron is most objectionable, rendering the temperature of the interior intolerable in hot weather, and producing an incessant and most unpleasant reverberation during the process of natural expansion and contraction (one or other of which appears to be always in progress), as also when affected by wind, or rain. I have also been assured by medical men that iron roofing for dwelling-houses is unhealthful, owing to the great variation of temperature occurring under it—the heat being excessive during the day in fine weather, while the cold at night is equally intensified.

Presenting a large surface with little or no proportionate weight, iron roofing-sheets, and indeed, entire roofs of this material are frequently carried away by the wind. To guard against this contingency, large stones or logs of timber are generally laid on them; but even this is often an insufficient precaution. Mr. Tytler, a successful Ceylon planter of very long standing, thus describes his difficulties from this cause. "If," says he, "the sheets were fastened down at both ends, the simple expansion and contraction of the iron very soon drew out the nails and rivets, and the sheets became loose. The manager of the estate became annoyed beyond endurance by the wind blowing off his store-roof, and in desperation he screwed them to the rafters. The result was, that one blowy night the rafters and all were lifted off."

"John Gordon, the pulper maker," he goes on to say, "conceived the idea of rivetting slips of iron to one end of each sheet of iron, into which he slipped the end of the over-lapping sheet, nailing the other end to the rafter or reeper. One end (the lower one) being free, slid up and down within the slip according as the iron contracted or expanded, and thus he kept the iron firm and secure. Recently, on an emergency, I had to cover a store with iron. I could find none of Gordon's iron, but only plain sheets. I mentioned the difficulty to a gentleman in Kandy, who, tearing off the cover of a price current, at once showed me how, by pieces of stiff hoop iron, bent in three, to slip over the end of the upper sheet, and under that of the lower, the object might be effected; so I procured these from Walker and Co., and nailed the upper end of the sheets to the rafters, and holding the lower ends of the next overlapping sheets by means of these slips; the roof is all I could desire."

The description of bungalow to be built must, of course, depend on the amount to be expended on its erection. In most localities a suitable residence might in my time be put up for between £300 or £400. Probably, however, in the present position of the coffee enterprise (the value of estate property being enormously increased, in consequence of the high prices ruling during the last few years in the European markets), the planter's views on this subject may have become more ambitious, while the advance in wages will also probably tend further to necessitate an increased estimate. It is, however, beyond the scope of a work like the present to consider the erection of anything beyond a plain, comfortable, and substantial dwelling; it being neither prudent nor desirable in my opinion to burden the accounts of a young estate with expenditure on merely ornamental architecture. The only objects I would be disposed to keep in view are *comfort*, stability, neatness, and economy.

In 1855, I superintended the erection of a little bungalow, in the Swiss cottage style, raised on pillars three feet from the ground, and entirely of wood, with thatched roof. This contained a sitting-room, two bed-rooms and a verandah, the principal room being provided with a masonry fire-place and chimney, and the entire cost was about £100. In houses thus raised off the ground on pillars, dryness and salubrity are secured, but the boards of the floor should be dove-tailed into each other, otherwise the wind will find its way up through the interstices, and render it unpleasantly cool, especially at night.

Bungalows may be floored either with bricks, paving-tiles, plaster, asphalte, or boards. The most durable of these materials is asphalte, the most comfortable, in my opinion, boards.

Asphalte is a mineral product, somewhat of the nature of pitch, which, being reduced to a liquid state by boiling, is largely mixed with sand, and laid down about an inch or a couple of inches thick, being then allowed to harden as it cools into a solid, smooth surface. A great point in favour of asphalte is its being impervious to the operations of white ants, if laid of the proper thickness.

Chunam plaster, though very nice to look at when *new*, soon gets broken up when trampled on, and is then very dirty and objectionable.

Dutch tiles for flooring are very durable and neat, but also *very expensive*, having to be brought from a distance; common bricks, however, form a good substitute, the joints being neatly pointed with mortar containing a large proportion of lime.

When wooden floors are adopted, it is necessary to see that the boards are well seasoned in the first instance; they should also be narrow, not exceeding six inches in width, and not less than an inch and a half thick : their tendency to warp and shrink will, with these points attended to, have been reduced to a minimum.

Timber for sawing should, if possible, be found among the felled logs in the clearing, as it will in this case probably have lain some time, and be more or less seasoned, and consequently better adapted for immediate use than trees felled for the purpose in the forest. In Ceylon, the sawyers are very expert, and usually fell and hoist the logs for themselves; but in South India this has usually to be done by the estate coolies, the sawyers rigidly restricting themselves to sawing, according to the most approved "caste" principles. This is a great source of additional trouble and expense to the planter, who often in consequence prefers doing without sawyers altogether, especially where there is anything approaching a scarcity of labour.

The charge for sawing in Ceylon is so much per hundred superficial feet.[1] In Western India the cost is so much per *candy;* a candy being equal to 12 *coles*, and a cole to 24 Malayalim inches, or $28\frac{1}{2}$ inches English.

The following is the most simple way of measuring sawyer's work in Ceylon, where the English terms of measurement are in use. Take, for example, a timber 6 inches by 5, and 21 feet in length; add 6 to $5 = 11$; then multiply 11 by $21 = 231$; next divide 231 by 12, and the result is arrived at, or say 19 feet 3 inches. Or, take a board 9 inches wide, 1 inch thick, and 24 feet long; here, it will be observed, the thickness, being *no more than one inch*, is not counted; multiply 9 by $24 = 216$; divide by $12 = 18$ feet, the correct result.

In Malabar the method differs, the cuts of the saw, and not the dimensions of the pieces sawn, being calculated; the result is arrived at as follows: A log of timber having been intersected by 6 cuts, say 11 inches (Malayalim) in width, by $5\frac{1}{4}$ *coles* in length; 11 must be multiplied by $5\frac{1}{4} = 57\frac{3}{4}$; multiply this again by $6 = 346\frac{1}{2}$; divide by 24 (to bring the sum into *coles*) $= 14$ and $10\frac{1}{2}$ over, and

---

[1] 12*s.* to 14*s.* in my time.—AUTHOR.

again by 12 (so as to reduce to candies), and the result is 1 : 2 : 10½, or 1 candy, 2 coles, and 10½ inches. Or, again, take a log with say 17 cuts, measuring 3½ inches (Malayalim) in width, and 5½ coles in length; multiply 3½ by 5½ = 19¼, and again by 17 = 327¼; divide this by 24 = 13 and 15¼ over, and again by 12, and the result is = 1 : 1 : 15¼, or say 1 candy, 1 cole, and 15¼ inches.

For *Coolie Lines*, the planter should be most particular to select a healthful situation, well-drained, and airy without being exposed. They should be sheltered in particular from the land-wind, which in India seems to be charged with injurious influences (arising, no doubt, from its passage over an immense area of country, reeking with the malarious exhalations called forth by a tropical sun). The situation of the lines is too often made dependent on the vicinity of some stream or spring, but instead of this, the water ought to be conveyed by a channel or pipe to the spot decided upon as most eligible. Ravines and hollows are always to be avoided, as the unhealthful gases float down and settle in them.

Ventilation must also be attended to, and this may be arrived at in the following manner. Each set of lines should be provided with a verandah six or seven feet wide, running along its entire length, the verandah posts being the same height as the back wall; the front wall facing the verandah should then be run up so as to leave a space of six inches or more between it and the roof, to allow of the escape of impure air and smoke. Coolies like a good wide verandah, finding it useful to sit in in hot weather, for storing firewood, and for drying their clothing in in wet weather.

Sanitation must of course be attended to as far as possible, no impurities being allowed to collect near the lines. It will not be possible to prevent this altogether, and it will therefore be well to employ a scavenger specially to clean up all round the immediate neighbourhood. A cangany may be specially deputed, with a small extra allowance of pay, to see that this duty is properly carried out.

Coolies should always be provided with raised "charpoys," or sleeping benches, and will generally be found only too willing to fix these up for themselves if provided with a few boards. Each hut or apartment should also have a wooden door swung on strong hinges.

The walls should be frequently re-coated with mud or clay to keep them in repair, and plastered with cow-dung. The latter is an excellent preventive of vermin, and once dried gives an exceedingly clean, neat surface. No cracks or interstices in the walls should be left open, or these will become populated by innumerable fleas, and perhaps other vermin, the moment the lines are left unoccupied. An occasional coat of whitewash will also be of use, both in discouraging vermin, and in rendering the dwellings clean and wholesome.

The coolies should be encouraged to make little gardens for themselves, for the cultivation of brinjals, Indian corn, beans, &c., and in order to admit of this being freely done, without an unnecessary sacrifice of land, the lines are always better placed on a grass hill or piece of open waste land, than in the midst of the coffee. When so situated, moreover, the coolies may keep pigs, sheep, and poultry to their heart's content without loss to the proprietor.

With regard to the number of rooms in each set of lines, I think twenty an extreme limit; where the number is so great as this, it will be better to have them in a double row back to back, otherwise the length will be inconvenient and unsightly. Small sets of six or eight rooms are preferable, the different castes being then less likely to interfere with each other. Moreover, in this case, should a fire occur, the loss and inconvenience are reduced. For the same reason, it is not desirable to have a number of sets in close contiguity, lest a spark some fine day should lead to the destruction of the whole. Considering the number of fires nightly in every occupied set of lines, and that in no case is there such a thing as a flue or chimney to conduct the smoke and sparks to the outer air, and also the extremely combustible nature of these buildings, &c., it seems very surprising so few accidents occur. If once a thatched building in these climates catches fire, especially in the hot season, there is little chance of extinguishing the flames. The only course is to destroy a portion of the building or roof, and thus, if possible, interrupt their course.

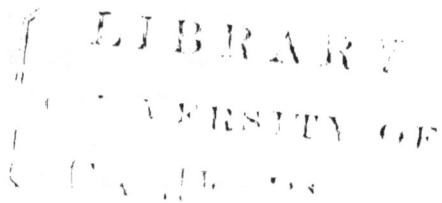

CHAPTER XIX.

The pulping-house—The cherry loft—The machine platform—The cisterns—Water supply—The pulper—The sieve—The crusher—Revolving buckets—Butler's pulper—Letter of a Ceylon planter, 1860—The Disc pulper—Setting the pulper—Improvements—Iron barrels—Walker's patent punching—Gordon's breasts—Letter from Mr. John Gordon—Stores—Iron stores—Objects required—Crop difficulties—Mr. Clerihew's system—Revolving fans—Hot-air apparatus—Barbecues—Macadam and plaster—Asphalte—Plenty of drying-ground desirable.

STORES, PULPING-HOUSES, &c.—Before the first crop season has arrived, it is necessary to make preparation for its reception; in other words, that we should provide suitable buildings for the safe keeping of the crop while still on the estate, and for its being prepared for despatch to the port of shipment. These buildings are usually treated of under the heading of Stores and Pulping-Houses. These should be placed as near the middle of the plantation as possible, so that the distance the crop will have to be carried may be reduced to a minimum. It will also be desirable that an elevated open position be chosen, where there will be plenty of air moving, so as to facilitate the drying of the coffee.

The first building that comes into requisition is the *pulping-house*, and it therefore merits the first description. This building comprises three departments—the cherry-loft, the pulping platform, and the cisterns.

The cherry-loft is the apartment into which the ripe coffee is first brought direct from the trees. As each crop-gatherer comes in, the sack of crimson produce is emptied into the measuring-box, and the quantity carefully recorded against his or her name in the pay list. Bushel after bushel is brought in, until at length a goodly heap is raised, sometimes filling the entire apartment, and rising in the centre well-nigh to the roof. This apartment must, consequently, be immediately over the platform on which the pulping machines are placed, or, at any rate, in such a position that the fruit can be conveniently run, by means of water, into the machines in question.

It is desirable that the pulping-house should be built, if possible, against the side of a cutting, or embankment, the cherry-loft being placed on the top of this, so that the coolies may be able to carry the ripe cherry (a bag of which is of considerable weight) straight in, instead of having a flight of steps to ascend.

The machine platform, again, must be in such a position that the coffee after being pulped can be run, by means also of water-pipes, into the cisterns; and the cisterns must be so placed as to admit of the coffee after being washed in them being conveniently conveyed to the drying-ground, and of the waste water and refuse being run off to the pulp-pit.

The cisterns must be at least three in number; that is to say, two "receiving cisterns" to receive the beans as they come direct from the pulper, and each of which must be large enough to hold the produce of the largest amount of cherry ever likely to be housed in a single day; the third cistern is for washing the parchment in as it comes from the receiving cisterns, and should be as large, superficially, as both the others put together, equal *depth*, however, being unnecessary.

These cisterns should all have a slight incline, to facilitate the water being quickly drained off; the gradient of the washing cistern should not exceed three or four inches in twenty-four feet. The receiving cisterns should be provided with a grating of perforated zinc at the lowest part, to allow of the water draining off as fast as it comes in. The washing cistern, on the contrary, should be water-tight, being provided with a sluice door at the lower end, which can be opened or closed at pleasure; both close and perforated or grated doors being adjusted to this for use as required.

The most important consideration in the selection of the site of the pulping-house is an ample supply of water, which is required in considerable quantity for both the operations of pulping and washing, and should also be available, if possible, as a motive power for the whole of the machinery.

The building should, therefore, be erected in the vicinity of some large stream, or at any rate in such a situation that water may be conveyed to it at a level at least 10 feet above that of the platform on which the machinery is to stand; this will admit of an over-shot water-wheel of 20 feet diameter (with its axle resting on the level of the platform) being employed to keep the pulpers, &c., in motion. Where there is no large stream which can be requisitioned for these purposes, its absence must be compensated for by a dam of adequate dimensions.

The operation known as "pulping" consists in the separation of the skin or pulp of the cherry from the seeds or beans it contains. This is performed by a machine the oldest and most common form of which is as follows: Suppose a framework of iron or wood some four feet in height, the same in length, and two feet wide. Across one end of this, and at about two feet and a half from the ground, a cylinder rests on its axles; it is covered with a sheathing of punched copper, being thus not unlike a nutmeg-grater on a large scale. This cylinder, which would be about one foot in diameter, is made so as to revolve inversely towards two bars or "chops" faced with iron, the one placed above the other with a space of about $\frac{5}{10}$ths of an inch between them. The upper chop is so shaped that while its lower edge is no more than the thickness of an ordinary lead pencil distant from the punched protuberances of the cylinder, its face slopes backwards so as to leave a rapidly widening space upwards, to allow the fruit to fall readily in between it and the cylinder. The lower chop, on the other hand, has its upper edge so close to the copper that nothing thicker than a sheet of brown paper would pass between the two. The effect of this adjustment is that, in course of rapid revolution, the cylinder compresses the berries sharply against the upper chop, by which means the beans are forced out, and pass out in front over the lower chop. The skin or pulp, on the contrary, being penetrated by the rough points of the copper, adheres to the cylinder, and is carried round past the lower chop (the space between which and the cylinder is too small to allow any of the beans to go with it), until washed off by the flow of water which is constantly passing into the machine from above, with the fruit.

The lower chop must be just near enough to the cylinder to admit the skins, while preventing the entrance of any part of the smallest bean. Should even the tips of the bean gain admittance into this space, the result will be a nip or "cut," which amounts to irremediable damage.

From this pulper the coffee is run into a sieve, which arrests any berries which have not been efficiently dealt with, and any skins which have not been got rid of, and throws them out in order that they be returned to undergo a second operation; the beans, however, pass through and are run off into the cisterns. The pulp is conveyed by a water-pipe at the back into a pit, where it is reserved for manure.

Another machine much employed, and with great advantage on large estates, in conjunction with and as an aid to the pulper, is what is called the "Crusher." The office of this, as its name implies, is simply to crush the ripe cherries with sufficient force to cause separation between the bean and the pulp of the larger berries, while giving the smaller ones such a squeeze as to make them at any rate very much more easily acted on by the pulper. The cylinder of the crusher is covered with overlapping steel plates instead of punched copper, and does not *get rid* of the skins as the pulper does, simply sending everything that has passed through it into the general sieve, whence all that is retained and thrown out is passed up, by means of buckets, into the pulpers. In general, a good deal of the coffee is actually pulped by the crusher, the beans passing through the sieve to the vat,—a fact which at once shows how much this machine lightens the work of the pulpers. The crusher was, I believe, the invention of Mr. J. Brown, formerly of Ceylon.

The operation of passing up the rejections of the sieve into the pulpers is usually, on large estates, and where there is sufficient water power, performed by buckets attached to revolving belts, by which means manual labour is economized—always a most desirable object in coffee-planting.

Butler's pulper was an ingenious contrivance, dispensing with both chops and sieve. It consisted of two cylinders covered with grooved metal, made to revolve inversely towards each other. I am informed, however, that this machine has now gone entirely out of use, having soon been put out of the field by the adoption of "Gordon's breasts," which also dispense with the use of the sieve, thereby effecting a large saving in motive power without any of the disadvantages complained of in the case of Mr. Butler's invention.

The following letter by a Ceylon planter, which appeared in the original work, although written so far back as 1860, possesses a certain interest, as giving a sketch of the history of this class of machinery:—

"Pulpers—until within the last few years—had undergone less change, and shown perhaps less improvement, than any other branch of the coffee planters' business. We had the same old rattle-trap machine, from the earliest introduction of coffee cultivation into Ceylon, with the modification of cast-iron spur and fly wheel, for the wooden ones at first in use with belt and drum. Then came, about ten years ago, and almost simultaneously, the crusher of Mr. Brown, and the pulper of Mr. Wall. The former has generally worked well, where there is plenty of water, but without that it is found heavy, and, therefore, not much used. The latter, as an article of merchandize, we hear little of now; and must therefore conclude that either it has not answered the expectation of its originator (who, by the way, took out a patent for it), or that it is too dear to get into general use, or is eclipsed by the more recent inventions. After it, the late Mr. Thomas Affleck was engaged on a new pulper, which was by his friends expected to supersede all that had gone before it. Mr. Affleck's death stopped midway this invention.[1]

[1] There is not, I am told, a single pulper on either Mr. Affleck's or Mr. Butler's principle, now in use.—AUTHOR.

Thereafter appeared in the field Mr. Butler, an old West Indian planter, who had been a few years on a coffee estate in this country, and Mr. John Gordon, of 3, Railway Place, Fenchurch Street, London, formerly Affleck and Gordon, Engineers, Kandy; and these are at present the chief rival competitors for fame and fortune. Mr. Butler's is a double cylinder covered with grooved brass of apparently a very simple construction, and which, with coffee of a uniform size, is said to work well, and do its work with little damage. But where the coffee is green, or black, or unequal, it crushes or peels. These are the objections we heard urged against it last year in many quarters; and we found that several of our friends, ere their crop was half through, had discarded this machine and resumed the old common pulper. This year we have heard it is working better, and that all those set up by Mr. Butler in person did well. Doubtless, like every other new invention, experience has enabled its patentee to remedy defects and improve on the primitive model. It is to be regretted that poor Mr. Butler died, just at the time that prospects for a career of usefulness and profit were open before him. His former supporters, we understand, are to carry on the business; but they will have considerably to reduce the charge for one of those machines before they will ever come into common use. £50 is a large sum to pay for a single pulper. Gordon's, on the other hand, excepting the barrel and the breast, is slightly different from the old machine. At least, it approximates it near enough to admit of the breast (which is the great merit of this invention) being applied to any ordinary pulper at a trifling cost. In fact, for £8 we believe any pulper can be fitted with one of Gordon's breasts, which those who tried last year have pronounced to work well. One gentleman, of great experience and intelligence, informed us that to an old pulper which could scarcely work through thirty bushels an hour last year, he had applied Gordon's breast, and now easily gets sixty bushels an hour out of it, without cutting anything perceptible, and without requiring a sieve. This adaptability of the breast, as well as the price of the whole machine, only £32, will always give Gordon the advantage in the market—supposing the other merits of the two machines to be equal, and it is not for us to say whether they are or not; each has its own admirers, and a little more experience will doubtless convince the planting community which is the preferable implement. For our own part, we prefer Gordon's as simple in construction, easy of application, cheap in price, and as far as we have yet seen, sufficient for every purpose by land or water.

"There are one or two others yet on the *tapis*, the invention of private planters; but, as neither has yet come before the public, it would be premature to notice them as inventions."

Since the above was written, Mr. Walker, of Walker and Co., Bogambra Mills, Kandy, has brought out his little machine, which has met with much favour and success; it is called the "Disc Pulper," and is exceedingly light, portable, and easily worked. I have been given to understand that the work of this pulper is very satisfactory and good, but have never had occasion to use it myself.

For my own part, however, I should always prefer a pair of the old pulpers, with crusher, circular sieve, and buckets, to any other arrangement of machinery I have yet seen or heard of; though this may probably to some extent be simply prejudice, partly due to natural attachment to old habits and associations, and partly to want of actual experience of the working of the more recent contrivances.

Driven by a twenty-feet wheel, with plenty of water, the double pulper, crusher, and circular sieve, will work off 180 Government bushels of fruit per hour, not cutting or pricking more than three or four per cent.[2] (always of course provided the

[2] Since the above was written, I have been told that this

pulper chops are properly set); while a man in the cherry loft and another on the pulping platform will suffice to keep all going. It is difficult to see what more can well be desired in the way of efficiency combined with the economy of labour.

A few words more about "setting" the pulper, which is a matter of some delicacy. By this is meant the adjustment of the chops with reference to the cylinder. At the beginning of the crop season, fix the chops as near as possible in the relative positions above prescribed, this being done by means of an arrangement of wooden wedges. Then try the result with a small basket of cherry coffee, pouring in a handful at a time, while causing the cylinder to revolve slowly. Should it be found that the large berries only are pulped, the smaller ones escaping nearly intact, the upper chop must be set closer to the cylinder; if, however, the beans are cut, it should be put farther out. Should the pulp not pass out freely behind, try lowering the upper chop slightly (remembering at the same time to observe the proper distance between it and the cylinder), and if this does not answer the purpose, move the lower chop out a little further from the

would now be considered a very large percentage of damaged beans, one to two per cent. being looked upon as quite as heavy as would come under the category of *good pulping*.

cylinder. Ample space must be allowed for the escape of the pulp, but the utmost care must be taken to see that there is not sufficient to admit the tip of a bean. The pulp that falls out behind must be examined to see that there is no chipped or broken coffee among it: should there be any, an improper space must exist *somewhere*, probably between the lower chop and the cylinder, or at the ends of the chops next the framework of the machine.

Since 1865, coffee-pulping machinery has been much improved, and planters can now pulp their coffee without having to reckon on a serious percentage being cut or pricked by the pulper. Greater care is taken to feed regularly than was customary before, and simple arrangements for this purpose have been very successful. The improvements have mostly been in the direction of construction and in turning the cylinder and disc pulpers to better account, no pulper on a new principle having come into general use. Cylinders and discs for pulpers are now almost invariably made of solid iron (instead of wood, as formerly), turned fair and then covered with punched brass or copper. This insures perfectly circular and plane cylinder and disc surfaces, obviating the inconvenience which used to arise from the warping of the woodwork in the old machines. Frames entirely of iron have also been introduced, with different arrangements of the working parts, giving increased durability, simplicity of structure, and facility in setting and adjustment. All these improvements combined have brought about much better work, a smaller proportion of the beans being cut and injured than formerly was the case.

This result has, I am informed, been very largely contributed to by the new system of punching the copper coverings of the discs and cylinders, invented by the late Mr. George Clarke (of the firm of John Walker and Co., and which was patented by that firm in Ceylon). This punch instead of producing sharp, rugged protuberances, causes merely small, round elevations without any open points, and when used, with the cylinder and chops correctly adjusted, the damage caused to fully ripe coffee is said to be really nothing, the quantity of work done being fully equal to that of the other punching. In fact this is looked upon as a most important improvement, and it will be evident that such is the case if, as is alleged, the old four or five per cent. of injured beans is by its means reduced to one or even two per cent. On the other hand, great care is required in *setting* pulpers covered in this way, as otherwise the projections may press against the beans so closely as to cause a bruise, which is the more to be feared, that the injury is not apparent at the time, and is only discovered when the coffee comes to be peeled.

Messrs. Walker inform me that unripe and black berries are no more liable to damage in passing through a pulper whose cylinder is thus covered, than would be the case with the "crusher;" and further, that a double pulper of this sort will do more work than a double pulper with ordinary covering and crusher combined.

"Gordon's Breast Pulper," so highly recommended by the writer above quoted, with the same inventor's patent iron barrel, both I believe, now in general use, are thus described by Mr. John Gordon himself (of the firm J. Gordon and Co., of London,) in a letter he has been kind enough to address to me on the subject at my special request: "The wooden barrel of the old 'Rattle-Trap' had the objectionable tendency to be always shrinking and swelling, and consequently never would keep to the true circle. This is entirely prevented in the arrangement of 'Gordon's Breast Pulper' with a patent iron barrel.

"The latter is cast and turned; then 500 holes bored taper through the iron; into each of these holes is driven a turned plug, which goes about half an inch through the web of the barrel. A wooden spike is next driven through the centre of the plug which splits that portion which extends within the iron web, and thus makes a rivet of the wooden plug, and prevents it from coming out. The copper or brass sheet is now fixed to the wooden plugs. The barrel does not require turning. Any common carpenter or planter can fix the copper sheet upon the barrel in about an hour. We have special machinery for punching these coverings. They are quite flat, and wrap round the barrel like a piece of paper. The late Mr. Donald Stewart, of Coorg, one of the most extensive planters in the world, used the 'breast' with a fluked iron barrel by the same maker, and he considered that a quarter per cent. of damaged coffee was quite enough. There is an opening in each side frame through which the man who sets up the breast can see when it is close to the barrel at both ends.

"If the machine is properly set up, the breast goes fair up against the barrel, but if the framing has not been correctly put together, one end of the breast requires to be raised a little by a piece of very thin hoop-iron. The breast should not be twisted by the force of the screws. This pulper if properly set is the safest machine of its kind in use, as the inclined recesses on the concave side of the breast protect the coffee from all damage. The breast pulper is the most easily set and managed pulper of any, having fewer parts than any other.

"Next in efficiency comes the 'Disc pulper,'

which should be made in double plates with a space between; the plates being bored, and the holes filled up in the same manner as the iron cylinders.

"Another pulper, sometimes used with power, has a crusher and a sieve between the crusher and the barrel, which works with chops. This is a very good pulper for ripe coffee. Then there is the large double pulper and crusher, with elevators, which is a good machine when there is an engineer near at hand in case of a break-down.

"Successful pulping depends greatly on the dryness of the season, or otherwise. One season the coffee may be all plump and ripe, and the pulpers will easily work through 90 or 100 bushels an hour, having plenty of water to run into the machines with the coffee. The next season may be a dry one, and the trees bearing heavily, very few of the berries becoming fully ripe. Now the difficulty of pulping commences, the pulp adhering to the parchment owing to the absence of saccharine matter. Should the pulper be set close, it will probably take off the parchment as well as the pulp. The greatest patience will now be required, as the same machinery as was used the preceding year will now be unable to pulp more than one-third of the quantity. The fault here, it will be seen, clearly lies with the coffee and not with the machinery."

Stores may be constructed of iron, masonry, or wood; those of the first-named material are, however, largely preferred, and have much to recommend them. In the first place, they are not liable to be burnt down; next, they are easily put up, being manufactured in numbered sheets which only require to be fitted together; then, they are comparatively inexpensive; and, finally, the material is well suited for keeping coffee dry and warm.

Iron stores are usually about 30 feet wide and 100 to 120 feet long, being of corrugated sheets, and in the form of an arch, springing from, and resting on, a foundation of masonry.

Coffee stores in general, whatever their material, have usually two storeys, the upper floor, and very often both, being made of iron gauze or coir matting, laid over reepers an inch or so apart, so as to admit of a free circulation of air through the coffee which may be laid on it; sometimes, however, the lower floor is of asphalte or boarded. The objects of a coffee-store may be summed up in two words, *dryness* and security. In Ceylon, the great difficulty in crop time is the wetness of the season, and various appliances have to be resorted to, to compensate for this. In some parts of Southern India, on the other hand, the weather is so dry at this season that many planters build no store at all, merely piling up the coffee on the barbecues until it can be sent off to the coast, and relying on the night watchmen and others for its safe keeping meanwhile.

In Ceylon the rain sometimes falls for weeks in the middle of the crop season, and I remember on one occasion having between 3000 and 4000 bushels of wet parchment lying piled up all over the barbecues, which had accumulated before we could get a day's sunshine. Some of my neighbours had larger quantities still, and those of us who had no appliances for artificial drying had an anxious time of it. The only resource was to keep constantly turning over the wet coffee, night and day, to prevent fermentation and germination as far as possible; but, in spite of all exertions, an alarming proportion of the beans had begun to throw out pedicles, indicating the commencement of the germinating process,—much in the same way as old potatoes will do in a damp cellar. Of course we all thought the coffee was ruined, but to our surprise and gratification it seemed to be thought rather better than usual by the brokers of Mincing Lane, judging by the prices realized.

In a case of this sort, a store constructed on Mr. Clerihew's principle is calculated to be of great advantage. This is an arrangement by which coffee only partially dried can be kept sweet and fresh, by means of a continuous current of air being made to pass through it in the store. I shall first endeavour to give an idea of the way in which this is brought about with air at its natural temperature.[3]

To begin with, the store being divided into two storeys, the floor of the upper apartment must be open, with coir matting laid over one-inch reepers (an inch apart from each other) which, in their turn, rest upon joists.

It is necessary that these joists should run with the length of the building.

In order to provide a *ceiling* for the lower apartment, cloth must now be tacked on the lower sides of these joists, and well washed with boiled rice-water (or "congee") and whitewash, in order to render it as near as possible air-tight. It will now be evident that above this ceiling-cloth, and below the coir-matting floor of the upper apartment, there will be a continuous space, or passage, some six or

---

[3] During the picking season of 1844, in Ceylon, they had rainfall on the Hunasgiria range that lasted for more than a month, during the thick of the picking. There were very large crops on the Hunasgiria estate, and Mr. Gordon (then estate engineer) informs me he erected a temporary building, and, applying hot air, dried the whole of the crop, while most of the estates in the neighbourhood lost half their crops. This was before Mr. Clerihew came to Ceylon. It is impossible for the planters to get their crops properly dried *during* the picking season, but if they can get them *partially* dried, then, with a close store through which a current of fresh air is allowed to pass, the coffee is always kept fresh and sweet.

nine inches in depth (according to the dimensions of the joists) between every two joists, along the entire length of the building.

About ten feet length of one end of the lower apartment should now be partitioned off from the rest, the sides of the chamber thus formed being as near as possible air-tight. It must, however, have no ceiling other than the floor above, so that the spaces just described—between the mat-covered floor of the upper storey and the ceiling of the rest of the lower apartment—may all open into it. In an opening in the wall of this chamber, a pair of large revolving fans must now be adjusted, exactly like the fans of a winnowing machine, but on a larger scale. These fans are connected by means of belts with the water-wheel, and when made to revolve rapidly draw out a continuous current of air from the inside, and as there is only one source whence this air can be derived, it is of necessity sucked out of the spaces under the floor of the upper storey on which the parchment coffee is heaped, and consequently through the coffee itself.

By this process the parchment coffee in store, once partially dried, can be kept thoroughly well-aired and free from fermentation, without any turning over. But for coffee that is still wet, something more is necessary, and this brings us to the hot-air apparatus. At the furthest end from the fan-chamber, and outside the building, should be constructed a large furnace, in the upper part of which are fixed a number of heavy iron tubes, opening at one end to the outer air, and at the other into a flue or chimney which communicates with and terminates in the upper apartment, which is appropriated for the hot-air process (and which of course must be close and air-tight, all except the floor). As soon as these tubes become heated by the fire, the air rushes into them from the outside, and passes up into this chamber at a considerable temperature, while the fans at the other end of the building, being meanwhile kept rapidly in motion, draw this heated air through the floor, and the wet parchment coffee which has been previously spread on it for this purpose is soon dried. The great difficulty with this process is that only a comparatively small quantity can be dried at a time, owing to the limited surface available within a building. This can, however, be remedied to some extent by using hand trays, similar to those seen on drying grounds in the open air, which can be piled one on the other six or eight deep if necessary. As soon as the parchment has become tolerably dry, it may be passed on to the cool-air chamber previously described, and can there be heaped up and left to the good offices of the fans, which should be kept going night and day.

The next thing to be considered is making the drying grounds, or "Barbecues," as they are frequently termed. These may be prepared in various ways. Some planters simply level a large piece of ground adjoining or around the store, laying down coir matting when there is coffee to be spread out to dry; others look upon this as too primitive and inexpensive a method, and prefer frames of woodwork, over which matting of gunny or coir is spread; while others use trays some six or seven feet long, and two feet wide, of the same materials, with or without wheels, and these certainly have the recommendation of being quickly got under cover on the sudden appearance of a squall of rain.

Barbecues, again, can be made with macadam several inches deep, covered with a layer of gravel and lime, with the further addition of a smooth coating of mortar. The great drawback to this kind of ground, however, is that although very nice *when new*, the surface is constantly becoming broken, and as soon as this takes place, it is no better than the natural ground, inasmuch as it can no longer be used without coir matting being spread over it. Some sort of asphalte preparation, similar to those used for the London streets, would no doubt be proof against this objection, but most of these compositions have a tendency to soften and become odorous under the influence of heat, which would render them entirely unsuitable for coffee drying grounds.

It is well known that coffee has an aptitude for readily acquiring the smell of anything with which it is brought in contact, and the resinous, bituminous smell of the asphalte might possibly prove highly injurious to the sample—though I am unable to speak with absolute certainty as to this.[4]

The great point is to have plenty of level space available, and if matting is to be used (and coir matting laid down on level ground forms in my opinion as good barbecue as any), let there be plenty of it.

[4] It is narrated that a ship, on one occasion, left Colombo loaded with rum in casks under coffee in bags. Several of the casks of rum having burst during the homeward voyage, the coffee above became so strongly impregnated with the fumes of the spirit that on its appearance in the London market it was at once designated "rum coffee."

CHAPTER XX.

Crop appearances—The blossom—The "set"—Ripening—Picking—Importance of allowing coffee to ripen fully—Green berries—Day's task—*Pro rata* wages—*System* required—Black berries—Iron spouting—Laying spouting—Immediate pulping necessary—Washing—Drying—Turning—Peeling—Sizing—Shipment.

ABOUT the end of December, the eye of the planter should be refreshed by the earlier indications of the forthcoming crop, as clusters of buds begin to make their appearance on every tree, springing from the axils of the opposite leaves; in the case of young plants, all along the primaries, and in the case of trees that have already passed their first or second crop season, along all those branches that have been trained for crop-bearing; that is, of course, supposing circumstances to be in favour of a good yield.

These clusters each contain from five to ten blossoms, which at this stage are little, dark-green spikes. As they increase in size, however, this hue soon gives place to a lighter tint, until they gradually become straw-coloured, and later still almost white. Finally, under the influence of the showers which usually fall in March, after filling out and becoming visibly whiter day by day, the advanced relay of buds bursts into bloom, and the planter rises one fine morning to find the entire estate profusely decorated with snowy garlands, and the atmosphere heavy with their perfume. To convey any adequate idea of a fine, heavily-bearing estate, in this condition, is beyond my power; suffice it to say, that the millions of snowy wreaths resting on their background of dark-green, luxuriant bushes, closely ranked in even lines, stretching away over hill and dale as far as the eye can reach, produce altogether an effect not readily to be forgotten.

There are generally two, sometimes three relays of blossoms before all the buds have arrived at maturity (which is no doubt owing to the numbers of buds in each cluster preventing their all coming out together), but the principal one is usually the first, which comes out in March. After a day or two the flowers gradually turn brown and fade away, and the slower and more gradual this process is the better. Rainfall while the blossom is out is much to be deprecated, but once the latter has *set*, a good shower will be beneficial rather than otherwise. This will wash off the withered flowers, leaving exposed to view the numerous pistils or fruit-germs upon which so much depends. These should have fresh, whitish tips to indicate a healthy appearance, and when this is the case, the blossom is said to have "set well," and a crop may be looked for proportionate to the abundance of the blossom. Sometimes, however, an ominous little black spot is discernible in the centre of the pistil, and where this is the case, fructification will not follow. This is most commonly the result of inopportune rain, while the flowers are out; or it may follow a prolonged season of drought, and be due to a weakly condition of the plant.

From this time forward the berries continue to increase in size, gradually after a time beginning to change from their original dark-green hue to a light yellow, which in its turn deepens into red. The latter change will take place about October, when every preparation ought to be complete for gathering in the crop. As soon as a sprinkling of red berries is seen, "picking" should begin; at first with a few hands, but afterwards, as the reddish tinge begins to get general, all hands should be put on to gather in as fast as possible. Of course if the estate is freely supplied with labour in proportion to the crop expected, a more leisurely course may be followed; but as a general rule all available hands are required to be hard at work from the time the berries begin to ripen (in October or beginning of November) until the middle or end of January. In some low-lying districts, however, the crop ripens more rapidly, and all must be got in within about a month or six weeks.

In order to insure the coffee arriving at perfection, and so earning a high character in the market, the berries ought not to be picked until *fully* ripe, as indicated by a deep purplish crimson colour. The beans may then be expected to have a rich flavour and a strong aroma when roasted. It is understood to be owing in great measure, if not solely, to their attention to this fact by the Arabs, that Mocha coffee, although so inferior in size and *appearance*, commands its high position in the European markets. The system followed is to allow the berries to become dead-ripe on the trees, and when they are ready to drop off, to spread cloths and mats on the ground, over which the crop is then shaken down. The Ceylon and East India *native* coffee, on the other hand, owes its inferiority of quality, and the comparatively low price it consequently realizes, to the fact that half of the berries are picked in an unripe state. The same may probably be said of the Brazil coffee, which being carelessly grown, gathered, and cured, stands in value even much below "native" Ceylon and East India. The following quotations, from a

Mincing Lane circular of February this year, may be taken as showing the comparative values of the respective descriptions :—

Ceylon Plantation. (Middling.)	Mocha.	Native Ceylon. (Good ordinary.)	Rio. (Good firsts.)
110*s*. to 113*s*.	108*s*. to 110*s*.	86*s*. 6*d*.	78*s*.

In order to gather the berries as they ripen, it will generally be necessary to go over the estate two or three times—the first and third pickings, however, being usually very light ones, and the bulk of the crop being got in on the second round. The crop but rarely ripens all at once, except on very young trees.

Should the planter be *short-handed*, it will probably be more prudent to get in at once all the berries which are sufficiently matured for *pulping;* time will thus be gained, and a loss of crop may be prevented, if at some sacrifice in quality. However it may suit the native cultivator, who dries the berries as they are, to pick the ripe and unripe together, the planter must be most particular not to allow any green berries to be brought into the pulping-house, inasmuch as in *passing through the pulper* they lose not only their outer covering, but also the inner coat or "parchment," as well as the "silver-skin." They also usually get crushed and broken, being tender and wanting in mucilage, and consequently ferment and rot away afterwards in the store; and so are not only wasted themselves, but infect the other beans with mildew, and spoil the sample generally.

For picking, each coolie is provided with a large and a small bag; the former being sufficiently large to tie up when containing an imperial bushel and a half or even two bushels of fruit, while the other need only be capable of holding an eighth of this quantity, it being worn round the waist of the picker, who drops each handful of berries into it, until nearly full, when it is emptied into the large sack, which meanwhile has been deposited on the nearest road. The picker knows the exact quantity he has gathered by the number of times he has emptied the small bag. In the height of the crop season, each coolie can gather a bushel and a half of ripe berries twice a day; a sack full being brought in at an hour before noon, and again in the evening. Men, women, and children are all paid *pro rata* at this time, fourpence per bushel being formerly the usual wage. It thus frequently happens that, at this time of year, little boys and weakly women can earn as much pay as strong, robust men, and even more sometimes. However, as all the earnings of the family usually go into the common purse, there is not much grumbling in consequence, as a rule. Still, there are at times strong, willing men, good at hard field labour, &c.,

who are bad pickers, and who, not being blessed with a "Mootamah" and her progeny to make up for their deficiencies, think it hard they should be left in the rear ; it will therefore be wise to pick out such men for curing and store work, or for cutting grass for the cattle-sheds, &c., and thus by turning their capabilities to the best account, to guard against murmuring and discontent.

In consequence of this *pro rata* system of wages in crop time, the coolies are sadly tempted to go off and choose spots for themselves to pick in, where the crop is thickest and where they can fill their bags in the shortest time ; it is to the imperative interest of the planter, however, to see that the whole estate is gone over *in due order*, field after field from beginning to end, and so on the second time, and the third ; otherwise, it will inevitably happen that some parts will be left too long without picking, and crop will be lost. Consequently all such erratic, desultory proceedings must be vigilantly guarded against.

When the crop is large and the hands to gather it in comparatively few, and especially if the season is wet, the berries are apt, when over ripe, to burst and drop their contents, or to fall bodily themselves off the trees. Should the ground be free from weeds, much of this crop may be recovered, but otherwise the loss must be put up with, much as it may be lamented. On the other hand, in hot weather, the berries are more likely to dry up, and will then hold on to the trees for a long time. If this has proceeded to only a moderate extent, the berries being shrunken, but still comparatively soft and moist inside, they may be pulped after having been soaked in water for a few hours, to prevent their being cut or broken in the machine; but if they are very dry, it will be better not to attempt pulping them at all, but rather just to complete the drying process, sending them to the coast in this state, or after having had them pounded out and "peeled" on the estate. In either case they should be fully equal in value to the best *parchment* of the season.

On large estates, where the cherry has to be carried a long distance to the store, it has been found to effect a great saving of labour to lay down *iron spouting*, through which, by means of water, to run the coffee picked in distant fields down to the store.

The pipes are made of galvanized iron in eight-feet lengths. The store works being, perhaps, at the distance of a mile or more at the foot of the hill, a receiving cistern is erected in a central situation in which water is available, and into this the coffee is measured. A man is placed in the cistern to regulate the quantity of cherry that is to go down, and thus prevent the spouting from getting choked. With a sufficient supply of water some 100 to 150 imperial bushels an hour may, in this manner, be despatched to the pulping-house.

In laying spouting for this purpose, it is necessary to see that the gradient and curves are even and equable. If one portion be very steep, and the next nearly level, the cherry will rush quickly down the first, and get choked up in the latter part; and the same difficulty will be liable to happen at every curve of too angular a nature. It will often be necessary to raise the spouting on posts, in order to bring it across nullahs and hollows to the next rising ground. Where it lies on the ground, it must be firmly pegged down to prevent its rolling out of position. Two stakes driven firmly into the ground, one at each side, crossing and tied together at the top, will effect this object.

That part of the cherry-loft of the pulping-house into which the coffee is thus immediately conveyed, must, of course, be provided with a grating to allow the water to escape; and, moreover, should water not be particularly plentiful, that which has thus far done duty may be still further utilized by being turned in either to help the water-wheel, or to feed the pulpers.

Ripe cherry coffee should always be pulped as soon as brought into the store. If left heaped up in the cherry-loft for only a single night, a certain amount of fermentation will ensue, and the parchment become discoloured in consequence.

After being pulped, the parchment, as the coffee is now called, should be left undisturbed in the receiving cistern for from thirty-six to forty-eight hours, to allow the saccharine mucilage enveloping the beans to become decomposed. The parchment should then be shovelled out into the washing cistern, and there be well trodden out by coolies, so as to free the beans from any pulp or slime still adhering to them. Water may now be turned in, the whole contents of the cistern being violently churned and stirred until the latter is nearly full. In the course of this process all the light and worthless berries and beans will float to the surface, whence they may be skimmed off in a basket or sieve, and thrown in a heap by themselves. All the dirty water may now be allowed to flow off, together with all the skins, which, being lighter than the parchment, will have a tendency to drift towards the lower end of the cistern. This escape runs into a lower cistern provided with a grating at one end, the skins and any stray parchment in their company being thus retained for subsequent treatment.

The washing cistern must now be partially refilled with clean water, the previous operation being repeated; any remaining skins or other refuse being gradually raked down with the escaping water as before. The operation of washing is now complete, and the parchment being perfectly clean and free from foreign matters, is carried out and allowed to drain, previous to being spread out to dry.

As soon as the coffee has been washed it must be spread out to dry in the sun, over a large surface, and not more than, say, an inch and a half to two inches deep. Coolies should then be appointed to walk up and down through it, turning it with their feet into straight furrows about four inches wide, which greatly accelerates the drying process. Once the coffee has been got partly dry, the greatest care must be taken not to allow it to get wet again, and should rain threaten, it must be quickly raked up into heaps and covered over with mats or tarpauling, or, if sufficiently dried, put into the store. But it is not desirable that this drying process should be very rapid, nor should the wet coffee be immediately exposed to the rays of a hot sun for a great length of time, as this causes the parchment covering to shrink and burst, laying bare the bean before it has been sufficiently dried to withstand discolouration, and which consequently becomes bleached. Before being bagged up for despatch to the coast, the parchment should, if possible, have undergone three full days of sun-drying on the estate, in order to insure its escaping fermentations during transit.

Probably, however, before being sent off, it may have to be kept some considerable time in store, in which case it must be kept either constantly turned over, or else acted upon by the fan process before described; otherwise it is certain to become musty.

As soon as the beans are perfectly dry, and as hard as to break between the teeth like a piece of ivory, they are fit for being peeled. This operation is in Ceylon and S. India almost always performed at the port of shipment, but such is not the case in S. America, nor, I believe, in the West Indies, and elsewhere. Some account, therefore, of the process may prove useful in cases where the planter may have to set up and keep the machinery in operation for himself.

Peeling mills of great variety have been tried, and much time spent and expense incurred in trying to improve them, but so far no better machine has been found than the old edge runner. A trough, describing a circle of 15 feet diameter, will peel with ease 12 cwt. of market coffee per hour, and if properly made will not break any. After the coffee has been peeled it is placed in the fan and its parchment blown away. A badly-constructed fan will throw out a quantity of coffee along with the chaff, but this can always be detected by the sound which the coffee makes in falling (like the noise of small shot thrown against a board), and should at once be stopped.

From the fan the coffee passes into the sizing machine. The first sizing machine was made by Mr. Gordon on Hunasgiria, in Ceylon, and was awarded the Agricultural Society's prize in Kandy.

(Mr. Gordon also obtained a prize from the above Society, for the iron-framed pulpers he had brought into use at the meeting of 1845.)

The sizers have been greatly improved since then. The latest improvement has been to make them of steel wire, let into bars, and fixed very accurately and strongly, so that the wires cannot move about. This machine takes out the broken coffee, and separates the flat beans into three sizes, delivering the peaberry and malformed beans out of the end of the machine.

This operation finishes the preparation of coffee for the market, so far as it is treated by machinery.

The discoloured beans are picked out by hand from the coffee, which is spread upon a table for the purpose, after which it is ready for shipment in casks or bags.

SHIPMENT.—The general cargo in a ship's hold steams and sweats, and as the deck is air-tight the steam cannot escape, and it becomes condensed on the top of the cargo, the top bags getting damp. This discolours the coffee beans, which become of a grey, mottled hue, and are thus described as "country damaged." This cannot be covered by insurance. It is, therefore, necessary that all ships carrying coffee should have several wooden tubes about four inches square inside, perforated with holes, running from the keel to, say, four inches above the deck, to allow the escape of the evaporation and gases. In bad weather the top of these tubes can easily be plugged up. Coffee in a well-ventilated ship will lose about $\frac{1}{2}$ per cent. in weight, but its quality will be superior to the coffee which has been carried in ships having no ventilation. In a ship badly ventilated the coffee generally gains $\frac{1}{2}$ per cent. in weight, but loses colour, and consequently in value.

CHAPTER XXI.

"Topping"—Objects of—Proper height—In exposed situations—In sheltered situations—The true criterion—Economy of space—Argument against high plants—General mean height—Suckers—Time for topping—Method — Handling — Objects of primary branches—Secondaries—Open centres—Early handling—Pruning—Form of plant described by Laborie—General objects to be kept in view—Single branches—Suppression of unnecessary growth—Maiden crop—Knife pruning first season—Next year's wood—Tertiary branches—Criterion of good pruning—Regular handling, easy pruning—Women and children—Pruning neglected trees—Gradual reclamation — Violent treatment — Heavy pruning—Opening out thickets — Primaries not to be cut — Care and intelligence indispensable.

As soon as the young trees have reached the proper height, it becomes necessary to check their further upward growth. This operation is termed "*topping*," as applied to coffee, and answers to what is known as "heading down" among English gardeners. The objects of topping are to restrict the height of the plant within limits at which it can be conveniently dealt with by the coolies, in the various processes of pruning, crop-picking &c., and to force it to throw out vigorous lateral branches, and form a compact, well-arranged and manageable bush.

The height at which the plants should be topped must depend on the climate, soil, and aspect of the locality in which they are situated; and also, to some extent, on the distance at which they are planted from each other. In a cold climate, or in wet, poor land, the trees would not be likely to reach any considerable size under any circumstances, and here they must, therefore, be planted more closely than in more favourable localities, or else be topped lower than usual, so as to enable them, by throwing out strong side branches, to come into something like contact with each other, and thus form a good cover for the ground.

In exposed situations, the trees, if allowed to get high, would be much shaken by the wind, and must therefore be topped in accordance with the probable violence of the prevailing wind. Thus, for a field exposed to the south-west monsoon a height of from 2 to $2\frac{1}{2}$ feet will be sufficient. I have even had occasion to keep coffee which was much blown during the monsoon, down to a foot and a half, and with very satisfactory results. At this height a plant will usually still have from five to seven pairs of "primary" branches.

In a sheltered situation, where the soil is good and the climate moderately warm and humid—in other words, under conditions the most favourable to the growth of the coffee-tree,—a maximum height of five feet may be adopted. It must be remembered, however, that very rarely is such a combination of favourable conditions to be met with, and that, consequently, this will not often be found a suitable height.

The great point is to get the trees to a height at which they will neither be too much crowded together, nor too much separated, when planted at such a distance apart as is best suited to the character of the climate and soil. It is of importance that the ground should be properly covered, and this ought to be effected as much by the plants being at a proper distance from each other, as by their being topped at the proper height, and *vice versâ*. The lower a tree is cut down, the wider will be the area over which its branches are likely to spread, for the simple reason, that supposing that a given amount of nourishment is taken up from the soil and atmosphere by the roots and leaves, this is bound to result in growth *one way or other*, that is, either in height or in lateral redundancy.

Another consideration is, that the more space is occupied by trees (in consequence of their being kept low) the fewer of them will be accommodated on a given area of land, and hence it will evidently be more *economical* to grow high trees planted close together, where the richness of the soil will admit of it; but this is a system which may very easily be carried to excess, inasmuch as the closer and higher are the trees, the greater the demands made upon the soil, and the sooner will it, and the trees upon it, become exhausted and worn out.

A further objection to high trees is, that their lower branches, in consequence of being almost entirely excluded from light and air by the foliage above, have a tendency to die off, or at any rate to become weak and "whippy." Thus, high trees are frequently found, when old, to have lost all their lower branches, and to have assumed much the form of an umbrella. This can only be prevented by careful "handling," such as is hereafter described. Taking all points into consideration, the conclusion generally arrived at is, that three feet to three and a half is, under ordinary circumstances, the best height that can be adopted; anything over three feet and a half may be considered *high*, and anything under three feet, *low* topping.

Should it be found subsequently that the trees have not been topped sufficiently low, this is a mistake which can easily be rectified; while, on the other hand, if they have been cut down too low, the error may also be repaired to a certain extent, by allowing a "sucker," or young vertical shoot, to grow from below one of the top primaries. Of such shoots there will be no lack, as every tree once topped will make constant efforts to increase its stature by throwing these out. At the same time it is safer to err rather in the former than in the latter direction.

The plants should be topped *as soon as* they have reached the desired height, which can, at this stage of their growth, easily be done by a pinch between the thumb and finger. As, however, some of the plants will be found more forward than others, a knife will be required for use in cases where the wood is more matured. Each coolie should be provided with a measuring stick cut to the proper length, and holding this against the stem of the plant, be instructed to snip off the pair of young primary branches next above the stick, at about an inch from the stem, the latter being then also cut off above them. By this means, the joint or point of union of the amputated branches will form a sort of band, and prevent the stem from being subsequently split by the weight of the next branches pendant on either side when laden with crop.

I have heard it argued that plants should not be topped early, lest the growth of fruit-bearing wood should be forced on prematurely ; but, it must be remembered, the entire system of cultivation is more or less one of artificial forcing, and it appears to me, that to allow a young plant to produce a foot or so of stem and branches, merely in order that this may be subsequently cut away, involves a waste of vitality and time not compensated for by any reasonable consideration.

It having now been explained that one of the main objects of topping is to induce the plant to throw out strong primary branches (or those which grow directly from the main stem), the next process to be described, namely, "*Handling*" (or pruning by hand), as will be seen, is one having a decided tendency in the same direction. The branches next in order, those which proceed directly from the primaries, are called the "secondaries."

These also grow in pairs, the first of which is thrown out within an inch or two of the parent stem; the next pair an inch or more farther out, and so on. It will now be evident, that if each primary were allowed to produce two or three pairs of secondaries within a few inches only of the stem of the plant, the result would soon be a disorderly mass or thicket, completely impervious to light and air; while in addition, the sap being thus distributed and directed into so many channels, nothing approaching to strong healthy primaries could be looked for. To guard against such a state of things, we now proceed to take off, and to keep off, all the young secondaries within six inches of the main stem on every side, as soon as ever they make their appearance. The sap is thus allowed to proceed uninterruptedly along the primary to the point at which the secondaries can be trained with advantage, and (which is a further most important object), an open space of at least one foot in diameter is preserved down through the heart of the bush, for the free admission of light and air; without abundance of both of which, healthy, vigorous, crop-bearing wood cannot be produced.

Begun at this early period, handling is a very simple operation, and if systematically pursued with sufficient frequency, will always continue so. On the regularity with which it has been attended to will depend the simplicity of knife pruning, which must be resorted to after the first full crop, and which may otherwise become a very complicated and delicate operation.

Before laying down rules for *Pruning*, it will probably be advisable, with a view to making my remarks as clearly intelligible to the reader as possible, to describe the form and economy of the plant at the stage of its history at which we have now arrived. This I cannot do better than in the words of a very much earlier coffee planter than myself; I therefore borrow the following extract from Laborie's interesting work, the " Coffee Planter of St. Domingo : "—

" The sapling rises, always bearing leaves, and

afterwards boughs above them, by pairs or in axillary form and opposite; these boughs lengthen themselves in the same manner and proportion; and, as they grow, they always end as the trunk, in a sharp point, which divides itself into two leaves, which also spread out at a proper distance, and so on.

"In their turn, *secondary* branches shoot out, directly above every leaf of the primary ones. These make their growth as the former; and bear *tertiary* branches if the tree is luxuriant.

"Here a material observation is necessary, as it is in a measure the foundation of the whole system of lopping or pruning. The vertical sapling or trunk has been shown, bearing its boughs or primary branches in opposite pairs; so that the inferior (or lower) ones exhibit the figure of a cross with the superior (or upper), thus the four branches spread in four different directions; and this is necessary, that the tree may be garnished all round without being embarrassed. Exactly on the same principle of avoiding encumbrance, the arrangement of the secondary and tertiary branches is different. They are all placed by pairs on both sides of the mother branches, so that all spread out horizontally and with a direction in some measure towards the circumference. If any should grow upward or downward, they would become intricate, and the tree embarrassed, but Nature makes no such blunders; and if such happen to be the unintentional effects of art, Art must redress them, as we shall see in its place. It must also be observed that, the tree being in its natural state, two branches seldom grow from the same eye or bud.

"Now I suppose the tree to be about four or five feet high. The boughs near the ground will extend wider, as they are nearer the source of vegetation, so that the shape of the tree is pyramidal. All those branches of three orders or more garnish it richly, but as all are horizontal from below upwards, all diverging from the centre more or less; all placed either at the four faces of the trunk (and these at distances at least eight or nine inches from each other at the same face), or both sides of the mother branches, the profusion of Nature can neither be perplexed nor intricate."

All shoots produced by the main trunk, other than lateral branches, are known as *suckers*.

With the above picture of the coffee-tree in a state of nature, the object of the pruner in all his operations should be to preserve as much as possible this symmetrical form and arrangement, or to restore it as far as may be practicable when that form has been marred or lost under artificial treatment, the additional consideration being borne in mind, i.e., the desirability of inducing the tree to yield a richer crop than Nature herself would demand. Mr. Rhind summarizes the objects of pruning as: the "promotion of growth, lessening of bulk, modifying form, promoting the formation of crop, and the removal of decayed branches."

All the secondaries growing within six inches of the main trunk having been removed, the next operation should be to take off every alternate opposite secondary of those that remain, so that there shall be *no pairs*, but only one issuing from each joint of the primary, and no two consecutive joints producing secondaries from the same side. It will be evident that attention to this point tends greatly to encourage the development of the boughs that are left, as they get double the share of sap they would receive in a state of nature. We must take care also to see that in no case are more than one branch or shoot allowed to proceed from a single axil, and that all twigs growing cross-wise or backwards (towards the centre of the tree), also any tending in a vertical direction, either up or downwards, and, finally, all "suckers" are summarily and systematically suppressed. I use the latter word advisedly, as conveying the idea of *removal as fast as the shoots appear*. This to my mind is a great point, as protecting the tree as much as possible from all *waste* of power and energy.

Once a tree has been topped, it is no easy matter

to keep down the "suckers;" these persistently burst forth in clusters from the lower axillaries of the primary branches (generally the first two or three from the top), immediately after the operation referred to, as if in indignant protest against the arbitrariness of artificial treatment. They should always be *pulled off by hand*, in order that by the probable extraction of the germ or bud, further growths may be discouraged. Where the knife is used, the sucker will seldom be so completely removed but that two or more new shoots will spring out from its base.

The young tree having been thus trained, is now in the most favourable condition for the production of its maiden crop. This will probably proceed entirely from the primaries, with perhaps the addition of the lower and more matured parts of the secondaries on the lower part of the tree. While the crop is ripening, everything should be done to enable the young tree to bring it to maturity with the least exhaustion, by keeping off all useless or superfluous shoots.

The season for the annual knife-pruning arrives as soon as the crop has been gathered; but provided the system above described has been carefully followed from the first, there ought to be *very little* knife-work required, for the first few years at any rate.

Some planters recommend the removal of all secondaries that have once borne crop, but I am opposed to any arbitrary rule of this kind, preferring to see them left for a second season, unless, indeed, withered throughout their greater length, and manifestly exhausted. The pruner must look a-head, and endeavour to provide suitable wood for next year's crop, and even for that of the second year. With this object in view, a young secondary shoot must now be trained on the opposite side of the primary to that which has to be cut off the year following. By this means when the old branch has been taken away from the one side, a young and vigorous one will be left as a substitute on the other. It may not of course always be possible to carry out this programme strictly to the letter, but the *system* should be followed as closely as circumstances will allow.

Should the distance between the joints be greater than usual, *tertiary* branches may be allowed to grow in the same order as the secondaries, i.e. alternately on opposite sides; but, as a general rule, and where the primaries and secondaries are fairly numerous, tertiaries are better dispensed with altogether.

The true criterion of good pruning, in my opinion, is that the tree should produce fair crops every year evenly, in addition of course to the preservation of the tree in vigour and symmetry of form—which must be a necessary accompaniment of such a result. To insure the first object, trees should *never be heavily pruned*, nor will those that have been consistently treated in the manner above prescribed ever require it.

It should ever be remembered that regular and systematic handling insures easy pruning—and handling can never be done too carefully or too often. Some planters who are fortunate enough to have sufficient labour at their disposal, make a point of going over the estates in this way once a month; and if this can be done from the first, the work will be found both simple and light—in fact a monthly handling can be accomplished with a comparatively small gang of women and boys, while a bi-monthly or less frequent operation will prove more than twice or thrice as tedious and costly. Of course the longer any wood that is useless and intended to come off, is allowed to remain on the tree, the greater is the waste of vitality and sap. Considerable instruction and intelligence are required to make women and especially children good handlers, but this can be done nevertheless—and it *must* be done, as it is obvious that if shoots and twigs are plucked off at random, or without a proper selection being made, the greatest mischief may be done. Care must always be taken to leave enough wood for next year's crop, and wood of the nature and in the position *required*.

When an estate has been long neglected and badly pruned, the planter should never try and restore the trees to order and symmetry all at once, but rather extend the process over two, three, or even more seasons. By this means loss of crop will be avoided, and the trees will be saved from much loss of vitality. Heavy pruning is often attended with the most serious and injurious results. Its immediate effect is to cause the tree to throw out quantities of new wood, involving a drain on its resources beyond its strength. Violent treatment of this kind must always be avoided as much as possible in cultivation, as has of late years been discovered to be advisable in other domains. Where, however, the planter has determined, come what may, to "cut up" a field of old neglected trees, let the operation at least be immediately followed up by careful handling, so as to repress superfluous growth, and, what is more important still, by a liberal application of *nourishing* manure,—from the cattle-shed if possible.

Some planters have an idea of pruning weakly, or "shuck" trees heavily, in order to *strengthen* them, but never was a greater mistake; the effect is often to *kill* trees in this condition, whereas a milder course of treatment might have gradually produced the desired result. The more weakly a tree is, the less capable it is of undergoing a heavy pruning, and the more healthy and well trained it is, the less it will require such treatment. In fact, I am opposed to heavy pruning at any time, and could almost shudder when I look back upon the ghastly spectacles I have seen in Ceylon and elsewhere, where this sort of thing has been practised, whole fields of fine trees having been reduced to "bare poles and whips,"—poor skeletons of their former selves.

In beginning to prune a tree which has been allowed to become an impenetrable thicket, the first thing to be done is to *open out the centre*, that is to say, as formerly explained, to remove all secondaries within six or eight inches of the main trunk, and to take off all "suckers" springing from the main stem. It will, as a rule, be better to do nothing more than this the first year. The year following, the open space having been meantime strictly preserved, the branches can be carefully examined, and a liberal selection of wood made. This gradual treatment will be positively as beneficial and strengthening to the tree, as the old-fashioned cutting up process would have been injurious.

As a rule, primary branches must *never be cut*, except in cases where they have become too long, whippy, and straggling, when the end may be docked, or cut off, just beyond a good secondary, which latter will naturally take the place of leader. But primaries must never be cut on such grounds as their having become leafless, or sickly after crop, a more far-sighted policy will rather be to remove a secondary in order that its parent branch may have a more liberal supply of sap. Where the *ends* have died, there is no harm in breaking off the part that is dry and rotten, but it is much better even to leave these dry ends than that the coolies should get into the babit of cutting the primary branches. If the dead part be left, the branch will only die back as far as the next healthy secondary, which will then supply its place, and no great harm is done.

More than any other operation in planting, pruning should be done carefully and intelligently. The best men should be reserved for this work, and are better not hurried, it being preferable to have a small number of trees judiciously treated, than that the whole estate should be badly and slovenly gone over.

CHAPTER XXII.

Manuring—Its necessity early recognized—The objects of—Chemical constituents of plants—Mucilaginous and fatty fluids—Decomposition—Liebig's theory—Organic matter—Analysis of West Indian Coffee—Mineral constituents—Analysis of Ceylon plantation—Combustible constituents—Cattle dung—Duration of effects—Mr. Wilson's opinion—Sir Humphrey Davy on fermentation—English farmers' view—Method of making liquid manure—Dr Shortt's suggestion—Method with pigs—Another plan—Economizing transit with bulky manures—Cultivating grass—Putting out—On flat land—On slopes—Old method—Green vegetation—Woody fibres—Dead animals — Coffee pulp — Poonac — Bones — Castor-oil cake—Guano—Wood ashes—Lime—Sal ammoniac—Mâna grass—Ground thatching—Ceylon Prize Essays (1875).

THE absolute dependence of the ultimate success and permanency of crop cultivation upon manuring, has been universally recognized from the earliest times. Xenophon recommends enriching land by applying to it soil from the bottom of rivers and lakes, while the subject has also been enlarged upon by Theophrastus and Cato. Strange to say, however, it would appear to have been only within recent years that the attention of the planting community of India and Ceylon has been given to the subject in downright earnest, and its vital importance to have been practically admitted by them. This it is not very difficult to account for. While land remained cheap and plentiful, the simple but wasteful method of opening up new estates as soon as the old ones began to be exhausted, seemed always preferable to an intricate and laborious study of the best means of preserving land already under cultivation; and even *now*, planters pursuing their avocation in comparatively new districts openly advocate the system referred to. In Ceylon and elsewhere, however, where the forest and other land still available for cultivation is yearly diminishing in extent, and, under the influence of high prices for the staple in the European markets, increasing in value, so that instead of from £2 to £5 per acre, it has now become a question of from £10 to £25, the subject begins to assume a different aspect, and can no longer be evaded.

Treated generally, the object of manuring is to return to soil originally fertile, those constituents in which it has become deficient by cultivation; or, in some cases, to add certain constituents which the soil has never possessed, but without which it is unsuited for some particular growth. It will thus be seen, that soils naturally sterile are capable of being improved, to a certain extent, by the application of manure, but as this is a process involving more or less labour and expense, it is obvious that those which are originally the most fertile are the most economical to the cultivator. Moreover, soil which is *naturally* rich will always be more productive and lasting, than that which has *had to be made* fertile by artificial means.

Another object of manuring is to restore to plants, through the soil, those particular constituents which have been unduly wasted by a preternatural fruitfulness, induced by artificial culture, and in consequence of which the plants are threatened with premature decay.

The chemical constituents of plants are hydrogen, oxygen, nitrogen, and carbon, and some few earthy salts; and, therefore, bodies containing these elements, arranged in a manner suitable for absorption by the roots of plants, are those best adapted for use as manure. Decaying animal and vegetable matter, and a few mineral substances, answer this description, and consequently make up the various manures used in cultivation; and the more fluid and gaseous the nutritious parts of these are, the more easy of absorption will they be. Mr. Rhind, in his "History of the Vegetable Kingdom," says, "The great object in the application of manure should be to make it afford as much soluble matter as possible to the roots of the plants, and that in a slow and gradual manner, so that it may be entirely consumed in forming their soft and organized parts."

Substances composed for the most part of mucilage and gelatinous or fatty fluid, contain nearly all the elements of life in vegetation; but, as these are always combined with masses of woody fibre, a chemical change is necessary to render such substances suitable for food for plants. This change is produced by decomposition. Animal matters decompose more quickly than vegetable, and those which are glutinous and albuminous more quickly than woody fibre. Some manures, such as those consisting principally of matter soluble in water, decompose *too* rapidly, and this has then to be prevented; it being borne in mind that decomposition is *only* required to bring about a separation between the organic constituents and the woody fibre with which they are combined.

Undue decomposition may be prevented in manures by keeping them dry and cool, and by protecting them from the atmosphere: while the opposite result may be promoted by moisture and a warm temperature (from $55°$ to $80°$).

Liebig's opinion that the true theory of manuring consisted in adding to the soil the constituents of the *ash* of the plant, is now generally discredited, being found incorrect in practice. This seems much as if we should undertake to produce a man, by combining in due proportions in the laboratory the various constituents of the human body. The vital principle at least always remains absent in such experiments (if nothing more), and so it is in agriculture; soils often seem to be rendered more productive for a time by the addition of merely chemical manures, but the effect is transitory, and the plant which has thus been stimulated afterwards falls back into a state of more hopeless weakness and depression than ever.

The necessary *vital principle* of nutriment for plants seems only to be found in organic matter (or in other words, in decayed vegetable or animal bodies), and this it should always be the aim of the cultivator, in some form or other, to combine with the required mineral constituents, in order to render manure permanently beneficial and effective.

It now devolves upon us to inquire what are the chemical constituents of the *ash* of coffee? In "Ferguson's Commonplace Book" for 1860, we find the following analysis of West India Coffee berries (made about ten years previously by Mr. Herepath, of Bristol). Deducting the carbonic acid, 100 grains of ash gave the following result :—

Phosphate of Lime	45·551
Phosphoric Acid	12·801

Potash	16·512
Soda	6·787
Magnesia	5·942
Lime	2·329
Sulphate of Lime	1·751

with small quantities of sulphuric acid, chloride of sodium, and silicic acid.

"Consequently," remarks Mr. Herepath, "for every ton of dried coffee beans that is raised on a plantation, the proprietor must consider about the following quantities of the various mineral substances as having been removed from his land :—

	lbs.	oz.
Phosphoric Acid	27	14½
Sulphuric Acid	0	13½
Potash	11	4
Soda	4	10
Chloride of Sodium	0	7
Lime	18	14
Magnesia	4	1
Silicic Acid or Silica	0	5
	68	5

"When bone-dust, cow-dung, and wood ashes can be obtained and applied cheaply, of course nothing can be better; a little pounded gneiss might be an improvement. Failing bone-dust and cow-dung, then recourse must be had to ammoniacal manures (such as guano), and to lime. The dolomite of the interior contains, according to

Dr. Gygax, the proper proportion of phosphoric acid in the shape of apatite or phosphate of lime."

In 1858 the Ceylon Planters' Association obtained from the same chemist a new analysis, this time of Ceylon Plantation Coffee. This is given in the following letter, addressed to Mr. W. H. Walters, Bambra Ella Estate:—

"Sir, I have studied the subject of your letter, through the Rev. Walter Marriott, and having made the necessary experiments and calculations, I have to report that 1000 lbs. of raw coffee berries of Ceylon Plantation growth contain as under of mineral ingredients:—

	lbs.
Potash	37
Lime	$2\frac{3}{4}$
Magnesia	$5\frac{3}{4}$
Peroxide of Iron	$\frac{1}{4}$
Sulphuric Acid	$2\frac{1}{2}$
Chlorine	$\frac{3}{4}$
Carbonic Acid	$11\frac{3}{4}$
Phosphoric Acid	7
	$67\frac{3}{4}$

"I do not know the exact analysis of your granitic rocks, but presume they must contain a little potash, lime and iron, and possibly magnesia; but the ash is too alkaline for me to think that all the potash comes from that source, the principal portion of it must come from the felled wood; the carbonic acid of course comes from the atmosphere, but the principal ingredients you require as manure I conceive to be phosphoric acid, sulphate of lime, and carbonate of magnesia. About 100 lbs. of Peruvian guano, with 7 or 8 lbs. of ground gypsum, 10 lbs. of magnesian limestone, and 11 lbs. of salt, mixed up with your vegetable (sic), or the ashes of the wood clearance, and some of your granite or quartz pounded, would, I think, make a good manure for 1000 lbs. of raw berries. I cannot calculate what would be necessary to supply the woody matter of the trees with nourishment, as I do not know their chemical analysis, but should imagine that if the whole of the woody matter or their ashes were returned to the land it would be sufficient; but if any part of the vegetation is not economized, of course that loss must be made up by manure.

  I am, Sir,
   Yours respectfully,
    (Signed) W. HEREPATH, F.C.S.,
     Professor of Chemistry."

(5 *Guineas.*)

It would thus appear that for every ton, or according to the later analysis, for every 1000 lbs. of dried coffee beans produced, about 68 lbs. of certain mineral ingredients are lost to the soil. In addition to which we have to consider not merely the combustible constituents of the berries, but also the materials composing the wood and leaves of the tree. The principal mineral waste obviously consists of phosphoric acid, potash and lime, and it is consequently substances containing these, in combination with organic matter, which are required as manure for Coffee, if the soil is to be maintained permanently as far as possible in its original condition.

Although no land is capable of going on yielding crop during a succession of years without renovation, still land really suitable for coffee ought to be able to dispense with manure till after the second crop, or say for at least three years and a half from the time of planting. Of course poor lands, such as produce merely scrub jungle or grass, require manure at the outset to render them suitable for cultivation at all.

However authorities may differ as to the value and effect of different manure substances, there is one of these upon the merits of which no variance of opinion has ever existed. I refer to *cattle-dung*. In his well-known Essay on this subject, written in 1857, Mr. George Wall of Ceylon says, "It would be mere waste of time to descant on the virtue of this manure; its value being universally acknowledged. I believe that a cooly load, that is an ordinary basketful, of cattle manure applied to each tree in the usual way, gives an increased crop, varying from two to five cwts. per acre, according to the soil and climate, and its effect lasts from two to four years." In 1868 a sub-committee of the Ceylon Planters' Association, appointed to consider the manure question, recorded their opinion that "cattle manure is *par excellence* the best and most lasting, the effects remaining over two to three years." Mr. Arnold White, in an Essay on the same subject, written in 1875, remarks in reference to the foregoing extracts, "The lapse of years has added little or nothing to our knowledge of the subject." Mr. J. H. Wilson, Analytical Chemist of Bombay, in a letter written in the same year for the *Ceylon Observer*, thus writes, "Ever since coffee planting, or I may say since farming commenced, and in every part of the globe, *there has been but one opinion* respecting the value of farmyard manure, and when the amount of crop obtained by the use of cow-dung or farmyard manure is compared with that obtained where the ash or mineral ingredients of an equal quantity of the same manure was used, it is evident that the use of cattle manure effects something more than the restoration of ash constituents to the soil."

In fact all experience proves that there is no manure superior to, if indeed there is any equalled by, the product of the cattle-shed. It evidently contains all the elements necessary to restore fertility to the soil and vigour to crop-bearing vegetation in general; and it is certainly the only manure which enables coffee-trees to bear an increased crop for several years in succession. It may be *more* efficacious in combination with bones, lime, and guano, but for my own part, if I could obtain a sufficient permanent supply of farmyard manure, pure and simple, I should be little inclined to trouble myself with mineral or artificial compounds.

There appears to be some diversity of opinion as to the manner in which cattle manure should be treated previous to application. Sir Humphrey Davy was of opinion that only slight fermentation was necessary to render it suitable for use. He says, "It is better that there should be no fermentation at all, than that it should be carried too far."[1] In violent fermentation much of the gaseous properties are lost, and it has seemed to myself that the fresher the manure when applied to the soil the more eminently successful have been the results. A reckless waste of valuable manure is too often permitted by simple exposure to the sun. Sometimes coolies are sent out to collect old cattle droppings, that, after lying exposed on the roads or hill-side, have been reduced to a condition suitable enough for fuel purposes, but totally worth-

[1] Loudon's "Encyclopædia of Gardening."

less as manure—unless the woody fibre (which is about all that evaporation has left remaining) is decomposed by the aid of lime.

English farmers undoubtedly prefer using cattle manure *considerably* fermented, and in the state known by them as "short muck," so that it can be cut with the spade; on the grounds that in this condition it contains more *humic acid*, which with carbonic acid gas constitutes, according to Mr. Loudon, the chief food of plants. That writer remarks, "It has been proved that rotted dung contains more humic acid and carbonic acid gas, weight for weight, than fresh dung."

Drawing a line between the slight fermentation recommended by Sir Humphrey Davy, and the excessive decomposition required by the English farmer, we may perhaps arrive at the happy medium on this point.

Mr. Loudon describes a method of manufacturing liquid manure, practised by the farmers in German Switzerland, which might be practised with advantage occasionally on estates. The animals are stalled on a boarded floor, having a downward inclination of four inches to the hinder part of the cattle, whose excrement falls into a gutter behind, fifteen inches deep and ten wide. This gutter is so formed as to be capable of receiving water from a reservoir at pleasure, and communicates with four or five tubs or pits, fitted with boarded coverings to facilitate fermentation. These tubs or pits should of course be water-tight, and there should be five, in order that the liquid may be left undisturbed in each to ferment for four weeks, one being closed up every week. Every evening water is let into the gutter, and in the morning the cattle-keeper carefully mixes with it the excrement that has fallen during the night, breaking up all lumps, and working the whole into a liquid of uniform density: on the manner in which this part of the operation is done mainly depends the quality of the manure. The mixture may contain three parts of water to one of excrement.

This liquid is now fit for use, or may be poured over the bedding in the general collecting pit.

Dr. Shortt, in his work on Coffee Culture, recommends a pit communicating with the cattle-shed, into which the product of the shed, and all the rubbish, ashes, offal, &c., of the bungalow, lines, &c., should be thrown; a layer of lime being once a week sprinkled over the whole, followed by an inch thickness of earth. A rich compost would thus no doubt be created.

A Ceylon planter of my acquaintance used to adopt the following plan: the cattle-shed, an oblong building with a properly plastered (or asphalted) floor sloping towards one side at about six inches in every ten feet, is bounded outside along its entire length by a pit, into which the bedding and excrement are daily emptied. This is of course carefully roofed over, and in it are kept a number of pigs (fed on green grass, chickweed, and poonac), whose continual tramping on the entire mass of bedding with their sharp-pointed hoofs, soon works the whole into a rich and compact mass, easily cut with the mammotie when required for use. In order to keep the pigs in health, a considerable quantity of bedding ought to be daily thrown in; and, if possible, clean spaces round the sides should be provided for them to retire to at night.

Another plan, less satisfactory, is as follows :—
The cattle-shed is a large oblong building, having the floor excavated to the depth of say three feet below the surface of the ground surrounding, bricks being laid in and around this with the plastered joints well coated with tar. Clean bedding being laid well over the whole floor, the cattle are turned in for the night (being allowed to graze out all day), a supply of fodder having previously been placed in racks round the sides. Every morning the cattle are turned out to graze, and before their return in the evening a fresh layer of dry bedding sufficiently thick to keep them clean and comfortable when lying, and night fodder are provided,

the dung deposits of the night previous being left undisturbed. This system may go on for any length of time, or until the mass has risen two or three feet *above* the level of the outside ground, when it will be some six feet in depth. The shed may then be emptied, the cattle in the meantime being housed elsewhere. By this process the urine is being constantly added to the mass, a too rapid decomposition is prevented by the exclusion of air, and yet there is sufficient fermentation to convert the manure into a state in which it can be readily absorbed by the trees.

On estates in the vicinity of a public road, all cattle-droppings, &c., should be collected as fresh as possible, and added to the dung-pit under cover.

The chief difficulty in connexion with cattle manure (as with all others equally bulky), is the expense and labour of applying it to the land. In order, therefore, to obviate this, as far as possible, the sheds should be situated as centrically as possible ; and if on a hill slope, they should, of course, be *above* the coffee-field. Where the estate is large and straggling, a number of small sheds and manure depôts, with ten or a dozen head of cattle to each, should be established in different parts of the estate.

Some planters plead inability to keep cattle, owing to their being without grass-land for grazing.

Where this is so, cattle should be stalled, and grass for fodder *planted* and *cultivated* in the immediate vicinity. Let it not be supposed that land is *wasted* when thus planted with grass. If the estate is to be kept up *permanently*, manure is a *necessity;* and it is far better to have five acres of healthy crop-bearing trees and five acres of "Guinea grass" adjoining, than ten acres of "shuck" coffee, yielding no crop worth mentioning, and, nevertheless, gradually dying out. Moreover, grass can often be grown in swamps and ravines, where coffee-trees would not flourish. In such spots "Mauritius grass" grows so luxuriantly that a sharp look-out has to be kept to prevent its overrunning the bounds to which it is desired to restrict it. This grass is too succulent and sappy in its natural state to feed cattle on entirely (it being apt to bring on purging), but this difficulty can be, in great measure, obviated by drying and chopping it up in the chaff-cutter; or, better still, let the cattle be fed on half Mauritius and half Guinea grass. The latter is a most useful and valuable food for both horses and cattle, and can be grown without difficulty. It should be planted in rows (the roots being put in some two feet apart each way), and must be kept free of weeds, and dug round occasionally, and thinned out and manured every couple of years or so.

In putting in manures the points to be considered

are, how they may be best brought and retained within reach of the roots, and, secondly, how they may be distributed through the soil with the least possible waste. No manure for coffee ought to be more than one foot below the surface of the ground, the lateral or " feeding " roots of the plant seldom extending much beyond that depth in search of nourishment.

On flat land, where there is no danger of wash, the most judicious method is to spread the manure, well broken up, generously and uniformly over the surface, and then immediately to dig it well in with the forked hoe or the pick, delving to the depth of from nine inches to a foot, and up to within say a foot and a half of the tree ; though *not nearer*, so as to avoid unnecessarily wounding or injuring the leading roots.

Flat land, however, as a matter of fact, is not often met with on coffee estates ; and therefore, *on slopes*, continuous parallel trenches are more usual. These should be one foot deep on the *lower* side, should run *level* across the face of the hill, and be about fifteen inches wide. A man may be set between each line of the bushes, so that the length of each trench made by him will be five or six feet, according to the width of separation between the lines, the trench opened by him being continued by his neighbour on each side. Of such trenches an able-bodied cooly will make from twenty-five to thirty daily. When the first has been made (beginning always at the *bottom* of the hill, of course), a layer of green vegetation, "mana grass," or bracken, some six inches deep, should be laid in it, and on this the manure should be carefully strewn, at the rate of not less than one basketful or cooly load for each tree: all lumps should be broken up, and the whole spread evenly over the grass, &c., in the trench. The trench next above may now be begun, the earth dug out of which will naturally roll down into that below, covering over the valuable deposit.

Manuring in this manner, which of all others I consider the most efficacious and satisfactory, will not probably cost much less than £7 or £8 per acre, at any rate should the materials have to be carried any distance. If, however, as is calculated by trustworthy authorities, an increase of some three and a half cwts. per acre in the crop for at least three years, may, under ordinary circumstances, be looked for as the result, it will be seen that even this outlay would be highly remunerative.[2]

The old common method of applying cattle manure by simply digging a small hole close to each tree, smashing the principal feeding roots

---

[2] Mr. Wall's Essay gives an estimated increase of from two to five cwts. per acre for from two to four years.

without scruple, tumbling in a basketful of dung, and then covering this over, is a slovenly method now well-nigh obsolete. The ground in this case has not the advantage of a good digging up, which in itself is a method of manuring, nor is the manure *distributed* over the surface as it should be, the consequence being that it is *in great measure wasted*. Another fatal objection to manure being put in in great clods or lumps, is the certainty that in this condition it will breed numbers of grubs, worms, &c., only too ready to attack the roots of the trees.

Green vegetation of any kind may be applied to the soil with advantage. The best plan is to put it in trenches, as above, or dug in on *flat land;* the more succulent and green it is the better, and the sooner it should be buried after being cut, as decomposition will proceed more gradually under ground than when it is exposed to the atmosphere. It should not, however, be covered over too deeply. Green vegetation, however, may be used to much greater advantage, in combination with mineral manures, and after having been reduced to compost in the heap.

Woody fibres, it may be again mentioned, are useless as food for plants, unless first decomposed. Under this heading may be classed the bark of trees, wood shavings, sawdust, &c.

Dead bodies of animals, when buried under five or six times their bulk of earth, and one part of lime, will impregnate the surrounding earth, so as to convert it into excellent manure after the lapse of two or three months. This should be borne in mind when deaths occur among the cattle.

Coffee pulp is usually preserved in a pit below the curing-houses during crop time, and put out with the other manures subsequently. It is not, however, generally considered to be of much value by itself. Possibly were it applied fresh it might yield better results, especially as it contains large proportions of sugar, mucilage, and other properties useful as food for plants. Applied fresh it should at least be as beneficial as green herbage, if not more so, containing as it does but little woody fibre, and being itself a product of the plant.

Poonac—oil-cake made from the cocoa-nut—is a valuable manure, containing oily or fatty fluid. Its effect is to produce wood and foliage rather than crop. Before application it should be moistened and pulverized; it may then be put in small trenches near the trees, care being taken to mix it up carefully with the earth, handful by handful, until the trench is filled. It is better adapted for hot than cold climates, its oily parts being more soluble in the former case. Ten cwts. of poonac to the acre will allow of about a quart of the pounded

S

flour being applied to each tree, and this should produce a healthy show of dark-green foliage within a few months. Wild hogs have a strong predilection for poonac, and therefore unless it is carefully pulverized and mingled with the soil they are sure to grub it out of the trenches. Poonac should always, if possible, be used in combination with—

Bones.—These contain a large proportion of earthy salts, such as phosphate of lime, magnesia, and carbonate of lime, as well as fat, gelatine, &c., and are therefore peculiarly valuable. Bones will be found to produce crop rather than foliage or wood. Mr. Wall thinks that the effect of one application should be apparent for six years, and that one pint of the crushed "dust" per tree, or say, five cwts. per acre, is sufficient. There is, however, a strong impression that bones are of questionable advantage *for application alone*, causing as they do a forced yield for a time, only to throw the trees back subsequently into greater weakness and exhaustion than before. No doubt a combination with poonac would in some measure reduce this tendency, but *reduce* it only, I fear. What is really wanted is to add, as previously recommended, a due quantity of real *organic matter*, either in the form of decayed vegetable substances, or better still in the form of the product of the cattle-shed. These combinations are best arrived at in the *compost* heap. The same remarks apply to—

Castor-oil cake, which is coming more and more into use in Ceylon.

Guano is the excrement of sea-birds, and is brought from the Islands of Chinca, Ilo, Iza, Arica, &c., off the coast of Peru. When exhibited for manuring purposes it has the appearance of a fine brown powder. It contains uric acid, ammonia, potassa, phosphoric acid, a little fat, and silica. Guano is a very valuable manure, its effect being to produce both foliage and crop, but it should be applied with some more bulky substance.

Wood-ashes, when containing charcoal, and not too much burned, are useful as manure. Mr. Wall informs us:—"I have used wood-ashes with marked advantage. This manure has the advantage of being both cheap and abundant. As *we* use the ashes they contain much soluble alkaline matter, which in England is almost always previously extracted for the manufacture of soap. For this reason ours are peculiarly valuable, and cannot fail, when judiciously used, to give very beneficial results."

Lime.—Ferguson's Ceylon Commonplace Book for 1860 contains the following:—" Lime, if it could be procured cheaply and in quantity, is of course one of the best applications for coffee estates, for it forms sixty per cent. of the ashes of the plant. Doctor Gygax, who analyzed the wood as well as the berries, was of opinion that one cwt. per acre of lime would generally suffice. The difficulty is to get the lime; for, although excellent dolomite abounds in many parts of the coffee districts, the expense of burning, carrying, and applying, has hitherto in most cases been found too high. It, however, becomes quite a different matter where planters are told that the quartz and gneiss, which are found on every coffee estate, are when pounded valuable as constituents of manure. This accords with experience, for the finest coffee grows among masses of gneiss, gradually decomposing from the influence of the climate from its felspathic constituents."

Sulphate of ammonia and other *chemical salts* are all valuable manures, entering as they do largely into the constituent parts of vegetation, but, as Mr. Wall observes, "their solubility and affinity for water makes them liable to be carried down below the reach of the roots, or swept away by the rain before they have been absorbed." They should be used in combination with vegetable matter, which they would rapidly assist in decomposing.

Māna and other hard long grasses, consisting principally of woody fibre, are in their natural state but of little use as manure, but when put in with cow-dung, as previously described, or with other substances by which their decomposition is promoted, they become valuable. In any case, however, even if it will do no more, digging in grass of this nature will greatly improve stiff, clayey soils, by rendering them loose and friable. In wet, exposed situations, with cold, stiff soils, it is an excellent plan to cover the ground under the coffee trees with a stratum of māna grass; the ground by this means is kept warm, throws off excessive rainfall, while weeds are kept down and wash entirely prevented. Mr. Wall writes on this plan:—"I have applied it to a cold, heavy, yellow soil, in which coffee bushes could scarcely exist, and where their scraggy branches had only a few small, yellow leaves upon them, and the effect was most surprising. Not only were the trees soon clothed with fine dark-green foliage, but even the soil appeared to be changed, and to the depth of three or four inches became friable and dry."

This "ground-thatching" may be tried with equal prospect of benefit in *hot, dry* situations, to enable the ground to retain its moisture; but great care must be taken to guard against *fire*, especially in the neighbourhood of grass hills or jungle likely to be burned in the dry season. A spark falling on this ground-thatch might set a field of coffee in a blaze, as has indeed occasionally happened.

As space will not admit of my entering more at large into this very important branch of my subject, I must refer the reader to those brochures on manuring which have of late been written by some of the Ceylon planters, under the auspices and in response to the invitation of their Association, and more particularly to the Prize Essay by Mr. Grigson (1875), which, I have been informed (not having myself had an opportunity of reading it), carries off the palm for completeness and practical excellence.

CHAPTER XXIII.

Diseases incident to plants—Classification by Tournefort—Enemies of coffee—Bug—The black bug—Mode of propagation—Treatment recommended—The white bug—Affects dry situations—The borer—Its appearance in Coorg—Treatment—Probable causes—The leaf disease—Its character—Its effects—Its causes—Pellicularia—"Stump"—The rot—Grubs—Rats—Grasshoppers.

LIKE the members of the animal kingdom, plants are subject to diseases. They have, likewise, numerous enemies, which attack and prey upon them in various ways. Protection is, therefore, required against these hostile influences, or remedies where prevention has failed, and the discovery of such remedies, or means of prevention, should be one of the pursuits of every cultivator.

The first step in this direction, it is clear, must be to obtain as close and accurate a knowledge as possible of the nature of the enemies and diseases by which plants are assailed.

A deranged circulation of the sap is brought about by such causes as unsuitability of soil or climate. The soil may be swampy, or, possibly, deficient in organic matter; or, the climate may be too cold, too hot, too dry, or too wet. Again, diseases often in reality result from the attacks of external enemies, such as insects or fungi, and in this form are commonly vaguely termed "blights."

Tournefort divided the diseases of plants into the following classes: those arising from over-abundance of sap; those caused by too little; those arising from sap of bad quality; those from its being unequally distributed; and, fifthly, those due to external causes.

An excess of sap is produced where the climate is too wet, and is understood to be most readily remediable by the application of organic manures, such as cattle-dung. Where plants are deficient in sap, on the other hand, owing to a want of organic nourishment, or of moisture, the natural remedies are, again the application of manure, irrigation, repression of weeds, and, above all, *shade* culture.

The principal external enemies of the coffee-tree are BUG, WORM (or BORER), LEAF-DISEASE, ROT, GRUBS, and STUMP.

Bug (*Coccus Coffeæ*, or *Lecanium Coffeæ*) has been fully described by Mr. Nietner, of Ceylon, in his interesting work, entitled "Enemies of the Coffee-tree." The pest may be divided into two species, the black and the white bug. The black bug is a minute insect, which attaches itself to the tenderest shoots of the plant; the females having the appearance of small scollop shells, of a brown colour, adhering to the leaf or twig in the same manner as the scollop shell to a rock. Each of these formations is said to contain several hundred eggs undergoing incubation. In a short time the whole of the green wood of the tree will become covered with these, and coated over with a black soot-like powder, which is an excretion of the insects. This excretion renders a tree affected by the disease easily discernible at a distance.

From one tree the bug will soon spread over whole fields or whole estates, entirely checking the growth of the trees, the fresh young shoots being always first attacked, and such wood as is allowed to mature producing hardly any crop. The berries, moreover, are in their earliest stage destroyed by these insects, which seem to cut them off at the stalk from the mere love of destruction.

The following description of the coffee bug is taken from Sir J. Emerson Tennent's work on Ceylon:—" A number of small wart-like bodies may be seen studding the young shoots and buds, and occasionally the margins of the under sides of the leaves. Each of these warts is a transformed female, containing a large number of eggs (about 700), which are hatched within it. When the young ones come out of their nest, they may be observed running about, and looking like wood lice. Shortly after being hatched, the males seek the under sides of the leaves, while the females prefer the young shoots as their place of abode. The larvæ of the males undergo transformation in pupa beneath their own skins; their wings are horizontal, and the fact of their possessing wings may probably explain the comparatively rare presence of the male on the bushes. The female retains her power of locomotion till nearly her full size, and it is about this time that her impregnation takes place.

"The coffee bug first appeared on the Luhallagalla estate (Ceylon) in 1843."

This scourge cannot well be overcome and destroyed unless taken in a very early stage, i.e., when found only on a few isolated trees. Each tree on which it first makes its appearance may be well dusted with a mixture of pounded saltpetre and quicklime in equal parts. Some planters recommend brushing, or sponging the parts affected with a mixture of soft soap, tar, tobacco, and spirits of turpentine, in about equal quantities. A coolie, with a bucket and a piece of rag, can perform the office effectually. If the first application is insufficient, it may be repeated.

Once the presence of bug has been detected, it will be worth while to keep one or two intelligent persons regularly on the look-out for a time, in order that, if possible, its depredations may be checked at the outset by some such treatment as the above.

From personal observation, I should say that the black bug has a decided partiality for cold, damp, elevated situations. It generally makes its first appearance under the shelter of some large rock, near a belt of forest, or at the bottom of a damp ravine, or "nullah." It will sometimes hang about for one season only, and then disappear as mysteriously as it came ; on some high, cold estates, however, it seems to establish itself permanently, setting all attempts to dislodge or exterminate it at defiance. At other times, a hot, dry season appears to destroy it temporarily, while it reappears on the return of the rains.

White bug appears in reality to be a distinct species of insect. It is a small, flat, oval insect, about one-sixteenth of an inch long, covered with a white down or fur, and having parallel ridges running across its back from side to side, like the wood-louse, though on a much smaller scale. It takes up its quarters at the axils of the leaves and among the stalks of the crop clusters, which it mercilessly cuts off wholesale, either during the blossom stage or just after the young berries have been formed ; in the latter case, its operations may easily be recognized by the large quantities of young green berries with which the ground beneath the trees will be strewn. It is also easily discovered by a white, flour-like excretion which it deposits around the axil nooks which it has made its abode.

The prescriptions above recommended for black bug will be here found equally efficacious, though, in either case probably, a decoction of common tobacco might be sufficient, while much more easily prepared.

The white bug appears to have as decided a preference for hot, dry situations as its black *confrère* has for wet ones, and generally disappears in the wet season; too often, however, only to return as soon as the blossom has "set," when it at once recommences its work of destruction.

The *Borer*, formerly known as the "worm," and subsequently as the "coffee fly," first began to attract considerable notice, amounting in some parts of Southern India (especially in Coorg) to consternation, in 1865 or 1866. A great deal has been written about it, and naturalists for some time differed as to its character. It has been variously stated to be the *Sirex Gigas*, one of the *Tetramera* of the *Coleoptera*, and one of the *Zenzera*; finally, however, from its exact correspondence with a specimen placed in the British Museum by

M. Chevrolat, it has been identified as the *Xylotrechus Quadrupes.*

Whole estates in Coorg and other districts have been entirely destroyed by this scourge. In its complete stage, the insect appears as a fly or winged beetle; it is from half to three quarters of an inch in length, rather finer in shape than a wasp, with a hard, shiny coat, in colour red and black, or in other cases yellow and black, in alternate transverse lines. (The difference of colour is believed to indicate the sexes.) This fly or beetle *bores* a passage into the stem of the coffee-tree, usually some few inches above the ground. This passage, at first horizontal, soon takes an upward spiral direction and proceeds for a certain distance, until a safe retreat is found in which the larva may be deposited. The tree soon begins to droop, and in a short time dies down to the point where the entry has been effected, at which part it can be easily broken off by a sharp pull at the upper part.

The only course is to break off the tree in this manner, and then to burn the stem with the larva secreted in its centre. The borer *always works upwards.* Young shoots will, in most cases, proceed from the stump (if the perforation has not begun too near the roots), and one of these may be trained to succeed the original stem.

There is a general impression among the Southern Indian planters that the advent of the borer was in some way due to effects on the coffee plant of want of rain, and I am firmly of opinion that it can only be kept out of estates in hot, dry situations like the Bamboo districts of the Wynaad, by providing the coffee estates with suitable *shade*, if indeed irrigation to some extent be not also necessary during the long dry season.

The natives connected the borer visitation with the dying out of the bamboos, which, occurring once in every sixty years, or some such period, took place throughout Coorg and Wynaad in the very year, 1865, in which the borer began to be so well known. It seems highly probable, supposing the borer to have been previously accustomed to find its home and food in the green bamboo stems, that as soon as these withered and died it might have betaken itself to the coffee plant for sustenance. For further particulars regarding the "borer visitation," the reader cannot do better than refer to Dr. Bidie's Report to the Madras Government (1867), and to the late Col. C. P. Taylor's "Campaign against the White Borer." (Madras).

It may here be added that the ravages of the borer were most felt on *weedy, neglected plantations;* so that it is fair to infer that much, in the way of prevention at least, may be accomplished by careful and judicious cultivation.

Leaf disease.—Since the first edition of this work appeared, yet another scourge has been added to the planter's already formidable list of troubles. The leaf disease seems first to have been observed in Ceylon in 1869, in the Madoolsema district, though it did not cause much alarm until later. In S. India its appearance began to attract notice about the close of 1871, though, as is often the case, some persons subsequently came forward to show that they had been acquainted with the blight for many years previously.[1] The *Ceylon Observer*, moreover, states that the disease has been known in Brazil for many years past.

By the year 1875 whole districts in Ceylon and S. India had become devastated by "leaf disease," and the Ceylon planters, thoroughly alarmed, brought the subject under the notice of Government, who at once took steps to have it investigated. A list of questions was drawn up by Mr. Thwaites, of the Kandy Botanical Gardens, and circulated among the planters; as also through the

[1] Mr. W. G. McIvor, Superintendent of the Government Cinchona Plantations on the Neilgherries, reports, "The disease at Hoolicul and Kartairy has been observed for upwards of twenty-six years, but only developed to an alarming extent within the last two years, when it has spread more or less over the whole extent under cultivation."

medium of the Madras Government, among the planters of Wynaad and the Neilgherries. From some of the statements thus elicited, and from other sources I gather the following summarized conclusions.

The leaf disease is a fungus, scientifically described as the *Hemeleia Vastatrix*, which first attacks the under side of the leaves, causing spots or blotches, at first yellow, but subsequently turning black. These blotches are, on examination, found to be covered with a pale, orange-coloured dust or powder, which easily rubs off. The blotches gradually increase in size, until at last they have spread over the leaves, which then drop off, leaving the trees in a short time perfectly bare, in which state they are, of course, unable to produce crop, or to bring that which may already have been produced to maturity.

After a time, but more particularly after the trees have been carefully pruned and manured, the disease seems to retire; too often, however, only to return the following season with renewed virulence. Mr. Cockerell, commissioner of the Neilgherries, reports that the trees "apparently recover in the spring of the year, and throw out fresh foliage, which is in its turn attacked." The trees produce little or no crop the first year after being affected, and the amount of loss caused by the visitation will be appreciated, when it is stated that the yearly crop of Ceylon has been diminished some 300,000 cwts. since its appearance.

Hopes are entertained that the disease is now on the decline, but whence it came, and what are the conditions under which it finds most encouragement, appear to be questions as to which nothing is known with anything approaching to certainty. The idea in one place that the visitation is caused by, or at least connected with, drought, or an exposed situation, is immediately disproved by its appearing, with equal destructiveness, in some sheltered valley where moisture abounds. On the whole, however, the weight of evidence, so far, seems to favour the conclusion that the disease is most prevalent in dry, exposed situations, with poor soil, and where, consequently, the trees are weak in constitution; while there is even great unanimity of opinion that its ravages, though not altogether prevented by high cultivation, may be at least checked by it. By the term "high cultivation," I mean careful pruning, manuring, shade, where required, the entire suppression of weeds, &c.

A Bombay paper states that coffee-leaves from Mysore have been submitted to the Royal Agricultural Society, affected with a new kind of fungus, different from that which is above described, and to which the name of *Pellicularia Koleroga* has been given. A report on the disease was written by Mr. Berkeley.[2]

When visiting Coorg some years ago, my attention was called by a planter residing on the Mangalore Ghaut to a new form of blight, which, he assured me caused much mischief in that district.

This disease is there known as *stump*, from its being due to decay of the stump of a particular forest-tree peculiar to the district, felled in the process of clearing; sooner or later all the coffee-trees in the immediate neighbourhood of these stumps begin mysteriously to die out, and the only remedy for the mischief is to remove the offending stumps as quickly as possible.

Rot is a disease said to exist where the young coffee-leaves and shoots turn black and wither. This is generally caused by too much wet and cold. The best remedy is draining the ground well, laying down also, if possible, māna grass two or three inches thick over the surface. This ground-thatching has a marvellous effect in qualifying sour, stiff soils, and counteracting the effects of a cold, wet climate. It will also be desirable to prune the

---

[2] While going to press, I am informed that a Ceylon planter claims to have discovered some means of checkmating the leaf disease. Not having any details, I make no comment on this announcement, which I sincerely hope may prove true.—AUTHOR.

trees moderately, so that the sun and air may play freely through the foliage.

Grubs.—Coffee-trees, previously the finest in a field, not uncommonly die off in the most disheartening manner, without any apparent cause, and just after exhibiting the perfection of luxuriant growth. This is most frequently the case in rich soils, full of organic matter, or where cattle manure has been generously bestowed. On digging round the tree, it will almost invariably be found that the roots, or, to speak more precisely, the tap-root, has been attacked by grubs.

A Ceylon planter, many years ago, determining to have a field of coffee that would surpass in luxuriance and productiveness anything previously known, half-filled each hole, before the plants were put in, with manure. To his great surprise and chagrin, in the second year some 25 per cent. of the plants died off. In order to discover the reason, he had these all dug out, and found that in every case, the tap-root had been partially destroyed by large, yellow grubs, which had been generated by, or, at any rate, had congregated in, the decaying manure. The only thing that can be done when such symptoms appear, is at once to set to work and dig out the offending causes.

Rats, especially a description known as the Golonda Rat, sometimes make raids on the coffee, attacking the branches and severing the stems of young plants. In some districts they are exceedingly destructive. These creatures, as well as squirrels, monkeys, wild cats, and other animals, also purloin the ripe berries, during the crop season, in considerable quantities. They should, therefore, be destroyed when met with. The same remark applies to—

Grasshoppers, which are also addicted to cutting down young trees close to the ground, and to sawing off the branches of older trees. What the particular source may be of the gratification which they derive from these operations, I have never been able to discover. The fact, however, remains, that they cause considerable loss and annoyance to the planter in this way, and have therefore established their claim to rank among the enemies of the coffee-tree.

CHAPTER XXIV.

Estimates—Difficulties in the way of accuracy—Cost of land—SOUTHERN INDIA, First year—Second year—Third year—Fourth year—Fifth year—Sixth year—Seventh year—Balance-sheet.—CEYLON, First year—Second year—Third year—Fourth year—Fifth year—Sixth year—Remarks—Crop—Market value—Balance-sheet—General result.

A BOOK such as the present would be incomplete without estimates of the cost of bringing a coffee estate under cultivation, and of maintaining it in that condition, as against the returns which may reasonably be looked for.

To furnish accurate statements of this nature is now more difficult than ever, owing to a variety of causes. In the first place, it is almost impossible to say what sum per acre might have to be paid for land at the outset. Looking at Ceylon, we find prices for forest ranging from £8 to £25 per acre, while, if we embrace the districts of Southern India in our survey, the figures may be almost anything, from 10 rupees upwards. As shown in a previous chapter, in some districts the Government upset price is a merely nominal sum, representing the cost of survey and demarcation, an annual assessment being levied subsequently. In others, the assessment is commuted on payment of a sum of 50 rupees per acre. As a matter of fact, however, the cost of Government lands in S. India need hardly be taken into account, comparatively little land suitable for planting purposes now remaining in the hands of Government in either the Neilgherries, Coorg, or Wynaad, while there is great difficulty in securing what there is at any price, except under the most stringent conditions. The same remark will also soon become applicable to Ceylon. It is thus more a question of what private landholders will accept, and here the margin is perplexingly wide. Natives are fully alive to the keenness of the inquiry among European capitalists of late years for this kind of property, and have not been slow to take advantage of it, any more than have Europeans in their position. Consequently, we hear of 100, 150, and 200 rupees an acre being asked for forest land, which a few years ago could have been got at 15 or 20 rupees.[1] These prices, however, are practically prohibitory,

---

[1] Some natives being asked last year at what price they would dispose of a block of 150 acres of forest in the Wynaad, at once demanded 30,000 rupees = £20 per acre!

as few capitalists are willing to pay more than £10 or £15 an acre.

Having thus described the actual situation, it becomes practically of little moment what the cost of land is stated at below. The sums I fix upon, for convenience sake, are 50 rupees per acre for forest-land in Southern India, and £10 for Ceylon; should the intending planter pay more, he must amend the estimate for himself accordingly; if less, so much the better for him. Grass-lands for pasturage, I shall state at 25 rupees and £4 respectively.

SOUTHERN INDIA.

Estimate for the purchase of 300 acres of forest-land, and 200 acres of grass-land, bringing 200 acres of the former under cultivation, and into full bearing. Labour calculated at 4 annas per day, exclusive of Maistries' wages.

First Year.
(October 1st to 30th September following.)

	Rs.	a.	p.	Rs.	a.	p.
300 acres of forest @ Rs. 50	15,000	0	0			
200 ,, ,, grass-land @ Rs. 25	5000	0	0			
				20,000	0	0
Purchase of tools, &c. (A)	350	0	0			
Felling and clearing 50 acres @ Rs. 20 (B)	1000	0	0			
Coolie lines, writer's house and temporary bungalow	1200	0	0			
Carried forward	2,550	0	0	20,000	0	0

	Rs.	a.	p.	Rs	a.	p.
Brought forward	2,550	0	0	20,000	0	0
Nursery containing say 1 lac of plants, for 2nd year's extension	250	0	0			
Roads, to the estate and on the clearing (C)	230	0	0			
Lining out 50 acres @ Rs. 3	150	0	0			
Pitting, 50 acres @ 5 ft. × 6 ft., say 1452 pits per acre @ 4 as. for 20 (D)	907	8	0			
Filling in pits (E)	151	4	0			
Plants bought, 75,000 @ Rs. 7/8 per 1000 (F)	562	8	0			
Planting up 50 acres	90	12	0			
Cleaning up and weeding till 30th September 50 acres @ Rs. 6 (G)	300	0	0			
				5192	0	0

Management.

	Rs.	a.	p.	Rs	a.	p.
Superintendent's salary and allowances (H)	1320	0	0			
Writer's pay	360	0	0			
Maistries' pay, 10% on coolie labour	418	0	0			
				2098	0	0
Contingencies				500	0	0
Outlay, first 12 months				Rs. 27,790	0	0

(A) The *Tools* required at first starting will be, say, 50 bill-hooks, 50 axes, 50 mammoties, 25 crowbars, besides a few other articles.

(B) *Felling and clearing* usually cost in the Wynaad from Rs. 15 to Rs. 22/8 per acre. On bamboo land a clean burn is the exception, and clearing up is consequently expensive. The contract rates are Rs. 15 for felling, and Rs. 7/8 for clearing up.

(C) *Roads;* the clearing is hardly likely to be just on the high-road, and I have therefore calculated on a communication with it having to be made through the jungle. This should be a good ride-able road, some 5 or 6 feet wide, and will cost Rs. 120 to Rs. 150 per mile.

(D) *Pitting;* this provides for pits at 6 feet × 5 feet apart, (1452 to the acre), of one foot and a half *cube;* the cost being at the rate of 20 per 4 annas.

(E) *Filling in,* costing 4 annas per 120.

(F) *Plants;* although nurseries are made at the outset, they will not furnish plants till the second year; consequently the first season's requirements must be bought from native cultivators or elsewhere; prices varying from 5 to 10 rupees per 1000.

(G) *Cleaning up.* In bamboo clearings where the second growth is very rapid and luxuriant, this "cleaning up" is a laborious and expensive business, a great deal of grass having to be dug out, and green jungle to be cut down. 6 rupees per acre may hardly cover it. On forest-land, after a clean burn, 3 rupees may more than cover the cost of all weedings between the 1st of July and the 30th September.

(H) *Superintendence.* For a young European in sole charge, 100 rupees a month is the usual salary to begin with, while there will be a further sum allowed to pay for a "waterman."

SECOND YEAR.

Cultivation (50 *acres*).

	Rs.	a.	p.	Rs.	a.	p.
Weeding for 12 months (A)	900	0	0			
Filling up vacancies (B)	69	8	0			
Thatching and repairing buildings	150	0	0			
Repairing roads and surface trenching	100	0	0			
Re-planting nursery (C)	133	5	4			
				1352	13	4

Extension (50 *acres*).

	Rs.	a.	p.	Rs.	a.	p.
Additional lines	350	0	0			
„ tools	250	0	0			
				600	0	0
Carried forward				1952	13	4

		Rs.	a.	p.	Rs.	s.	p.
Brought forward	. . .				1952	13	4
Felling, clearing, lining, pitting, filling, and planting, cleaning up and weeding 50 acres at last year's rates	. . .	2599	8	0			
Roads and surface trenching	. .	120	0	0			
					2719	8	0

Management (D).

		Rs.	a.	p.	Rs.	s.	p.
Superintendent's salary and allowances	. . . .	1800	0	0			
Purchase of horse	. . . .	400	0	0			
Writer's pay	. . . .	420	0	0			
Maistries' wages reckoned as before		407	0	0			
					3028	0	0
Contingencies	. . . . . .	500	0	0			
Outlay in the second year	. . .	Rs.	8199	5	4		

(A) *Weeding* on bamboo estates is always expensive; the grass is in the land from the first, and it is difficult to get it under. The above estimate is Rs. 18 per acre per annum.

(B) *Filling up Vacancies.*—This provides for 10 per cent. of failures on the new planting, which may be exceeded should the rains be unpropitious. Cost is thus arrived at:—

Re-opening, 40 pits @ 4 as. .	Rs. 45	6	0
Re-filling 120 ,, ,, . .	15	2	0
Planting 200 ,, ,, . .	9	0	0
	Rs. 69	8	0

(C) The Nursery must be fully re-stocked so as to provide plants for the following year's extension, and for supplying vacanies over an increased area.

(D) An annual increase of salary for both superintendent and writer will not only be fair but judicious. Have thoroughly efficient employés, and pay them *well*.

THIRD YEAR.

Cultivation (100 acres).

	Rs.	a.	p.	Rs.	a.	p.
Weeding for 12 months	1800	0	0			
Filling up vacancies 10% on 50 acs.	69	8	0			
And 5% on 50 acres	34	12	0			
Thatching and repairing buildings	225	0	0			
Trenching and repairing roads	150	0	0			
Re-planting nursery, &c.	166	10	8			
Topping and handling 50 acres (A)	125	0	0			
				2570	14	8

Extension.

Additional Coolie-lines, tools, and roads, as before	720	0	0			
Felling, clearing, lining, pitting, filling, planting, and cleaning up and weeding 50 acres, as before	2599	8	0			
				3319	8	0

Crop.

Pulping-house, store, and pulpers				4000	0	0
Gathering 1250 bushels Cherry (say 125 cwts.) @ 4 as.	312	8	0			
Curing @ 8 as. per cwt.	62	8	0			
Despatching to coast @ 10 as. per bushels parchment	390	10	0			
				765	10	0

Management.

Superintendent's salary and allowances.	2620	0	0			
Writer's pay	480	0	0			
Maistries' wages	555	0	0			
				3655	0	0
Contingencies				500	0	0
Outlay in the third year				Rs. 14,811	0	8

(A) *Topping and Handling.*—The 50 acres planted in the

first year should now be ready for topping, and will then require to be handled once or twice.

(B) *Pulping House, &c.*—A mere platform and set of cisterns roofed over with thatch, can of course be run up for much less than is here set down. My intention, however, is to provide for a neat, strong building, with iron roof and water-wheel, costing in all some Rs. 2000 or more. Some planters look upon a store as a superfluity in districts where there is no rain from which to protect the coffee; my view, however, is decidedly in favour of a moderate-sized building, with brick or stone pillars and an iron roof, costing something like Rs. 2000 or 3000. Part of the outlay under the above heading may be extended over the following year.

(C) *Crop.*—A first crop of 2½ cwts. per acre is here calculated on, from the 50 acres first planted.

FOURTH YEAR.
(October 1st to September 30th following.)

Cultivation (150 *acres*.).

	Rs.	a.	p.	Rs.	a.	p.
Weeding for 12 months	2700	0	0			
Filling up vacancies.	139	0	0			
Thatching and repairing buildings	400	0	0			
Repairing roads and trenching	250	0	0			
Keeping up nursery (A)	100	0	0			
Topping, handling, and pruning	425	0	0			
				4014	0	0

Extension (50 *acres*).

	Rs.	a.	p.	Rs.	a.	p.
Additional coolie-lines, tools, and roads, as before	720	0	0			
Felling, clearing, lining, pitting, filling in, planting and weeding 50 acres, as before	2599	8	0			
				3319	8	0

Crop.

				Rs.	a.	p.
Completing store and pulping-house				2000	0	0
Carried forward				9333	8	0

	Rs.	a.	p.	Rs.	a.	p.
Brought forward				9333	8	0
Gathering 4250 bushels Cherry (say 425 cwts.) @ 4 as. (B)	1062	8	0			
Curing @ 8 as. per cwt.	212	8	0			
Despatching to coast @ 10 as. per bushel parchment	1328	2	0			
				2603	2	0

Management.

	Rs.	a.	p.	Rs.	a.	p.
Superintendent's salary and allowances	3120	0	0			
Writer's pay, &c.	540	0	0			
Maistries' wages	788	0	0			
				4448	0	0

Stock.

	Rs.	a.	p.	Rs.	a.	p.
Building cattle-shed	1000	0	0			
Buying cattle, 75 head @ Rs. 30	2250	0	0			
Keepers, &c. (6 men)	432	0	0			
				3682	0	0
Contingencies				500	0	0
Outlay in the fourth year				Rs. 20,566	10	0

(A) The cost of keeping the nursery may now be permanently reduced, no further extension being contemplated. It will only be necessary in future to provide a sufficient number of plants to fill up vacancies.

(B) Crop is estimated after the first year at 6 cwt. per acre.

Fifth Year.

(October 1st to 30th September following.)

Cultivation (200 acres).

	Rs.	a.	p.	Rs.	a.	p.
Weeding for 12 months	3600	0	0			
Filling up vacancies	173	12	0			
Carried forward	3773	12	0			

	Rs.	a.	p.	Rs.	a.	p.
Brought forward .	3773	12	0			
Thatching and repairing buildings .	500	0	0			
Repairing roads and trenching	400	0	0			
Upkeep of nursery . . .	100	0	0			
Topping, handling, and pruning	850	0	0			
Manuring 50 acres @ Rs. 40 .	2000	0	0			
				7623	12	0

Crop.

	Rs.	a.	p.	Rs.	a.	p.
Gathering 7250 bushels Cherry (725 cwts.) @ 4 as. . . .	1812	0	0			
Curing @ 8 as. per cwt. . .	362	8	0			
Despatching to coast, as before	2265	10	0			
				4440	2	0
Building permanent bungalow, &c. .				5000	0	0

Stock.

	Rs.	a.	p.	Rs.	a.	p.
Buying 25 head of cattle . .	750	0	0			
Keepers (6 men) . . .	432	0	0			
				1182	0	0

Management.

	Rs.	a.	p.	Rs.	a.	p.
Superintendent's salary and allowances.	3620	0	0			
Writer's pay	600	0	0			
Maistries' wages . . .	980	0	0			
				5200	0	0
Contingencies				500	0	0
Outlay in the fifth year . .				Rs. 23,945	14	0

Sixth Year.

Cultivation.

	Rs.	a.	p.
Weeding 12 months . .	3600	0	0
Filling up vacancies . .	175	0	0
Carried forward .	3775	0	0

	Rs.	a.	p.	Rs.	a.	p.
Brought forward .	3775	0	0			
Buildings	500	0	0			
Roads and trenching . .	500	0	0			
Nursery	100	0	0			
Pruning and handling . .	2000	0	0			
Manuring	2500	0	0			
				9375	0	0

Crop.

	Rs.	a.	p.	Rs.	a.	p.
Gathering 10,250 bushels .	2562	8	0			
Curing and despatching . .	3715	10	0			
				6278	2	0
Stock				1200	0	0

Management.

	Rs.	a.	p.	Rs.	a.	p.
Superintendent and writer .	4220	0	0			
Maistries	1000	0	0			
				5220	0	0
Contingencies				500	0	0
Outlay in the sixth year . . .				Rs. 22,573	2	0

SEVENTH YEAR.

	Rs.	a.	p.
Cultivation as before . . .	9375	0	0

Crop.

	Rs.	a.	p.	Rs.	a.	p.
Gathering 12,000 bushels Cherry (1200 cwts.) full crop @ 4 as. .	3000	0	0			
Curing and despatching . .	4350	0	0			
				7350	0	0
Stock, as before				1200	0	0
Management, as before				5220	0	0
Contingencies				500	0	0
Outlay in the seventh year . .				Rs. 23,645	0	0

BALANCE-SHEET.

Estate in Account with the Proprietor.

Dr. / **Cr.**

First Year.

	Rs. a. p.		Rs. a. p.
To Expenses . . .	Rs. 27,790 0 0	By Balance . . .	Rs. 27,790 0 0

Second Year.

	Rs. a. p.		Rs. a. p.
To Balance . . .	27,790 0 0	By Balance . . .	35,989 5 4
,, Expenses . . .	8,199 5 4		
	Rs. 35,989 5 4		Rs. 35,989 5 4

Third Year.

	Rs. a. p.		Rs. a. p.
To Balance . . .	35,989 5 4	By 125 cwts. crop @ Rs. 45 nett.	5,625 0 0
,, Expenses . . .	14,811 0 8	,, Balance	45,175 6 0
	Rs. 50,800 6 0		Rs. 50,800 6 0

Balance-sheet (S. India).

FOURTH YEAR.

	Rs.					Rs.		
To Balance	45,175	6	0	By 425 cwts. crop @ Rs. 45 nett.		19,125	0	0
,, Expenses	20,566	10	0	,, Balance		46,617	0	0
	Rs. 65,742	0	0			Rs. 65,742	0	0

FIFTH YEAR.

To Balance	46,617	0	0	By 725 cwt. crop @ Rs. 45	32,625	0	0
,, Expenses	23,945	14	0	,, Balance	37,937	14	0
	Rs. 70,562	14	0		Rs. 70,562	14	0

SIXTH YEAR.

To Balance	37,937	14	0	By 1025 cwts. crop @ Rs. 45	46,125	0	0
,, Expenses	22,573	2	0	,, Balance	14,386	0	0
	Rs. 60,511	0	0		Rs. 60,511	0	0

SEVENTH YEAR.

To Balance	14,386	0	0	By 1200 cwts. crop @ Rs. 45	54,000	0	0
,, Expenses	23,645	0	0				
,, Balance	15,969	0	0				
	Rs. 54,000	0	0		Rs. 54,000	0	0

CEYLON.

Estimate for the purchase of 300 acres of forest-land, and 200 acres of grass-land, bringing 200 acres of the former under cultivation and into full bearing. Labour calculated at 9*d.* per day, including Canganies' wages.

FIRST YEAR.
(October 1st to September 30th following.)

	£	s.	d.	£	s.	d.
300 acres forest-land @ £10	3000	0	0			
200 ,, grass ,, ,, £4	800	0	0			
				3800	0	0
Felling, burning, and clearing 50 acres @ £2 5*s.* per acre (A)	112	10	0			
Purchase of tools, &c.	35	0	0			
Coolie lines £80, conductor's house, &c., £50, and temporary bungalow £50 (B)	180	0	0			
Nursery to provide for *second* year's extension, &c., say 100,000 plants	37	10	0			
Roads to the estate, and on the clearing (C)	34	10	0			
Lining out 50 acres @ 5*s.*	12	10	0			
Holing 50 acres, @ 5 ft. × 6 ft., i.e. 1452 holes per acre @ 25 per 9*d.*	108	15	0			
Filling in, @ 120 holes per 9*d.*	22	13	9			
Plants purchased 75,000 @ 10*s.* per 1000	37	10	0			
Planting @ 200 per 9*d.* (72,600)	13	12	3			
Cleaning up and weeding till 30th September, 50 acres @ 10*s.*	25	0	0			
				619	11	0
Carried forward				£4419	11	0

First and Second Years (Ceylon).

Management.

	£	s.	d.	£	s.	d.
Carried forward . . .				4419	11	0
Superintendent's salary . £120						
Allowances 12						
	132	0	0			
Conductor's pay, &c. . . .	45	12	0			
				177	12	0
Contingencies				50	0	0
Outlay first twelve months . . .				£4647	3	0

Second Year.
(October 1st to September 30th following.)

Cultivation (50 acres).

Weeding, 12 months, by contract .	50	0	0			
Filling up vacancies . . .	10	8	6			
Thatching and repairing buildings .	20	0	0			
Surface trenching and repairing roads	15	0	0			
Replanting nursery	20	0	0			
				115	8	6

Extension (50 acres).

Additional lines	50	0	0			
„ tools	25	0	0			
				75	0	0
Felling and clearing, lining out, holing, filling in, planting 50 acres as before	270	1	0			
Roads, one mile	12	0	0			
Cleaning up and weeding as before .	25	0	0			
				307	1	0

Management.

Superintendent's salary and allowances	182	0	0			
Purchase of horse	40	0	0			
Conductor's pay	51	12	0			
				273	12	0
Contingencies				50	0	0
Outlay in the second year .				£821	1	6

THIRD YEAR.
(October 1st to September 30th following.)

Cultivation (100 acres).

	£	s.	d.	£	s.	d.
Weeding, 12 months, by contract	100	0	0			
Filling up vacancies	15	13	0			
Thatching and repairing buildings	30	0	0			
Surface trenching and repairing roads	22	10	0			
Re-planting and manuring nurseries	25	0	0			
Topping and handling 50 acres @ 7/6	18	15	0			
				211	18	0

Extension (50 acres).

Additional coolie-lines	50	0	0			
„ tools	25	0	0			
				75	0	0
Felling and clearing, lining out, holing, filling in and planting 50 acres, as before	270	1	0			
Roads, one mile	12	0	0			
Cleaning up and weeding, as before	25	0	0			
				307	1	0

Stores, &c.

Pulping-house, machinery, and store (first instalment)				400	0	0

Crop.

Picking 850 boxes cherry (125 cwts.) @ 7d.	24	15	0			
Curing the same @ 1s. per cwt.	6	5	0			
Carriage to the coast @ 1s. per bushel parchment	31	5	0			
				62	5	0

Management.

Superintendent's salary and allowances	262	0	0			
Conductor's pay	57	12	0			
				319	12	0
Contingencies				50	0	0
Outlay in the third year				£1425	16	0

Fourth Year.

(October 1st to September 30th following.)

Cultivation (150 acres).

	£	s.	d.	£	s.	d.
Weeding, 12 months, by contract	150	0	0			
Filling up vacancies	19	10	3			
Thatching and repairing buildings	40	0	0			
Repairing roads and surface trenching	33	15	0			
Partially re-planting nursery	12	10	0			
Topping and handling, 50 acres @ 7/6	18	15	0			
Pruning 50 acres @ 15s.	37	10	0			
				312	0	3

Stores, &c.

Completing store, &c.				400	0	0

Crop.

	£	s.	d.	£	s.	d.
Picking 2850 boxes (425 cwts.) cherry @ 7d. per box	83	2	6			
Curing @ 1s. per cwt.	21	5	0			
Carriage to Colombo @ 1s. per bush. parchment	106	5	0			
				210	12	6

Extension (50 acres).

	£	s.	d.	£	s.	d.
Additional coolie-lines	50	0	0			
,, tools	25	0	0			
				75	0	0
Felling and clearing, lining out, holing, filling in, and planting 50 acres, as before	270	1	0			
Roads, one mile	12	0	0			
Cleaning up and weeding, as before	25	0	0			
				307	1	0

Stock.

	£	s.	d.	£	s.	d.
Building permanent cattle-sheds	100	0	0			
Buying cattle, 75 head @ 3l.	225	0	0			
Keepers, &c. (6 men)	53	12	0			
				378	12	0
Carried forward				£1683	5	9

	£	s.	d.	£	s.
Brought forward				1683	5 9

Management.

	£	s.	d.	£	s.	d.
Superintendent's salary and allowances	312	0	0			
Conductor's pay and allowances	63	12	0			
				375	12	0
Contingencies				50	0	0
Outlay in the fourth year				£2108	17	9

FIFTH YEAR.

(October 1st to September 30th following.)

Cultivation (200 acres).

	£	s.	d.	£	s.	d.
Weeding, 12 months, by contract	200	0	0			
Filling up vacancies	23	9	6			
Thatching and repairing buildings	50	0	0			
Surface trenching and repairing roads	42	10	0			
Upkeep of nurseries	12	10	0			
Topping and handling 50 acres @ 7s. 6d.	18	15	0			
Pruning and handling 100 acres @ 15s.	75	0	0			
Manuring 40 acres @ 5l.	200	0	0			
				622	4	

Crop.

	£	s.	d.	£	s.	d.
Picking 4850 boxes of cherry (725 cwts.) @ 7d. per box	141	9	2			
Curing at 1s. per cwt.	36	5	0			
Carriage to Colombo	181	5	0			
				358	19	0
Building permanent bungalow				500	0	0
Buying stock (25 head)	75	0	0			
Keep of ditto (6 men)	53	12	0			
				128	12	0
Carried forward				£1609	15	6

Fifth and Sixth Years (Ceylon).

	£	s.	d.	£	s.	d.
Brought forward				1609	15	6

Management.

	£	s.	d.	£	s.	d.
Superintendent's salary and allowances	362	0	0			
Conductor's pay and allowances	69	12	0			
				431	12	0
Contingencies				50	0	0
Outlay in the fifth year				£2091	7	6

SIXTH YEAR.

(October 1st to September 30th following.)

Cultivation.

	£	s.	d.	£	s.	d.
Weeding, 12 months, by contract	250	0	0			
Filling up vacancies	25	0	0			
Thatching and keeping up buildings	50	0	0			
Surface trenching and roads	40	0	0			
Nurseries	12	10	0			
Pruning and handling 150 acs. @ 1*l*.	150	0	0			
,, ,, 50 ,, 15*s*.	37	10	0			
				565	0	0
Manuring 40 acres @ 6*l*.				240	0	0

Crop.

	£	s.	d.	£	s.	d.
Picking 6850 boxes of cherry (1025 cwts.) @ 7*d*. per box	199	6	6			
Curing the same, as before	51	5	0			
Carriage to Colombo, as before	257	10	0			
				508	1	6
Stock				150	0	0
Management, as before				431	12	0
Contingencies				50	0	0
Outlay in the sixth year				£1944	13	6

Seventh Year.

	£ s. d.	£ s. d.
Weeding, filling up vacancies, upkeep of buildings and roads, trenching, nurseries, and manuring, as before	617 10 0	
Pruning @ 1*l.* per acre	200 0 0	817 10 0
Crop-picking, curing and despatching 1200 cwts. @ same rates as previously		593 6 8
Stock, management, and contingencies @ same rates as previously.		631 12 0
		£2042 8 8

Remarks on the above.

Wages in Ceylon vary from 7*d.* to 9*d.* per day for able-bodied men, and from 4*d.* to 7*d.* for children and women, 1*d.* per day being added to cover the wages of the Cangany. It will, however, be noticed that, with one exception, the above calculations are based on the maximum rate, the idea being that the full day's wage should correspond to the full day's work. Where the work is performed by women and boys, who receive a lower remuneration, the amount of work will, in most cases, be proportionally smaller.

Felling and Clearing.—This will be done by Cingalese contractors from the low country.

Coolie Lines, &c.—Substantial, warm buildings of the usual character, and such as will stand for some years. The temporary bungalow, when superseded by a superior building, ought to be available for use as stables, rice-store, or for other purposes.

Roads.—The supposition here is, that not only will a mile of four-foot road be made on the clearing, but that a bridle-road may have to be made for a couple of miles through the jungle, from the nearest highway to the estate.

Plants, for the first season's planting, will be bought at or under this price, from some neighbouring estate, while the second year's requirements are being provided for by a home nursery.

Weeding.—£1 per acre per annum is not the lowest contract rate, 1*s*. 6*d*. per month being not uncommon. In Chena land[1] the cost will be greater, perhaps as high as 2*s*. 6*d*. per acre per month, for the first twelve or eighteen months, until the seeds begin to be eradicated.

Stores, &c.—My friend, Mr. W. Sabonadiere, estimates the cost of the pulping-house, with water-wheel and other usual machinery, at from £300 to £500; and of the store, with Clerihew appliances, at from £500 to £1200, according to the nature of the building. I have in both cases elected the

---

[1] Land which has been cleared for grain or other cultivation at some previous period, but allowed to grow up again into jungle. Such land is always more or less sown with weeds.

minimum amount, spreading the total expenditure until this heading (£800) over two consecutive years.

Crop.—In the first edition of the work, a maiden crop of 4 cwts. per acre in the third year was calculated on, and 7 cwts. peracre afterwards. I have myself picked a maiden crop (third year) of 9 cwts. in Ceylon, and have known a friend to get 13 cwts. in the Wynaad. Since then, however, there have been so many disappointments from one cause or other, and the "leaf disease" has so largely reduced the average yield of Ceylon, that I do not feel justified in adhering to these figures. The present calculations are consequently based on a first yield of 2½ cwts., followed yearly afterwards by one of 6 cwts. per acre. This is a sad "come down," looking back upon the glorious crops one has seen gathered in such districts as Kallibokka, Matale, Knuckles, &c., before the year 1863. One estate, also, in Hewahettie, yielded a crop of 22 cwts. an acre all over, one year, and one averaging 13 cwts. in the year following. One field on this estate (of which I was then superintendent) bore 27 cwts. of crop per acre!

The "Box" here referred to, is the usual measure used, and contains a bushel and a half. During the height of the crop season the cost of picking will not be more than 4*d.* or 5*d.* per box, but this cannot be kept up all through, and the average will, perhaps, be not much less than 6*d.*, with the canganies' penny added.

We next come to the most important question of all—the *value* of the crop. In the original work this was set down as 56*s.* per cwt., but the state of the case has here altered very materially for the better, and the actual value of good plantation coffee, in bond in London, is now exactly *double* that figure! If we deduct from this, 12*s.* as a set-off against cost of curing, and preparation for shipment, freight, loss in weight, &c., &c., this will leave 100*s.* per cwt., and no one, as far as I am aware, is at present in a position to say that a continuance of this value must not be looked for. There seems no reason to anticipate any very immediate large increase in the production, while the consumption is more likely to go on increasing than otherwise. The prospects of the market being, therefore, on the whole, decidedly favourable, I see no reason why 90*s.* per cwt. net may not fairly be set down as the realizable price during the next few years.

Topping, handling, and pruning.—The idea here is to allow 7*s.* 6*d.* per acre for the first year, 15*s.* for the second, and £1 for the third and subsequent years.

Stock.—As the entire estate should be manured once every five years, it will be necessary to begin keeping cattle during the fourth year, so as to have a supply of litter, &c., to put out the year following. Some planters estimate three head of cattle being required for every acre to be manured, but the correctness of this, or otherwise, will greatly depend on the care with which the process of *manure making* is attended to. Provided always there is plenty of pasturage and fodder, the more cattle the better, but it is useless having a larger number than can be well fed and cared for; seventy-five bought the first year, and twenty-five added every year or two afterwards, should be sufficient, with the various composts, to provide manure for forty acres.

Having arrived at the end of the seventh year, with the estate clear, and capable of giving an annual return of from £3000 to £3500—supposing all to be in first-rate order, and the coffee market to have kept up at not less than 100*s.* per cwt. in London—the estate may be valued at from five to six years' purchase, say—

For the coffee in bearing . . .	£18,500
For the forest-land (100 acres) . .	1,000
For the grass-land (200 acres) . .	1,000
	£20,500

This gives over £90 per acre for the cultivated portion; whereas, at the present time, from £100 to £120 is asked, and (I am told) *given* in Ceylon.

BALANCE-SHEET.

Estate in Account with the Proprietor.

Dr. | | | | | | | | **Cr.**

First Year.

		£	s.	d.			£	s.	d.
To Expenses	.	4647	3	0	By Balance	.	£4647	3	0

Second Year.

		£	s.	d.			£	s.	d.
To Balance	.	4647	3	0	By Balance	.	5468	4	6
„ Expenses	.	821	1	6					
		£5468	4	6			£5468	4	6

Third Year.

		£	s.	d.			£	s.	d.
To Balance	.	5468	4	6	By 125 cwts. crop @ 90s. net	.	562	10	0
„ Expenses	.	1425	16	0	„ Balance	.	6331	10	6
		£6894	0	6			£6894	0	6

FOURTH YEAR.

	£ s. d.			£ s. d.
To Balance	6331 10 6	By 425 cwts. crop @ 90s.		1912 10 0
,, Expenses	2108 17 0	By Balance		6527 17 6
	£8440 7 6			£8440 7 6

FIFTH YEAR.

To Balance	6527 17 6	By 725 cwts. crop @ 90s.		3262 10 0
,, Expenses	2091 7 6	,, Balance		5356 15 0
	£8619 5 0			£8619 5 0

SIXTH YEAR.

To Balance	5356 15 0	By 1025 cwts. crop @ 90s.		4612 10 0
,, Expenses	1944 13 6	,, Balance		2688 18 6
	£7301 8 6			£7301 8 6

SEVENTH YEAR.

To Balance	2688 18 6	By 1200 cwts. crop @ 90s.		5400 0 0
,, Expenses	2042 8 8			
,, Balance	668 12 10			
	£5400 0 0			

SUBSEQUENT YEARS.

To Expenses	£2000 0 0	By 1200 cwts. crop		£5400 0 0

CHAPTER XXV.

Durability of coffee property—Question one to be faced—Age of estates in Ceylon—Planting fifty years ago—The legacy of pioneers—Native coffee gardens—Difficulties—Dangers to permanency—Diseases, &c.—Conditions of durability—Climate—Soil—Culture—The Author's opinion.

THE question of the permanency or durability of coffee property is one which has long been agitating the minds of not a few of the Ceylon and South Indian planters, and I am inclined to believe it is one upon which, if truth were told, many of them entertain considerable misgivings, and would, consequently, be just as well pleased to defer, if not evade the discussion of. Such a course, however, seems to me a mistake, and moreover one from which nothing can possibly be gained, inasmuch as it must inevitably convey to outsiders the impression that the question of permanency as a proposition has been already privately brought up, examined, and dismissed as untenable. Now what are the facts bearing upon this subject?

On arriving in Ceylon myself, so long ago as

the year 1855, I had the advantage of becoming acquainted with a most worthy old gentleman, then a resident of some thirty-five years' standing in the island. This was Mr. George Bird, the pioneer of coffee planting in Ceylon. It will be apparent that any estates opened about the time of his coming to the island would now be upwards of half a century old, and as a matter of fact there *are* estates in the Kandian district, still under cultivation, which were first planted about that time. I believe I am correct in naming among these Sir Edward Barnes's Gangaroowa, and Condesalle in the Doombera Valley. At the same time, it must be admitted that most of the estates planted fifty years ago, or anything like that period, have either been long since altogether abandoned, or, if not entirely so, are at least very much the worse for wear. And this admission may be freely made without by any means involving any such doctrine as that it is impossible to keep up estates for fifty years, or, as far as that goes, for ever!

It is only natural to suppose that half a century ago coffee planting would have been carried on in a very rude and imperfect fashion. We know this to have been the case, to a very large extent, in even much more recent times. At the outset all must have been groping experiment. The conditions of soil, climate, &c., best suited to the plant had yet to be discovered; and we are told that the earliest planters commenced operations, in the first instance, near the coast at Galle, where, it is now known, the plant could not be cultivated with advantage. Thus it ever is with a new enterprise; the pioneer plods on, feeling his way amid darkness and difficulty, seldom himself reaching much beyond the dawn of information, before he is compelled to abandon his researches into younger hands.

Then even when some clear ideas had begun to be formed, and the plant was found to flourish best under given conditions, it was evidently thought to require but little further care or culture, and was left pretty much to itself. Proprietors, agents, and managers, one and all, were in general very different from those of the present day, even up to within the last five-and-twenty years. To lead a jovial, easy-going life, with plenty of conviviality and field sports, was often the first object of the superintendent; while to get through as much capital as possible in the form of estate outlay, without much inquiry as to how it had been expended, was as often the main idea of the agent. As for proprietors, they were either absentees, like the Irish landlords, or, if residing in the island, they themselves shared in the general recklessness, and contributed to the general mismanagement. Stories are told of proprietors who, having taken out specie from the bank in Kandy, to pay the coolies with, engaged in play on arriving at the manager's bungalow, until the whole amount had passed into the pocket of one or other; payment of the coolies being postponed until a fresh remittance could be obtained. While it is also narrated how Colombo agents have been known to remonstrate with the estate managers for not being sufficiently extravagant in their expenditure.

It would surely, therefore, be rather a matter for wonder than otherwise were all the estates opened in such days as those referred to, to be still under cultivation.

There seems, as far as I can see, to be no reason to apprehend a limit to the possible permanency of a coffee plantation, under favourable or even suitable conditions. Native plantings are to be found in many parts of Ceylon, Wynaad, Mysore, &c., containing trees of an age far beyond the power of the oldest inhabitant to define, and which have very probably been flourishing for generations.

At the same time, one is forced to admit that there may possibly be much still to learn, as to the conditions best calculated to promote the health and longevity of the plant. We of to-day are reaping the fruits of the painful experience sown by our predecessors; and may it not be that our successors may reap many fruits resulting from experience dearly bought by us?

Then, again, it has to be confessed that there are great and serious difficulties in the way of keeping up that constant, unremitting care and culture which appear necessary to maintain in a state of perfect health a plant which, however hardy in some respects, is after all an exotic in our Indian settlements, and is moreover being grown under a forced and artificial system.

Experience shows us every day how irremediable is the damage that may result from even a short temporary neglect of weeding, a contingency often unavoidable, owing to scarcity of labour; or from improper, reckless pruning, which may be the work of a few days, under an inexperienced or careless superintendent; or from a failure to supply the trees with due support, in the shape of manure, when they may have become exhausted from over-bearing.

Moreover, it is impossible to lose sight of the diseases, blights, &c., to which the plant itself is subject; which may, indeed, arise from circumstances unfavourable to the plant, which we shall become cognizant of by-and-by, but which are certainly, in the meantime, likely to prove to a greater or less extent a cause of decay.

The conditions upon which the permanency of

coffee property are dependent may be classed under the three headings of *climate, soil,* and *culture;* and I have long been of opinion, that of the three the first named is, perhaps, the most important.

I believe the majority of old planters will be found to agree, that coffee requires a *moderately warm* climate, possessing considerable atmospheric humidity. If such is the case, we have only ourselves to blame, if, when having planted it in situations where these conditions are totally wanting, we spend our labour for nought. And yet how often has this been done! Entirely ignoring the necessity of *warmth,* estates are opened at elevations with a temperature verging on frost, and where the plant can barely live in a state of perpetual barrenness; or, overlooking the equal importance of a moderate temperature and plenty of moisture, we domicile the plant hopefully on arid plains, where, during months, no drop of rain falls to mitigate the effects of a scorching sun. One might suppose that under the last-named circumstances the plant would at least be provided with some sort of shade protection, but (notwithstanding that coffee is known to be a shade-loving plant in a state of nature) this has seldom been done. In fact, instead of endeavouring to copy the arrangements of nature, the object too often seems to have been rather to compel the plant to conform to our crude and imperfect notions of what *ought* to be beneficial to it. It is not surprising if, under such a system, disappointment should have frequently attended the planter, and an idea have sprung up, and gradually gained ground, that a coffee estate is something to be planted and then parted with as quickly as possible.

I will not, however, enlarge further here upon the shade question, having treated it fully elsewhere in the present work.

We now come to our next heading, i. e. *soil*. Having in the first instance obtained a soil suited for producing coffee, the great object must be to *preserve it in that condition*. With this view there are three influences to be guarded against; the first is the loss of surface soil by *wash*, the second is impoverishment by exposure to a hot sun, and by the growth of weeds; and the third, exhaustion by the extraction from it of chemical constituents by the coffee itself. Unless these processes are either prevented or fairly compensated for, all hope of the estate's remaining permanently valuable must be given up.

As elsewhere shown at large, there are means by which wash may be prevented, such as terracing, cutting level drains across the hill face, and a careful avoidance of unduly disturbing the surface soil, when weeding, &c. Then, the ground can be protected from being burned up by the sun, by planting the trees sufficiently close to form a good cover, and from exhaustion otherwise by systematic weeding; while, obviously, exhaustion by cropping can only be remedied by *substantial manuring*.

It will perhaps be objected that my chapter on that subject does not lay sufficient stress on the value of those manufactured fertilizers which the advance of science has of late years brought within our reach; and, as a practical planter, knowing the dislike of practical planters generally to all that seems to savour of mere theorizing, I may not improbably have erred in this direction, as much as a practical chemist, in treating of the same subject, might have been inclined to do in the opposite one. Chemical manures, however, must by no means be lost sight of: indeed, where judiciously made use of, in composts and in conjunction with the produce of the cattle-shed, the refuse of the bungalow, lines, &c., and even with merely green vegetation, they will be found invaluable. Of late years chemistry, like every other branch of science, has made immense strides, and fertilizers carefully compounded in accordance with the chemical analysis of the product to be grown, are specially manufactured to an enormous extent for every species of cultivation.

In consequence of the increasing scarcity and the deterioration in quality of Peruvian guano, chemists and capitalists have combined with each other to seek for substitutes capable of yielding similar results, and boldly claim to have succeeded. Guano from the Chincha Islands formerly tested as high as 18 per cent. of ammonia; but this deposit has long since been exhausted, and the cargoes now imported contain no more than from 4 per cent. to (in rare cases) 12 per cent.

(The phosphates, which are of course *in*soluble, average about 20 per cent.).

Sulphate of ammonia, nitrate of soda, and super-phosphates (viz. dissolved bones, bone ash, and rock phosphate), with potash, magnesia, &c., are the fertilizers of the day, and immense quantities are exported annually, their value being fully appreciated by cultivators all over the world.

Nowhere is this more the case than with the English farmer, who, in the face of high rents, yearly advancing wages, and increasing foreign competing production, finds it imperative to get the largest possible return from his land. That the planters of India, Ceylon, and other fields of agricultural enterprise would (and *will eventually*) reap much larger returns by an increased adoption of these chemical fertilizers, skilfully compounded and prepared specially for the particular growth to which they are to be applied, there can be little question.

As regards *culture*, the word implies all those operations which it has been the object of the present work to describe, and due attention to each of which is equally necessary in turn.

It is upon such questions as the foregoing that the whole question of the permanency of coffee property seems to hinge. So far as I am aware, we know of no necessary limit to the life of the coffee plant in its natural state, and in fact I entertain a firm belief that, *under suitable conditions*, it may be considered capable of indefinite longevity as much as the English laurel, yew, or apple-tree. Even, however, should I be incorrect in this belief, the permanent value of coffee property will not be greatly affected, provided the soil is maintained in such a state as to be capable of supporting subsequent generations of plants.

APPENDIX.

INSTRUCTIONS FOR THE
MEDICAL TREATMENT
OF
COOLIES AND OTHERS
ON
COFFEE ESTATES
UNTIL PROFESSIONAL ASSISTANCE CAN BE OBTAINED.

Written specially for the present work by
R. S. MAIR, M.D., &c.,
Author of the Medical Guide for Anglo-Indians, &c.

FEVER (Simple).

Causes.—Exposure to cold or damp, indigestion, over-fatigue, a debauch, &c.

Symptoms.—Chilly sensation, with more or less shivering, pain in the head and back, loss of appetite, foul tongue, quick pulse, increased heat of skin, and general languor and weakness; distinguished from ague or jungle fever by the absence of remissions.

Treatment.—Rest in bed, warm foot-baths and warm drinks at bedtime, light farinaceous food, and, if necessary, a simple aperient, such as Gregory's powder, castor oil, or a couple of colocynth pills in the morning. If fever continues without intermission, give an emetic of twenty grains ipecacuanha powder in half a tumbler of tepid water, and one hour afterwards commence the following—

FEVER MIXTURE.—Take of nitre or saltpetre one dram, sweet spirits of nitre half an ounce, mindereris spirit, or aqua acetatis ammonia, three ounces; mix, and give a tablespoonful every three hours. Sponge the body with lukewarm water, containing a little vinegar, and apply cold wet cloths to the head. If fever persists two days after above treatment, and without remissions, give the following

FEVER PILLS.—Take of quinine ten grains, calomel six grains, rhubarb and jalap each fifteen grains; mix with sufficient honey to make a mass, and divide into twelve pills. Dose, two every four or five hours.

Pain in back, chest, and abdomen, may be relieved by hot-water fomentations, bran or linseed poultices, or turpentine stupes. *Diet*, soups, beef-tea, arrow-root, corn-flour, and, if much weakness is complained of, half wineglassful of port wine, or table-spoonful of brandy, or arrack, in water, may be given two or three times a day.

INTERMITTENT FEVER, AGUE, OR JUNGLE FEVER.

Cause.—Exposure to malaria.

Symptoms.—Sighing, yawning and stretching, languor, pain in head and back, quick pulse, violent shiverings and chattering of the teeth, followed soon after by great heat of skin and profuse perspiration.

Treatment.—Cover the body with blankets, apply hot sand, bran, or salt, or hot water bottles, freely, drink copiously of hot tea or rice water, and take a wineglassful of sherry or port, or half that quantity of brandy, whisky, or arrack, with hot water.

If tongue is foul, give at the outset an emetic of twenty grains ipecacuanha powder, or a tea-spoonful of mustard or common salt in water. In the hot stage, sponge the body with tepid water; apply cold wet cloths to the head, and drink freely of cold or iced water. One grain of opium, or twenty drops of laudanum, given in this stage will relieve the throbbing of the temples and promote perspiration.

In the sweating stage, encourage perspiration by covering the body with blankets, and by warm drinks; afterwards wipe the skin with dry towels, change the clothes and get out of bed, or go to sleep if so inclined.

Preventive Measures.—When an attack or paroxysm threatens, take a simple purgative; two compound colocynth pills, or twenty grains of jalap if the bowels are constipated; and after the purgative has ceased to operate, give fifteen grains of quinine in water, followed by smaller doses of three or four grains three times a day; or, for convenience, take the following

Ague Mixture.—Take of Epsom salts, one ounce; nitre, one dram; quinine, two scruples; diluted sulphuric acid, one dram (or the juice of one lime); and water one quart. Mix. Dose, a wineglassful three times a day. This mixture will be found especially suitable in removing the dropsical symptoms which frequently attack coolies after fever.

DENGUE FEVER.

Symptoms.—Sudden and severe pains all over the body, not unlike rheumatism, considerable fever, red-tipped, furred tongue, great depression, and on the fourth or fifth day a red or measly eruption, appearing first in patches, then spreading over the body, followed by swelling of the joints and glands, and subsequent shedding of the cuticle.

Treatment.—Rest in bed; warmth externally and warm drinks. Give ten grains of Dover's powder at bedtime, followed next morning by a simple aperient, if necessary, after which give the following: take of iodide of potass forty-eight grains, water one pint. Mix, and give half a wineglassful three or four times a day.

DIARRHŒA.

Causes.—Indigestible food ; unripe fruits or fruits in excess ; badly-cooked vegetables ; particular kinds of fish, as crabs, prawns, oysters ; exposure to cold ; suppressed perspiration ; worms ; liver disease, &c.

Treatment.—At the outset a teaspoonful of castor oil with or without ten drops of laudanum or a teaspoonful of Gregory's powder. If purging continues, take thirty drops of chlorodyne or twenty drops of laudanum with a tablespoonful of brandy or arrack in water, or a glass of port wine, repeating this dose in three or four hours if necessary. Or the following mixture may be used :—*Astringent Diarrhœa Mixture*, Tincture of catechu, four drams ; Tincture of rhubarb, two drams ; laudanum, one dram ; prepared chalk, one dram ; and peppermint water, three ounces. Mix. Dose, a tablespoonful every three or four hours. Diet, arrow-root, sago, corn-flour, toast, and tea. If much pain is complained of, apply mustard poultices or hot fomentations or turpentine.

CHOLERA.

Symptoms.—Rumbling in the stomach, copious stools, at first more or less dark, then becoming lighter till they resemble rice water, nausea and vomiting, followed soon after by cramps in different parts of the body, cold, clammy skin, sunken eyes, loss of voice, intense thirst, blueness of skin, and coma.

Treatment.—In the early stage and before collapse has set in, give thirty drops of chlorodyne or twenty drops laudanum, with half a wineglassful of brandy or arrack, repeating this in two or three hours, or the following may be kept always ready for use :—

Cholera Mixture.—Take of prepared chalk two drams, cinnamon powder one dram, sugar half an ounce, tincture of catechu one ounce, sal volatile two drams, chloric ether two drams, laudanum two drams, and water six ounces. Mix. Dose, a tablespoonful every two hours ; or the following

Cholera Pills.—Take of sugar of lead half-dram, camphor powder twelve grains, opium six grains, chillie powder six grains ; mix into a mass, and divide into twelve pills ; dose, one every two hours. Vomiting may be subdued by applying mustard poultice to the stomach, and giving small quantities of soda water or ice frequently.

For cramps, apply turpentine, mustard poultices, hot bran or ashes, and smart friction.

Diet.—Beef-tea, mutton or chicken broth, arrow-root, sago, corn-flour, rolong, but no solid food.

In collapses, discontinue cholera mixture, pills, or chlorodyne, and give small quantities of brandy or arrack or champagne, or a teaspoonful of sal volatile in water every hour till reaction sets in.

Note.—Avoid all saline or strong purgatives when cholera is prevailing. Bury all discharges from cholera patients in ground distant from wells or tanks, and do the same for a week or ten days with all clothes (worn by the patients) before they are washed.

DYSENTERY, ACUTE.

Causes.—Exposure to heat and cold, sudden variations in temperature, malarious atmosphere, unwholesome food, persistent constipation, disease of liver.

Symptoms.—Frequent evacuations of mucus or slime and blood, or both together from the bowels, severe griping pain, increased on pressure over lower part of abdomen, with great straining.

Treatment.—A teaspoonful of castor oil, with twenty drops of laudanum, to be given at once. If symptoms continue twelve hours after the above, then give the patient twenty-five to thirty drops of laudanum in a tablespoonful of water, fifteen or twenty minutes afterwards give thirty grains ipecacuanha powder, in a small wineglassful of water, and immediately after, apply a good-sized mustard poultice over the pit of the stomach for twenty minutes ; keep the patient on his back, and do not disturb him. Great nausea and depression will be complained of, but if vomiting comes on within an hour, and the powder is ejected, the same routine of treatment must be adopted in about three hours afterwards. This may be required to be repeated three or four times during the course of two or three days, but it ought not to be pushed further without medical advice. If it fails (which it very seldom does), twenty drops of laudanum in one wineglassful of water or thin arrow-root may be injected into the bowel, and repeated twice in twenty-four hours; poultices of bran or linseed meal should be kept constantly applied over the abdomen.

Diet.—Milk, chicken or mutton broths, sago, corn-flour, or rolong.

Chronic Dysentery.—Give ten grains of Dover's powder two or three times a day, or give as frequently the third of a teaspoonful of castor oil, and ten drops of laudanum beat up with a small quantity of powdered gum arabic and warm water, or the following

Dysentery Pills.—Take of quinine twelve grains, opium six grains, ipecacuanha powder four grains, extract of bael fruit, twenty grains; mix and divide into twelve pills. Dose, one three times a day. Decoction of the dried peal of the pomegranate or the bael fruit are sometimes most beneficial in chronic dysentery.

HEAT APOPLEXY.

Causes.—Exposure to a high temperature by night or by day.

Symptoms.—Giddiness, intense headache, with feeling of weight, tightness, and heat at back of head, hot burning skin, face flushed, thirst intense, breathing laboured, oppressed and sighing, followed sometimes by violent convulsions, ending in stupor.

Treatment.—Place the patient in a recumbent position in a cool place, with his head and shoulders raised; pour cold water, iced if possible, steadily and perseveringly in a small stream from a height on the head, face, and chest, *so long as*

there is preternatural heat and dryness of the skin; apply mustard poultices to chest, abdomen, calves of legs, and spine, and administer an injection of two tablespoonfuls turpentine and four tablespoonfuls castor oil, with a pint of tepid water. A dessert-spoonful of brandy, or a teaspoonful of sal volatile in water, should be given every hour when patient is able to swallow, till reaction sets in; he must then be kept quiet, and have milk or farinaceous food or broths only, and a simple purgative if necessary.

LIVER DISEASE.

Causes.—Cold, malaria, intemperance, high temperature, sedentary habits, constipation.

Symptoms.—Dull, aching sensation in right side, pain at top of right shoulder, loss of appetite, nausea, torpid bowels, sometimes diarrhœa or dysentery, and general debility.

Treatment.—Apply mustard poultice or turpentine fomentation over the right side, and take two compound colocynth pills, or the following antibilious or

Liver Pills.—Take of podophyllin three grains, compound extract of colocynth two scruples, quinine six grains, powdered ipecacuanha four grains, and extract of taraxacum six grains. Mix, and divide into twelve pills. Dose. One every night, followed early next morning, if necessary, by a teaspoonful of Rochelle salts in half a tumbler of water.

SNAKE BITE.

Apply a tight bandage two or three inches above the wound, cut out the bitten part, by pinching up the skin between the finger and thumb, or scarify it freely with the point of a sharp knife, by making small incisions all round, allowing blood to flow freely, or press the point of a red-hot iron, or some strong nitric acid or carbolic acid, into the bitten part. Give half a wineglassful of brandy or arrack, or half a teaspoonful of the strongest liquor ammonia, or a teaspoonful of sal volatile diluted with water every half-hour; apply mustard poultices over region of heart and along the spine, and keep the patient moving about to combat the drowsiness.

Scorpion Stings.—Apply to the part a paste made of ipecacuanha powder and liquor ammonia or sal volatile, or a saturated solution of iodide of potassium in liquor potassa. The bruised leaves of the jack-tree, made into a poultice, or the juice of a fresh onion or garlic applied to the part, often proves successful.

DROWNING

Remove all superfluous clothing. Place the patient on his face on the ground, turn him gently on his side, then briskly on his face, making uniform pressure with the open hands on the back between the shoulder-blades and on each side of the chest, removing the pressure immediately before turning the body again on its side. Repeat this process about fifteen times in the minute, and while it is being carried out let one person attend solely to the movements of the head and of the arms placed beneath it; should these measures not prove successful in the course of three or four minutes, commence the following. Place the patient on his back, with head and shoulders raised and supported on a cushion, and draw the tongue out; then standing at his head, grasp the arms just above the elbows, draw them steadily and gently upwards above the head, keeping them stretched upwards for two seconds, then turn down the arms and press them gently and firmly for two seconds against the sides of the chest. Repeat these measures alternately, deliberately and perseveringly about fifteen times in a minute, for some hours, if necessary, until a spontaneous effort to respire is perceived, when the body should be well rubbed with hot towels so as to induce circulation and warmth.

Cautions.—On no account hold the body up by the feet.

Do not place the patient in a warm bath till respiration is established.

Avoid rough usage, and do not allow the body to remain

on the back unless the tongue has been brought forward and secured.

WOUNDS.

Wash out all dirt or blood, bring the edges together with strips of adhesive plaster, and cover over with dry lint and light bandage. If large and gaping, apply one or more stitches in addition to the above, and in wounds on the scalp the hair should first be shaved off all round the part. In punctured or gunshot wounds apply lint soaked in cold water, and keep the patient on his injured side, and if the wound throbs, or is hot and painful, apply frequently hot-water dressing or a poultice. Ragged wounds are best treated by applying simple cold water dressing and a light bandage, but if there is much pain a light poultice or lint soaked in warm water may be applied. Note, do not change the dressings oftener than once in twenty-four hours.

BRUISES.—Rest, fomentations of hot water, or poppy water, afterwards gentle friction with soap liniment or oil, with or without camphor; an onion or garlic poultice, or cloths soaked in tincture of arnica, diluted with four parts of water, will remove discoloration as well as pain.

In severe cases, when the skin or tissues are torn apply lint soaked in warm water, covering it over with oiled silk, and changing this twice a day. Loose skin or other tissue not falling off spontaneously may be removed by a pair of scissors. If the part becomes inflamed, apply cloths soaked in a lotion, composed of sugar of lead, half dram; brandy, one dessertspoonful; and water, half a pint.

If the wound looks dark-coloured, and discharges offensive matter, apply poultices every three hours, made with linseed-meal and charcoal, or grated carrots, or yeast (Indian toddy fermented), and if insects (maggots) appear, dust over the wound a powder composed of equal parts of calomel and camphor.

SPRAINS.—Keep the limb at perfect rest, and apply cold

or hot water till pain and swelling are reduced, then apply gentle friction with hand or with soap liniment, and afterwards a bandage. Sprains of the ankle are best treated by careful application of adhesive plaster all round, and the immediate but cautious use of the limb. If there is much swelling or redness, and pain, apply the same lotion as that referred to for bruises, and observe perfect rest.

BOILS.—When beginning to grow, paint with tincture of iodine, or rub over with lunar caustic, or if small apply spirits of camphor two or three times a day; or use the following *Boil* ointment. Take of extract of belladonna one dram, opium powder half a dram, and lard one ounce; mix and spread on leather sufficient to cover the boils. If, however, there is redness and swelling, apply poultices till the boil bursts, or is opened and until the core comes out.

Whitlows are treated in the same way.

If there are a number of boils over the body, give the following mixture. Take of Epsom salts two ounces, quinine half-dram, water one pint. Dose, half a wineglassful night and morning.

ULCERS and SORES.—When of a bright red colour, apply lint soaked in warm water and cover over with oil silk, changing this night and morning. If surface looks dark or is discharging profusely, touch lightly with blue stone or solid caustic, and apply charcoal poultices as recommended for bruises. Basilicon ointment or Turner's cerate may be applied when the sores are beginning to heal. If maggots appear, dust in a little powder composed of equal parts of calomel and camphor, and give two grains of quinine with half-teaspoonful of sulphur twice a day.

BURNS and SCALDS.—When slight apply lint or cloth soaked in oil, or the smooth side of the plantain leaf covered with oil, or the part may be covered with cotton wool and a light bandage. In more severe cases cover the parts with a paste made of finely powdered chalk (chunam), or flour, or violet powder, and over this cotton wool and light bandage. Do not remove the dressings for two or three days, after which apply bread or linseed poultices, and when the surface looks clean and free from loose skin, apply simple water dressing covered with oil silk, or Turner's cerate, or zinc ointment may be used. Burns of face are best treated by anointing the parts with salad oil.

FRACTURES.—Send for surgical aid at once; meantime make patient lie down, place the limb in a straight position apply splints made of split bamboo or thick millboard on each side, retaining them in position by broad tapes or pieces of bandage, not tightly tied, but sufficiently firm to keep the limb at rest, and prevent the broken ends of the bone from moving against each other. Place the limb on a pillow or cushion, and if there is much pain or swelling apply cloths soaked in lotion composed of equal parts of vinegar, arrack, and cold water.

BLEEDING or HÆMORRHAGE may be arrested by applying a compress or firm pad made of rag or dry lint over the bleeding part, retaining it by adhesive plaster or a moderately tight bandage, and leaving this undisturbed for two or three days. When the bleeding is from the mouth or nose or from large open surfaces, where pressure cannot be employed, apply powdered alum or tannin, or tincture of steel and ice, if procurable, and keep at perfect rest.

POISONING.—Clear out the stomach at once by giving an emetic of one teaspoonful of common salt, and one teaspoonful of mustard in a tumblerful of warm water, or twenty grains of sulphate of zinc in the same quantity of water. Repeat this three times at intervals of ten minutes till free vomiting is induced, assisting this, if necessary, by tickling the throat with a feather.

In cases of poisoning by arsenic, corrosive sublimate, sugar of lead, copper, and most other mineral poisons, give raw eggs and milk, or milk alone, after the above emetics have cleared the stomach.

In poisoning by opium or stramonium, give a tablespoonful of animal charcoal in water every ten or fifteen minutes, and use every possible means to combat the drowsiness by keeping the patient constantly on the move, by splashing cold water on the face, by beating tom-toms, by snuff to the nostrils, and by strong ammonia; strong coffee in small quantities may also be given frequently.

In poisoning by vitriol or other strong mineral acid, the best antidotes are soda, chalk, or soap-suds.

SELECT ADVERTISEMENTS

FOR

INDIA AND THE COLONIES.

R. D. SMYTHE AND CO.,

SUCCESSORS TO

LESLIE, RIVINGTON, & CO.,

EAST INDIA AGENTS,

32, ST. MARY AXE, LONDON, E.C.

ORDERS EXECUTED FOR EVERY DESCRIPTION
OF GOODS AT WHOLESALE PRICES.

Packages Forwarded to or from all parts of the East.

NEWSPAPERS, PERIODICALS, & BOOKS
For Libraries, &c., arranged for at Lowest Rates.

AGENTS
For the Northern Assurance Company.
INDIAN RATES FAVOURABLE.

COUPER, McCARNIE, & Co.

LIVERPOOL OFFICE,
8 B, RUMFORD PLACE.
CHEMICAL WORKS,
LANGBOURN WHARF
MILLWALL.

PHOSPHATED GUANO,
BONE SUPERPHOSPHATES,
MINERAL SUPERPHOSPHATES,
NITRATE OF SODA,
SULPHATE OF AMMONIA,
MURIATE OF AMMONIA,
CARBONATE OF AMMONIA,
SAL AMMONIAC,
&c.

17, FENCHURCH STREET,

LONDON, E.C.

To the export of FERTILIZERS for the culture of the Sugar-Cane, Coffee, and Tobacco Plants, &c., we give our special care, and find all practical Planters turning their attention to highly CONCENTRATED MANURES, as saving packages, freight, labour, &c.

COUPER, McCARNIE, & Co.

Quotations, Samples, &c., on application.

MACKAY BROTHERS,
Agricultural Chemists,
155, FENCHURCH STREET, LONDON.

ESTABLISHED 1857.

The advertisers (formerly of Inverness, N.B.), having in 1867 transferred their business to London are prepared to supply Chemical and Bone Manures of the *highest class*, and in the *most concentrated form*, for the cultivation of *Coffee, Sugar, Cotton*, &c., &c.

Their experience for the past ten years in the London Wholesale Trade in materials for the manufacture of Vitriolized Manures, enables them to offer carefully prepared Special and General Manures for these and other crops, on very favourable terms.

MACKAY'S "EXCELSIOR" COFFEE MANURE
(Registered).

MACKAY'S PURE DISSOLVED BONES
(Guaranteed).

MACKAY'S BONE, MINERAL, AND GUANO SUPERPHOSPHATES.

SULPHATES OF AMMONIA, POTASH, AND MAGNESIA,
&c., &c., &c.

ALL QUOTATIONS MADE F.O.B. IN THE THAMES.

ANALYSES GUARANTEED.

London, March 1st, 1877.

PERUVIAN GOVERNMENT GUANO

DISSOLVED BY

OHLENDORFF & CO.

IS SPECIALLY ADAPTED FOR

TEA, COFFEE,

AND

OTHER COLONIAL PRODUCE.

Sold with Guaranteed Analysis.

Opinion of Dr. VOELCKER, F.R.S., Consulting Chemist to the Royal Agricultural Society of England, &c.

"The highly concentrated state and fine condition of Dissolved Peruvian Guano render it peculiarly valuable to Planters, as they obtain in it the largest amount of the more expensive and efficacious fertilizing matters in the smallest compass, without the admixture of materials which merely increase the bulk and add nothing to the intrinsic value of the manure."

Report from the Manager of the Ramgurh Tea Company, Limited, Hazareebagh :—

"With reference to the three barrels of Dissolved Guano received from Messrs. Ede & Hobson for trial on the Tea plant, I beg to say that the result has been highly satisfactory. I think I may safely state the increase to be at the least 200 lbs. of green leaf, or 50 lbs. of Tea per acre, as compared with other manures or fairly treated cultivation."

For further particulars apply to

OHLENDORFF & CO.,

15, Leadenhall Street, London, E.C.;

Or their Agents—

Messrs. VOLKART BROTHERS, Bombay, Kurrachee, Cochin, Colombo.
Messrs. EDE & HOBSON, Calcutta.

THIRTEEN INTERNATIONAL PRIZE MEDALS

AWARDED TO

JAMES GIBBS AND COMPANY

FOR THEIR

AMMONIA-FIXED GUANO,

AND HIGH-CLASS

CHEMICAL MANURES.

SPECIAL COFFEE MANURE.

Wherever these Manures have been used, they have produced the most abundant crops, and they are universally admitted to be the cheapest and best sold.

HEAD OFFICES.
16, MARK LANE, LONDON, E.C.

BRANCH OFFICES.
KING STREET HALL, BRISTOL, AND GEORGE STREET, PLYMOUTH.

WORKS.
VICTORIA DOCKS, LONDON, & CATTEDOWN, PLYMOUTH.

THE HIGHEST AWARDS GRANTED FOR
ARTIFICIAL MANURES.

LONDON, 1873.

LONDON, 1862.  **PARIS, 1867.**

RIGA, 1865.   **LYONS, 1872.**

MEDAL for PROGRESS, VIENNA, 1873.

BRUSSELS, 1876.   **NORKOPING, 1876.**

The largest Producers of Chemical Manures in the World, the Annual Sales being upwards of 76,000 Tons.

EDWARD PACKARD & CO.,
IPSWICH, ENGLAND,
Manufacturing Agricultural Chemists, Producers & Dealers in
RAW PHOSPHATES.

Nitro-Phosphatic or Ammonia Fixed Guano, a Special Preparation for the Coffee Plant, being very rich in all the fertilizing ingredients necessary to promote the growth and development of the Plant. Price £11 per Ton, in casks delivered alongside vessel in London.

Concentrated Guano Super-Phosphate of the highest class, containing 44 per Cent. Soluble Phosphate of Lime, specially prepared and adaptable to Colonial use. Price £9 per Ton, in casks delivered alongside vessel in London.

WORKS—Ipswich; Bramford; Cambridge; Wetzlar, in Germany; Villefranche, in France; and Londonderry, Ireland. HEAD OFFICES—6, Princes Street, Ipswich, and 155, Fenchurch Street, London.

E. PURSER & CO.'S
COFFEE MANURE.

The gradual decline of the Coffee Estates has been for some time a source of extreme anxiety to all interested in their cultivation.

Messrs. PURSER and Co. have been frequently consulted on the subject, and having carefully investigated the causes of the failure of the crops, prepare a manure containing all the organic and inorganic substances so necessary for supplying the elements removed by repeated cropping.

In preparing a fertilizer containing the mineral constituents of a plant, it is not enough that these constituents be present, but it is further necessary that they be in an available form; that is, in such a form that they can easily enter into assimilation and be readily taken up by the plant in every stage of its growth.

In the COFFEE MANURE prepared by Messrs. PURSER and Co., special regard has been had to this; the Manure is also in a concentrated form, thus causing considerable saving in freight and labour.

This MANURE has been used since 1870 with great success in the Madras and Mangalore districts, as well as in Ceylon.

The quantity per acre should be from 4 to 6 cwt.

E. PURSER & CO.'S
PREPARED DISSOLVED BONES.

THE value of Bones as a Manure for Coffee has been well known and proved; but Bones are slow in their action, *particularly on heavy soils*, and the expense of collecting and crushing them very great.

Messrs. PURSER and Co. have for many years manufactured the PREPARED DISSOLVED BONES, an article well known and extensively used in the Coffee districts. The fine state of subdivision of the Bone, and the fact that portions of it have been acted on by certain acids, make it available at once for the food of the plant.

The quantity used per acre 5 to 8 cwt.

E. PURSER & CO.,
AGRICULTURAL CHEMISTS,
116, FENCHURCH STREET, LONDON.

COFFEE PULPING
MACHINERY.

THE undersigned are prepared to supply PULPERS and WATER-WHEELS as under, of the best description, made by themselves at Bogambra Mills, Kandy, Ceylon.

Single Disc Hand Pulpers, suitable for new Clearings or small Estates.
Double do. Hand or Power
Treble do. for Power only } suitable for Estates of any size.

In all these PULPERS the Discs are of solid Iron, and various improvements have been introduced, so that as now made they are simple, durable, and effective, and the Single and Double Machines can be had on a very compact and portable frame, which makes them convenient where transport is difficult.

Single Cylinder Pulpers, for hand or power, and with or without Elevators.

Double do. do.
Treble do. do.
Double do. do.
    with Crusher
} All these, as well as the Single Cylinder Pulper, have solid Iron Cylinders covered with our "Patent Punch Copper," Elevators and circular Sieves. They combine simplicity, convenience, durability, and effectiveness.

12 ft., 16 ft., 20 ft., and 24 ft. all Iron Overshot **WATER-WHEELS**.

THEY ARE ALSO PREPARED TO RECEIVE ORDERS FOR

TURBINES AND STEAM ENGINES

For driving Pulpers or for any other Coffee Machinery.

Orders for Disc Pulpers for India received and executed by

Messrs. PEIRCE, LESLIE, & Co.,
CALICUT AND COCHIN,

Who generally have some of our Double and Single Disc Pulpers on hand.

JOHN WALKER & Co.,
BOGAMBRA MILLS, KANDY, CEYLON.

WALKER BROTHERS,
LIME STREET SQUARE, LONDON, E.C.

JOHN GORDON & CO.,
Inventors, Patentees, and Manufacturers of every Description of
COFFEE MACHINERY.

COFFEE PULPERS WITH GORDON'S PATENT BREASTS.
GORDON'S SINGLE AND DOUBLE DISC COFFEE PULPERS.

DOUBLE DISC PULPER.

GORDON & CO.'S "Native" Coffee Pulper. This handy little iron "Pulper" was designed by Mr. J. Gordon, for the use of Native Cultivators on small patches or holdings; it is strong, but light for carrying readily from place to place, the barrel or cylinder is cased with copper, two natives can work it with ease, and it will be found in every way suited to its purpose. Price, with Two Winch Handles, complete, £20.

GORDON'S Improved Patent Coffee Pulper. This Machine will be found a substantial piece of work, carefully fitted without unnecessary cost; the barrel is well cased with stout copper, provision is made for freely carrying off the pulp, for delivery of the beans, and for preserving the copper surface of the cylinder from damage by small stones, &c. A better Pulper is not made; it will be found in every way adapted for its purpose, turning its work out thoroughly well, and not being liable to break down. Price, complete with Two Winch Handles, £32. Hand or Power.

GORDON'S Improved Disc Coffee Pulper. These simple and durable Machines are made with single and double discs; all the parts are strong but light, and may be carried on the backs of mules with ease. They are carefully made and marked, being easily put together, and not liable to break down. They are easily worked by hand. Price, including a set of spare copper sheets for discs, Single Disc Pulper, £20. Double Disc Pulper, £30.

GORDON & CO.'S Coffee Separator, best yet introduced. Price £21.
GORDON'S Improved Coffee Iron Fans. Price £15.

J. GORDON & Co. also manufacture Peeling Mills from £60 to £140, for Cattle, Water, or Steam Power; Water Wheels, Cattle Gearing, Steam Engines, and every description of Machinery and Tools required for the cultivation and preparation of Coffee, Rice, Arrowroot, Sugar, Fibres, &c.

Boring Tools, Mining Machinery, and Pumps.

Offices—No. 8, NEW BROAD STREET, LONDON, E.C.

BROOKER, DORE, & CO.,

2, ROOD LANE, LONDON,

SUPPLY

ESTATE TOOLS

OF BEST QUALITY,

ALSO,

GALVANIZED CORRUGATED ROOFING,

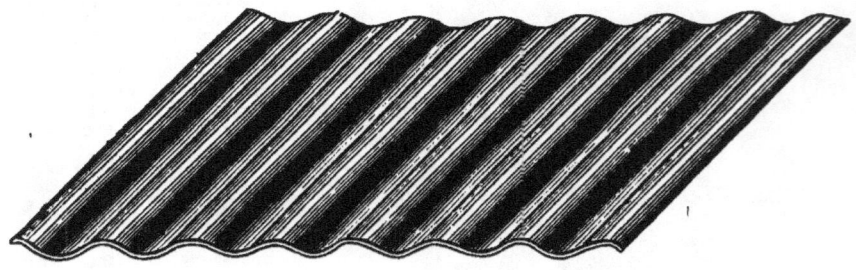

RIDGE CAPPING,

COFFEE SPOUTING, &c., &c.

Hoop Iron, Nails, Rivets, Screws, and every description of Hardware required by Planters.

BROOKER, DORE, & CO.,
METAL AND HARDWARE MERCHANTS.

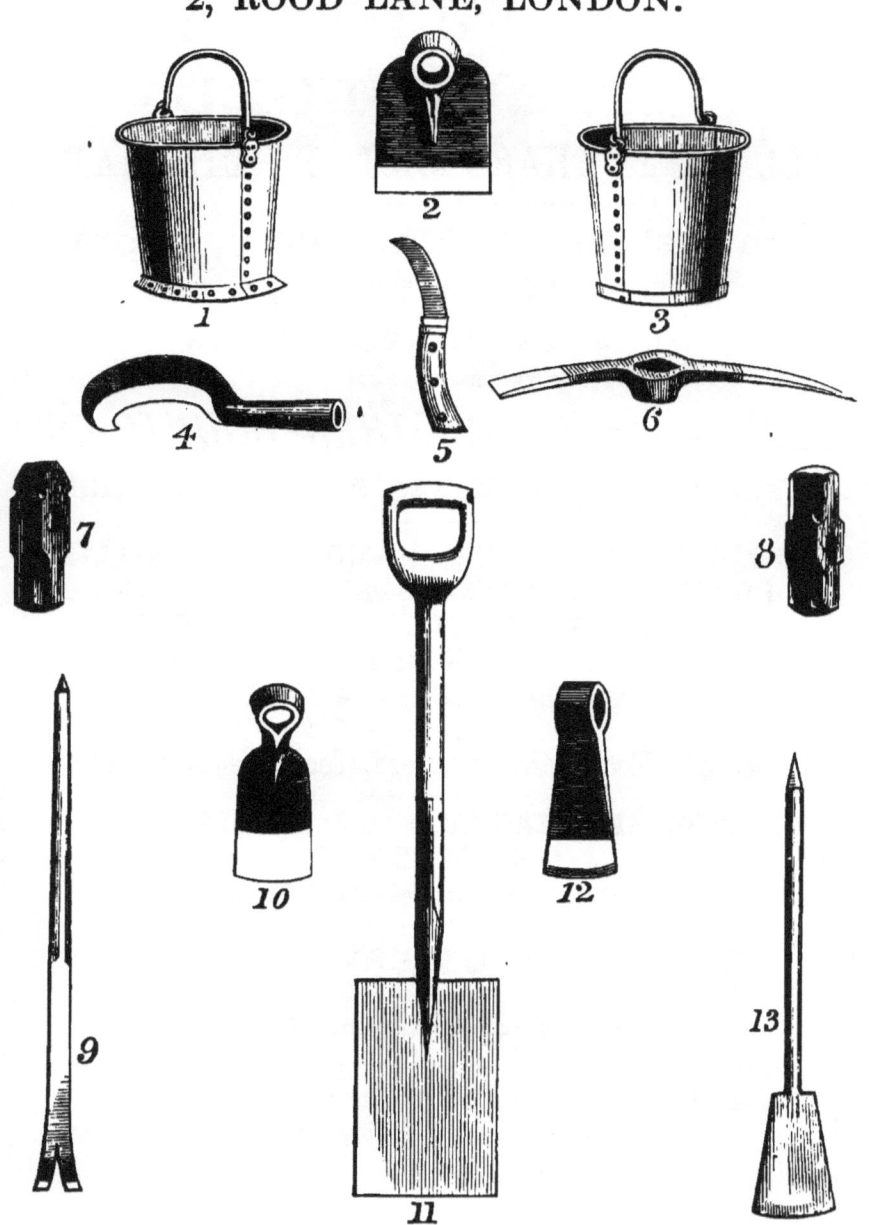

Registered Trade Mark.

J. C. & W. LORD,
142, GREAT CHARLES ST., BIRMINGHAM.

Planters' Tools, Machinery, Stores, and Hardware,

OF SPECIAL PATTERNS,

FOR THE REQUIREMENTS OF

CEYLON, INDIA, & OTHER COUNTRIES'
COFFEE, SUGAR, COTTON, TEA, & RICE PLANTATIONS.

HOES, CATTIES, DHAWS, MAMOOTIES, KODALIES, PLOUGHS, PLANTING BARS, HOOKS, CANE KNIVES, MATCHETS, REAPERS, AXES, ADZES, PRUNING SAWS, SPADES AND SHOVELS, SUGAR PANS.

Carpenters' Tools, and Planters' Tool Chests complete.

SUPERIOR SPORTING GUNS, £16; RIFLES, £17 10s.; REVOLVERS, £6,

Complete in Cases with Implements.

SADDLERY.

Orders through London Agents.

R. D. SMYTHE & CO., 32, St. Mary Axe, London, Merchants and Shipping Agents.

SADDLERY FOR INDIA AND CEYLON.

HENRY PEAT & CO.,

(Late of 14, Old Bond Street)

173, PICCADILLY, LONDON,

MANUFACTURE EVERY DESCRIPTION OF

SADDLERY, HARNESS,

AND

HORSE CLOTHING

SPECIALLY ADAPTED

FOR INDIA AND THE COLONIES.

PRICE LISTS SENT POST FREE.

All Orders from Abroad must be accompanied by a Remittance.

7½ per Cent. Discount allowed for Cash.

MEDIUM CHOKED GUNS.

12-Guage Central Fire 7¼lbs. ⎫ Made in four brands or qualities,
16   „   „   6¼ „   ⎬ beginning with our well-known
20   „   „   5¾ „   ⎭   £13 13s. Gun.

Prices, £13 13s., £17 17s., £20, £25.

The 16 and 20 bores give shooting fully equal to a 12-guage upon the old system of boring. They are much handier, and economize ammunition, have less recoil, and therefore do not produce such exhaustion, especially in hot countries, or with gentlemen who are not in robust health, or who are no longer young. The 12-guage on the new system is a most powerful weapon, and makes a first-rate pigeon gun.

EXPRESS DOUBLE RIFLES.

·360 Bore, Weighing 7lb. ⎫   ⎧ ·500 Bore, Weighing 9¼lb.
·450   „   „   9lb. ⎬ PRICE £25 ⎨ ·577   „   (6 drs.) „ 10½ lb.

These Weapons are kept in stock for the convenience of gentlemen who cannot wait to build, and they will be sent on receipt of order.

TESTIMONIALS (from a Large Number).

"Messrs. J. & W. Tolley.—The double rifle you sent me acquitted itself well; it made the highest score, standing position, at 150 yards, in the Northern India Rifle Association, Second Sportsman's Contest for 1874, and that without having had any practice with it whatever.
"Adam Smith,
"Poona, Jan. 28th, 1876." "Honorary Secretary, Poona, Rifle Club.

"Messrs. Tolley,   "Athlone, May 20th, 1872.
    "I yesterday fired with the Rifle without raising the back sight, from 25 to 200 yards, and almost every shot struck its fellow from the other barrel.
"J. E. Baines, Capt. 45th Regt."

"Little Shareham, Ootacamund, Neilgherry Hills, Madras, April 16th, 1874.
"Messrs. Tolley,—I beg to acknowledge the receipt of two 'Express' Rifles, and box of ammunition; everything correct and in first-rate order. The Rifles are in every particular what I required, and I am greatly pleased with them; they shoot accurately, and there is absolutely no recoil.
"F. H. Winterbotham, Capt. Sappers and Miners."

"Belgaum, India, July, 1875.
"Sirs,—My 'Express' is thought highly of here, both as regards finish and accuracy; I was much pleased with it during my shooting trip in North Canara, in April and May. My average of kills was higher with it than with any other rifle I ever used, and I don't recollect losing any beast I hit with it; the effect was most deadly, and, to my thinking, equal to those of a 12-bore. I am sorry I cannot give you my experience of its effects on bison, as the season was altogether unfavourable for those animals—there was no rain, so stalking them was all but impossible; I however got a shot at one with the 'Express'—the shoulder-blade was completely smashed to pieces, and I need not have fired again, except to put the beast out of pain. I tried at 100 yards a bran-new ·500 bore 'Express' by ———, against yours, using same ammunition in both. Your Rifle made a mean deviation of 0·38 inches, and his 0·51 inches; both Rifles were fired at same time and place.
"Yours faithfully, "W. H. McMath, Lieut. 66th Regt."

J. & W. TOLLEY,
Pioneer Works, St, Mary's Square, BIRMINGHAM.

Advertisements

"Lansdown House, Bath, May 17th, 1876.

"To Messrs. J. and W. Tolley,

"Sirs,—I have much pleasure in informing you that the 'Express' Rifle which you made for me has come up to my expectations in every way; I have fired with it, and find it very accurate and well balanced. I shall be very glad to recommend you to my friends in India.

"Yours, &c.,
"C. W. Douglas, Lieut. 92nd Highlanders."

·577 BORE EXPRESS DOUBLE RIFLE,

WEIGHING 10½ POUNDS.—PRICE £25.

The following extract will explain the wonderful power possessed by this the largest Bore Express Rifle, using either 5 or 6 drams of Curtis and Harvey's No. 6 Powder, and an Express bullet of ·480 grains weight :—

Extract of a Letter from Lieut. A. J. Lister, to Messrs. King, King, and Co., Bombay, dated Susi, the 27th April, 1876.

"I have lately had a few opportunities of trying the Rifle with five drams of Powder, and the following are some of the examples of the, I may say, awful effects:—

"1—A Panther shot through the head: small hole on near side, the whole of the far side blown off.

"2—Small Jungle Deer shot through centre and fleshy part of body: intestines bodily blown out, and body cut in half all but spine.

"3—A couple of Sambur shot through centre of body: first one, *inside*, a mass of blood and bones, about as big as a soup plate; the other shot through the shoulder, smashed the bone of near leg to atoms, and *inside*, a mass of jelly.

"4—With 5 drams therefore it is very deadly, but with 6 drams I don't believe anything but an Elephant or a Rhinoceros would be able to disregard a bullet in its body."

Pro forma Bill of a useful Battery for Indian Sport—

	£	s.	d.
Express Double Rifle	25	0	0
Gun-Case and Fittings	5	0	0
Central-fire 12-guage Shot Gun	13	13	0
Gun Case and Fittings	5	0	0
Tin-lined Case	1	0	0
Freight, Insurance, &c., to Bombay	2	7	0
	£52	0	0

TERMS.—One half the amount at least to accompany the order, the balance immediately on receipt.

J. & W. TOLLEY,

PIONEER WORKS, ST. MARY'S SQUARE, BIRMINGHAM.

HUNTLEY & PALMERS,
Biscuit Manufacturers

BY APPOINTMENT TO

THE QUEEN, THE KING OF THE BELGIANS, &c.,

READING & LONDON.

The highest awards given for Biscuits to any English house were made to HUNTLEY & PALMERS, at the following Exhibitions, "for excellence of quality:"—

LONDON	1851
PARIS	1855
LONDON	1862
PARIS	1867
HAVRE	1868
AMSTERDAM	1869
LIMA	1872
LYONS	1872

VIENNA, 1873,
"MEDAL FOR PROGRESS,"
SANTIAGO, 1875,
"SPECIAL PRIZE."

Also the "Diploma of Honour," and the Gold Medal of the "National Academy of Agriculture, Manufactures and Commerce," Paris.

These Biscuits are made of the finest materials, and from their great variety of Shape and Flavour, acknowledged Superiority of make, and fine keeping qualities, they have obtained a very extensive and increasing sale in England, on the Continent of Europe, and the various Markets of the World.

They are packed in Tins containing 1lb. and upwards, to meet the convenience of the Trade and Shippers.

MOIR'S
SOUPS IN TINS.

MOIR'S
MARMALADE IN TINS.

MOIR'S
JAMS IN TINS.

MOIR'S
BACON.

MOIR'S
OX TONGUES.

MOIR'S
HAMS.

MOIR'S
SALMON.

MOIR'S
PICKLES.

MOIR'S
TART FRUITS.

MOIR'S
SAUCES.

HEAD OFFICE:
GLASSHOUSE FIELDS, BROOK ST., London, E.
AND AT ABERDEEN.

COPLAND & CO.,

ESTABLISHED 1832.

Provision Merchants, Importers of Foreign Produce, Manufacturing and Export Oilmen, Grocers, and General Purveyors.

TART FRUITS, PICKLES, SAUCES, JAMS, JELLIES, MARMALADE, POTTED MEATS, FISH, &c.

(Expressly Prepared for Use in Tropical Climates.)

TO PREVENT FRAUD, AND A GUARANTEE FOR THE GENUINENESS OF THE CONTENTS,

SEE THAT OUR TRADE MARK ON METALLIC CAPSULE, CORRESPONDS WITH THAT ON LABEL.

Special attention paid to the execution of Private Orders from Foreign Residents, which, however, must invariably be accompanied with approved Remittances or References for payment in London.

EXHIBITION OF THE WORKS OF INDUSTRY OF ALL NATIONS, 1851.

Prize Medal

Awarded.

Page 56—"COPLAND, BARNES & Co's collection of Fruits deserves Honourable Mention."

Page 64—"COPLAND, BARNES & Co. exhibit few Meats, but abundance of Fish, Hams, and Vegetables dressed in various ways."

"A PRIZE MEDAL has been awarded for these in conjunction with the admirable Tart Fruits referred to elsewhere."

Great

Exhibition, 1851.

Manufactory—**30, BURY STREET, ST. MARY AXE,**
Office—**3, MITRE STREET, ALDGATE,**
LONDON, E.C.

WILLIAM MORRISON & SONS,

ESTABLISHED 1823,

WHOLESALE EXPORT MANUFACTURING
Stationers and Printers,

96, LEADENHALL STREET, LONDON, E.C.

All Forms required on Estates, &c., kept in Stock.

ACCOUNT BOOKS
Specially made for Warm and variable Climates.

PRINTING IN LETTER-PRESS & LITHOGRAPHY
BY STEAM POWER.

ENGRAVING BY FIRST CLASS ARTISTS.

All descriptions of Stationery required in the Counting-House supplied on reasonable terms.

Messrs. W. MORRISON & SONS having been established for upwards of Half-a-Century guarantee that all Orders will be efficiently executed.

Remittance to accompany Order, or good References on opening Accounts.

GEORGE PHILIP & SON'S
LIST OF
STANDARD ATLASES.

PHILIPS' HANDY GENERAL ATLAS OF THE WORLD, a Comprehensive Series of Maps, illustrating Modern, Historical, and Physical Geography. With a complete Consulting Index. By JOHN BARTHOLOMEW, F.R.G.S. Crown folio, half-bound morocco, gilt edges, price £1 11s. 6d.

"Messrs. Philip have just issued what is, perhaps, the most generally useful Atlas yet published. They very properly call it 'THE HANDY ATLAS,' and handy it is, as every one who uses it will find. It contains thirty-nine useful maps, just those which the ordinary newspaper reader or merchant requires. They have been constructed by BARTHOLOMEW, and every recent discovery is chronicled. There is also an excellent index."—*Bookseller*.

PHILIPS' NEW GENERAL ATLAS OF THE WORLD. A Series of Original and Authentic Maps, delineating the Natural and Political Divisions of the Empires, Kingdoms, and States of the World. With Consulting Index. Edited by WILLIAM HUGHES, F.R.G.S. Imperial folio, half-bound morocco, price £3 3s.

PHILIPS' IMPERIAL LIBRARY ATLAS. A Series of Fifty-one New and Authentic Maps, engraved from Original Drawings, compiled from National Surveys and the Works of eminent Travellers and Explorers. With a valuable Consulting Index. Edited by WILLIAM HUGHES, F.R.G.S. Imperial folio, half-bound Russia, price £5 5s.

"The work is the result of careful labour, extending over many years. In drawing, in colouring, and in printing, it comes very near perfection."—*Athenæum*.

PHILIPS' FAMILY ATLAS OF PHYSICAL, GENERAL AND Classical Geography. Fifty-seven imperial 4to Maps, with introductory Essay on Physical Geography, and a copious Consulting Index. By the late Professor W. HUGHES, F.R.G.S. New and cheaper edition, revised to date. Imperial quarto, cloth gilt, gilt edges, price £1 1s.

PHILIPS' MAP OF INDIA. By WILLIAM HUGHES, F.R.G.S. Size—42 by 30 inches. Price, on sheet, 6s.; in case, 10s. 6d.; mounted on rollers and varnished, 12s. 6d.

PHILIPS' MAP OF INDIA, reduced from the above. By J. BARTHOLOMEW, F.R.G.S. Size—22 by 28 inches. Price, on sheet, 2s. 6d.; in case, 3s. 6d.; on rollers, 3s. 6d.

PHILIPS' AUTHENTIC MAP OF INDIA, in neat case, 1s.

LONDON: GEORGE PHILIP & SON, 32, FLEET STREET; Caxton Buildings, South John Street, and 51, South Castle Street, Liverpool.

R. D. SMYTHE & Co., 32, ST. MARY AXE, LONDON,
Merchants and Shipping Agents.

MILITARY, NAVAL, AND CIVIL TAILOR,
Ceylon, India, China, Japan, Colonial, & General Outfitter.

TROPICAL LIST ON APPLICATION.

GOY'S STORE for every description of Hosiery, Gloves, Ties, Scarves, Perfumery, Toilet Requisites, Shirts, Collars, Rugs, Portmanteaus, Bags, Umbrellas, Tailoring, Boots, Shoes, and Ladies' Underclothing, Camp and Cabin Furniture, and Bedding.

Great Variety, Moderate Prices, Newest Fashions, and Free Delivery to any part of England.

Goy's New Premises are No. 21, Leadenhall Street, and 54, Lime Street. The old Premises were at 36, Leadenhall Street.

ESTABLISHED 1817.

THE "TERAI" HAT.—ANDRÉ'S.
A SOFT DOUBLE HAT FOR WARM CLIMATES.

Can be folded and packed without Damage. Especially suited for Sporting, Riding, and Travelling, and Ladies' Wear.

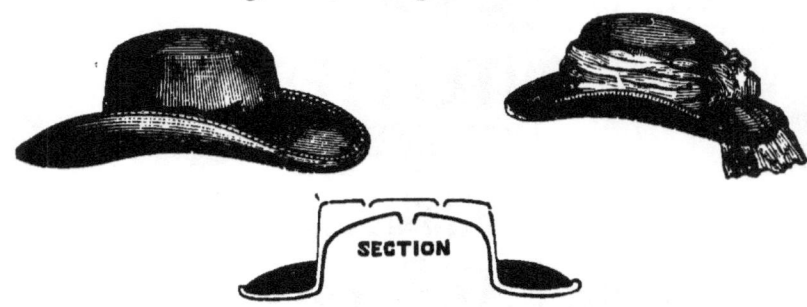

ANDRÉ & CO., HATTERS,
127, NEW BOND ST., LONDON.

CAUTION.—ANDRÉ'S "TERAI" HATS are sold by the principal merchants throughout India, Ceylon, &c. Ladies and Gentlemen are particularly cautioned to ask for "ANDRÉ'S 'TERAI' HATS," and, to avoid inferior imitations purchase only those bearing their Genuine Stamp, with Name and Address. Recommendations from—

HIS EXCELLENCY THE RIGHT HON. LORD LYTTON, Governor-General of India.
HIS GRACE THE RIGHT HON. THE DUKE OF BUCKINGHAM, Governor of Madras.
HIS EXCELLENCY THE RIGHT HON. SIR W. H. GREGORY, Governor of Ceylon.
HON. SIR JOHN STRACHEY, K.C.S.I., Lieutenant-Governor of the North West Provinces.
MAJOR-GENERAL SIR DIGHTON MACNAGHTEN PROBYN, C.B., K.C.S.I., Equerry to H.R.H. the Prince of Wales.
LIEUT.-COLONEL THE HON. SIR H. RAMSAY, C.B., K.C.S.I., Commissioner of Kemaoon.
LIEUT.-COLONEL OWEN TUDOR BURNE, &c., &c., &c.
And many Ladies of the highest distinction.

André's Sola Pith and Felt Sun Hats, Felt Air-Chamber Helmets, &c., &c.

COYLE & CO.'S
CELEBRATED BRANDY.

No. 1. WHITE LABEL, Crystal flasks, 44*s*. per Doz.
No. 2. BLUE   Do.   ...   ...   38*s*.   ,,

Certificate, dated 27th October, 1876 :—

We have had for many years the entire selection in this district of Messrs. COYLE & Co.'s Celebrated Cognac Brandies, and have much pleasure in Certifying, that their No. 1 quality is pure "Grande Fine Champagne" Brandy, fourteen years old —and their No. 2 quality, a very fine Brandy from a superior district, and is over twelve years old.

Signed,
The "Societé de Proprietaires,"
A Cognac.

Also **COYLE & CO.'S**

Finest DUBLIN WHISKY, 6 years old, highly recommended, 28*s*. per Doz.

Prices of Sherry, Claret, and Sparkling Wines,

Can be had on application to

31, LOWER ORMOND QUAY, **DUBLIN**.

GEO. THOMSON AND SON,
ABERDEEN, N.B.,
FINE OLD SCOTCH WHISKY
(FROM MALT ONLY).

As supplied to the London Clubs, the English Clubs in Paris and Brussels, &c. For Terms, &c., apply to

MESSRS. R. D. SMYTHE & CO.,
EXPORT AGENTS,

32, St. Mary Axe, London, E.C.

ESTABLISHED 1755.

C. GREATREX & SON'S

CELEBRATED

SADDLES, HARNESS, BRIDLES, WHIPS, &c., &c.

CAVALRY APPOINTMENTS,

AND FITTINGS OF EVERY DESCRIPTION.

AXLES, SPRINGS, LAMPS, BOLTS,

MADE UP CARRIAGES AND FITTINGS OF EVERY DESCRIPTION.

WALSALL, ENGLAND.

REASONS *why you should buy an* **American "Waltham" Watch** *in preference to any other:*

ALL AMERICAN WALTHAM WATCHES HAVE

FOGG'S PATENT PINION,

To prevent damage to the train by the accidental breaking of the mainspring.

- ALL AMERICAN WALTHAM WATCHES have hardened and tempered hairsprings, which secure a more uniform rate, and facilitate the regulating.
- ALL AMERICAN WALTHAM WATCHES have hardened and tempered pinions, which prevent wear.
- ALL AMERICAN WALTHAM WATCHES have a much longer and weaker mainspring than either Swiss or English watches, which reduces the wear and tear on all parts, and proves that the watch is properly constructed. In some instances the spring is 22 inches long.
- ALL AMERICAN WALTHAM WATCHES are made on the interchangeable principle, so that if one piece should break it can be replaced by a new one, to be obtained at the Wholesale and Export Offices of the

  AMERICAN WATCH COMPANY,
  Waltham Buildings, Holborn Circus, London, E.C.,

  saving time and cost.
- ALL AMERICAN WALTHAM WATCHES can be changed from a silver case to a gold one without loss of time or danger of having the movement spoiled by being taken down to make a new case for it.
- ALL AMERICAN WALTHAM WATCHES, even the keyless ones, are very simple in construction, and can be repaired by any watch-maker.
- ALL AMERICAN WALTHAM WATCHES are warranted by special certificate to be made on the most approved principles, of the best materials, and to possess every requisite of a reliable *Time Keeper.*
- ALL AMERICAN WALTHAM WATCHES are made on a principle spoken of by Sir EDMUND BECKET (late E. B. Denison) in his works on Clocks, Watches, and Bells, in which he says, "*although labour is dearer in America than here, this machinery enables them to undersell English watches of the same quality;*" and that the system of the American Watch Company of Waltham, of making watches wholly by machinery, *is perfectly correct,* this same eminent authority remarks that "*there can be no doubt in the mind of any one who understands machinery that this is the best as well as the cheapest way of making machines which require precision and uniformity.*"

The public are cautioned that there are quantities of worthless imitations of Waltham Watches being offered for sale, usually called Boston Levers, American Levers, and other similar names. Every Waltham Watch ought to have special certificate, signed by the Treasurer of the Company, and countersigned by the Company's Agents at London, and *for the good performance of which, under fair usage, the Company at all times hold themselves responsible, no matter where purchased.*

www.ingramcontent.com/pod-product-compliance
Lightning Source LLC
Chambersburg PA
CBHW031424230426
43668CB00007B/420